DEFUND FEAR

DEFUND FEAR

SAFETY WITHOUT POLICING, PRISONS, AND PUNISHMENT

ZACH NORRIS

WITH A FOREWORD BY VAN JONES

BEACON PRESS
BOSTON

BEACON PRESS
Boston, Massachusetts
www.beacon.org

Beacon Press books
are published under the auspices of
the Unitarian Universalist Association of Congregations.

24 23 22   8 7 6 5 4 3

This book is printed on acid-free paper that meets the uncoated paper
ANSI/NISO specifications for permanence as revised in 1992.

Text design and composition by Kim Arney

Defund Fear: Safety Without Policing, Prisons, and Punishment was originally
published under the title *We Keep Us Safe: Building Secure, Just, and Inclusive
Communities* (Beacon Press, 2020).

Library of Congress Cataloging-in-Publication Data

Names: Norris, Zach, author.
Title: Defund fear : safety without policing, prisons, and punishment / Zach Norris.
Description: Boston : Beacon Press, 2020. | Includes bibliographical
    references and index.
Identifiers: LCCN 2019026265 (print) | LCCN 2019026266 (ebook) |
    ISBN 9780807003022 (paperback) | ISBN 9780807029756 (ebook)
Subjects: LCSH: Human security—United States. | Public safety—United
    States. | Polarization (Social sciences)—United States. | Community
    organization—United States. | Democracy—United States.
Classification: LCC JC599.U5 N55 2020 (print) | LCC JC599.U5 (ebook) |
    DDC 363.10973—dc23
LC record available at https://lccn.loc.gov/2019026265
LC ebook record available at https://lccn.loc.gov/2019026266

CONTENTS

FOREWORD

This right here. This book.

What Zach Norris has done in his thoughtful and ambitious book is expand the story of justice further. He reaches back in time to the founding of our nation—*how did we get here?*—and he reaches forward, envisioning a compassionate future that promises much greater safety, particularly for all those who are most vulnerable in today's world.

The opposite of criminalization is humanization, treating each other like human beings, reclaiming the empathy and grace that seem to have fallen out of fashion.

Zach's own humanity has always been striking. He was just an intern when he came on board at the Ella Baker Center for Human Rights (an organization I cofounded in 1996): an intense young man who arrived at the office before everyone else each morning and stayed late most every night. I was reminded of a passage in *Letters from Prison* by the theologian and anti-Nazi dissident Dietrich Bonhoeffer:

> *What we shall need is not geniuses, or cynics, or misanthropes, or clever tacticians, but plain, honest, and straightforward men. Will our inward power of resistance be strong enough, and our honesty with ourselves remorseless enough, for us to find our way back?*

I came to find out that the real magic happened every time Zach would interact with the families of kids who were locked up. Zach's superpower is making people feel heard. Folks instinctively know they can trust him and rely on him. Around the Ella Baker Center, we all knew Zach was the secret to the success of our Books Not Bars campaign, which helped to shut down multiple youth prisons and kept a "youth super jail" from being built.

When Zach took on the executive directorship of the Ella Baker Center in 2013, it was clear that the country had reached an inflection point where liberals and conservatives were agreeing that prisons were a waste: a waste of money and a waste of lives. Zach had a vision for the opposite of the endless cycles of dehumanization, deprivation, and damage. He envisioned the hope and love of the Oakland community embodied in a building called Restore Oakland. He wanted to build a kind of monument to redemption.

As this book goes to press, his vision has been realized: Restore Oakland (a collaboration of multiple organizations) has opened its doors, offering conflict resolution through restorative justice, housing and tenant rights advocacy, and a hub to organize immigrants, formerly incarcerated people, students, LGBTQ people, and other community members. Making that vision a reality was no small feat, more proof of the powerhouse we have in Zach Norris. You'd be wise to take the model of safety presented in this book seriously as well. These are common-sense ideas whose time should have come long ago.

For twenty-five years I've been on the front lines of criminal justice reform. As an advocate, I've been in and out of more prisons than I care to count. I've attended too many funerals where the young people are in the caskets and the old folks are mourning in the pews.

I've seen firsthand the devastating impact that excessive incarceration has had on generations of families and entire communities—communities that were criminalized, that came to be regarded as dangerous and suspect. And I've seen the suffering of the survivors and the families who have been hurt, who rarely if ever have found healing—even when those who hurt them spend their life behind bars.

America's criminal justice system is based on retribution, the primitive notion of an eye for an eye that Gandhi says leaves the whole world blind. The damage done by an incident of violent crime is often horrific enough. But then society adds more damage with a system hell-bent on revenge. How is damage plus damage supposed to add up to justice and healing? That's an equation that's never going to work.

It is sometimes justified or necessary to place a human being behind bars. But incarceration is hardly the panacea—for the wrong-doer, for the victim, or even for society—that the public is led to believe it is. In fact we are far more likely to get to accountability and healing if we acknowledge each other's humanity and engage with each other—even when that is the very last thing we feel like doing.

My documentary series on CNN, *The Redemption Project,* is based on the understanding that the verdict in the courtroom is never the end of the story. The verdict may be the end in a bunch of TV shows featuring smart prosecutors, but not in real life. The real story keeps unfolding for years, often decades, after that moment—and it doesn't usually have a happy ending.

Just as there are no throwaway resources or throwaway species, there are no throwaway people or throwaway communities. Once we recognize the intrinsic value of every member of the human family, we can achieve justice, healing, and redemption.

—Van Jones

PREFACE TO THE 2021 EDITION

When this book went to press at the close of 2019, I was alarmed by the rise of fascism, white supremacy, and widening inequality, yet I never anticipated the levels of fear, dysfunction, and insecurity to which our country would descend in 2020—far too many to list but notably these:

- nurses forced to wear garbage bags as protection against the COVID-19 pandemic while police are outfitted in the best armor money can buy and actively engaged in suppressing protests across the nation

- surging domestic violence stirred by angry rhetoric that places blame on the least powerful, with the shelters for victims of violence, as for the homeless, desperately underfunded in a time of greatest need

- COVID deaths twice as high among people of color: a legacy of decades, even centuries of underfunded healthcare for these communities

- 45.7 million unemployment claims while the wealthiest 1 percent continue to post record profits

- the literal sacrifice demanded of essential workers—predominantly women of color

- thirty to forty million renters at risk of eviction; 80 percent of them black or Latinx, a direct result of the lack of educational, job, and advancement opportunities in those communities

- the shootings and murders of black men and women by police:

    Rayshard Brooks, twenty-seven, sleeping in his car

    Breonna Taylor, twenty-six, sleeping at home

    Ahmaud Arbery, twenty-five, jogging

    Jacob Blake, twenty-nine, with his sons watching in the back seat

    George Floyd, eight minutes and forty-six seconds, calling out for his mother

- lightning fires, 4.76 million acres burned, a direct outcome of the widespread refusal to address the impact of climate change

- forced sterilization of immigrant women in ICE custody and other inhumane actions against people seeking refuge

These incidents are not random nor merely the result of a really bad year. The dangers we face today are undeniably the result of choices made over four hundred years by politicians from both sides of the aisle and the interests that fund them. Their choices put into place the "framework of fear" that scapegoats black, indigenous, and other people of color while obscuring the real harms, from climate change to inequality to ongoing state violence.

Before the pandemic, seven hundred people a day died from poverty. Before George Floyd and Breonna Taylor, a black person was killed by police or vigilante violence every twenty-eight hours. Before 2020, we spent fifty-three cents of every federal dollar on the military. The lion's share of city and municipal budgets went to police departments. The very things that accelerated the suffering and death of black and brown people—policing and prisons—were recession proof. Meanwhile, after every recession since 1980, access to healthcare, education, housing, and meaningful employment—necessary for the lives of all people, black, white, and brown—was slashed and burned.

There is no denying that Donald Trump escalated the hateful rhetoric that animates the "framework of fear" while rolling back human rights advances and the rule of law itself. Still, this legacy cannot be laid at the feet of any one president, no matter how god-awful he has been. The man in 2020's White House is not the sole source of our suffering and insecurity. Regardless of who occupies the White House, we must defund the machine of fear and dehumanization. In its place, we must build a system of care that prioritizes public health and mental health, the restoration of relationships, and investment in our communities. Our overall community health can only ever be as good as the health of our most distressed communities.

If COVID-19 has taught us anything, it's that the lack of infrastructure and a lack of a culture of care can ultimately harm each and every one of us. As of October 2020, over two hundred thousand people had died due to COVID-19. Only the Civil War period exceeds this moment in terms of deaths due to a single cause: when three-quarters of a million people died in the span of four years. And only the Civil War saw as deeply divided a country as we have today.

I fear a new civil war is threatening. My wife and I have been committed nonviolent organizers all of our lives. For the first time, we have given thought to what for us is nearly unthinkable: do we need to get a gun to protect ourselves and our children? We have not done so. It is my fundamental belief that if a new civil war erupts, it is because we have never truly healed from the wounds of the last one nor from the harms that preceded and followed it. We must rally the nation now. But this time cannot be a call to take up arms but rather must be one to open our hearts. It can't be a call rooted in fear but one rooted in empathy. This is, in fact, a moment to Defund Fear and to turn away from a culture of policing, prisons, and punishment.

This book is about how we got here and how we can move forward together into a safer future, by rejecting the politics and practices of fear and by embracing a politics and practice of care and compassion.

This moment is so full of heartache and pain. But perhaps we can take solace in the words of the twelfth-century Persian poet Rumi, who wrote, "You have to keep breaking your heart until it opens."

DEFUND FEAR

US vs. THEM

June 2014

My family was out of town visiting relatives when someone broke into our house. I had received a call from our alarm company, but we'd had false alarms so often, like the Boy Who Cried Wolf, that I no longer knew whether to believe it or not. This time, however, it was for real.

We came home to find a window smashed, broken glass everywhere. It wasn't just any window in the house, either, but the window in the room shared by my two small daughters, who were two and four years old at the time. And it wasn't just any window in their room: it was the one right above the girls' bed. Glass had shattered all over the spot where my tiny, amazing, and precious daughters sleep at night. There might be worse nightmares for a parent, but this was up there.

What if we had been home?

Isn't that the horrifying thought that every parent has in this situation? It certainly was mine, and it got stuck on repeat as I set about cleaning up the mess. I collected the shards in a doubled-up paper bag. I had to be careful not to cut myself. The glass was jagged and sharp everywhere. One of the pieces was larger than my hand, and heavy, easily big enough to cause permanent if not fatal damage. It made a clanking sound when I dropped it in the bag with the rest. I picked up the next piece off my daughter's pillow.

It took me back to one of the first moments I ever held my older daughter. She was born one day shy of being premature and weighed

1

less than six pounds. Her skin bunched up at the knees and elbows as if to say, *I wasn't ready to come out! I'm still growing!* My wife had just gone through a thirty-nine-hour labor and was sleeping, deservedly so, while I held the tiny baby girl, in awe and in tears.

So much could have gone wrong. The United States has the worst rate of deaths from childbirth- and pregnancy-related complications in the developed world, and (across all levels of wealth and education) women of color—like my wife—are several times more likely to die than white women, due to racial and cultural bias in healthcare.[1] In America, premature delivery and low birthweight affect over 20 percent of children, the second-highest rate among developed nations, and the likelihood that a baby won't make it to their first birthday is also higher than in most similarly situated countries. This is because of our fragmented healthcare system and widespread poverty exacerbated by our weak social safety net.[2]

With my newborn daughter curled neatly across my chest, I had never felt so connected to life, nor the fragility of it. Overnight, an immense responsibility had settled on my shoulders. That's the deal when you make the choice to be a parent, right? You're supposed to keep them safe. It's the implicit promise:

We brought you into this world; we should keep you safe.

By the time the attempted break-in happened, my daughters had become sound sleepers—my wife and I joke that we had a second child mostly so the first one would stop waking us up in the middle of the night by crawling into bed with us, and in fact this has worked great since the girls started sleeping in the same bed. They sleep so deeply, their mass of curly hair intertwined, that they probably wouldn't wake until the brick was coming through the window, the shards of glass scattering over them.

If we had been home, what would the person robbing our house have done? What would have happened to my daughters?

As it was, we were all unsettled by the possibility that someone would even try to break in. For years my daughters refused to go downstairs on their own, and even now, years later, they won't linger. Even though the threat was averted before real harm was done, there was still trauma.

The girls had a hard time comprehending why anyone would want to take our stuff. I found myself trying to explain that sometimes people do the wrong thing for reasons that may make sense to them. The person who broke into our house may have had kids themselves that they were trying to feed. I thought of an incident that happened to me in 2002, during law school, while I was studying and doing internships in Buenos Aires: a kid younger than I was tried to rob me by waving a small knife at me. I had jumped out of the way of his knife and run across the street. For a fleeting moment, I considered myself brave. In hindsight, it was almost certainly this kid's fear and inexperience that saved me. He was probably fourteen or fifteen. Maybe he was a bit older: being malnourished doesn't help with your growth. He was so thin. Things were rough in Argentina. He was likely among the seven out of ten Argentine children who found themselves in poverty at that time.[3] The country was in the throes of a second Great Depression. Between 1974 and 1990, per capita income had fallen 20 percent and prices of goods increased by a staggering factor of 20 billion, followed by another economic downturn between 1998 and 2002.[4] In protests all over the country, people demanded work and social assistance.

That kid who pulled a knife on me saw me as a privileged foreigner. In *my* mind, he and I were so not different. He was also me. I saw myself on the side of those who were protesting. I had slept in the street outside of government buildings in Buenos Aires to protest for food aid, as part of the volunteer work I was doing. I volunteered with a group of unemployed workers striking for social assistance and with families fighting police violence. But the reality was—the kid who tried to rob me probably didn't have a choice about sleeping outside as I had. It was hard to blame him.

When I tried to explain the break-in to my daughters, I didn't want to demonize people I didn't know, but I wanted my kids to feel safe again.

My theories about safety were tested in that moment. And then they were confirmed. Here's the thing: the true threat in this story was not the would-be burglary, but the stuff in the margins—a fragmented health-care system with a racial bias, the radical wealth inequality that causes widespread poverty. Both are the calculated outcomes of a system that prioritizes profit over humanity, for the benefit of a powerful few.

Believe me, I understand the desire to keep your home and family safe. I want my family to be safe as much as you do. But safe from whom and from what? Who are the most dangerous threats to your family? Are they people in faraway lands, in the "inner cities," or people right next door? Are they people you know, from within your country, your community, or even within your family? And what really constitutes the worst threat to your family? Is it really crime? Or is it facing eviction because you can't make rent? Is it frequent hospital visits because you live near an oil refinery and your child has asthma, or because the water you drink is no longer safe? These daily realities are sometimes described as "cultural, political, and socioeconomic dynamics." But they are as real as your heartbeat. Decades of funneling money toward a punishment dragnet, instead of investing in a real social safety net, means that one lost job, one healthcare crisis, one traffic stop can be the end of a secure life. This is true whether you live in Oakland, New Orleans, Flint, or anywhere in between.

Powerful entities conceal the most pervasive and persistent harms, instead scapegoating and dehumanizing entire communities, calling them thieves and thugs, welfare queens and wastrels. When we allow those architects of anxiety to distract us from the real threats, we decrease our societal capacity to hold them—and their policies and institutions—accountable for the things that actually threaten and harm us.

My vision for a comprehensive model of safety for America is informed by my life and work in Oakland, California. Since 2013 I've been the executive director of the Ella Baker Center for Human Rights, which promotes investment in community well-being and safety, but I would argue that there is no greater motivation for making America a safer place than raising two children, perhaps especially those who represent a trifecta of vulnerability: being young, female, and brown. At this point in my life and my work, I feel the urgent need to find new and surer paths to safety for my family and for yours.

For the purposes of argument and clarity, in this book I use *safety* both in the sense of physical integrity, in the sense of not being harmed, as well as in the sense of *security*: do I have a roof over my head, do I have a job that pays me enough, can I start a family if I am young, can I retire if I am old? We can't divorce notions of security from safety. People feel at ease only if they are both safe and secure. You can't feel at ease, even if you have great wealth, if you are worried for your physical safety. And you can't feel at ease if you are physically safe but don't have enough to eat, don't have shelter, don't have access to healthcare. This is why the Universal Declaration of Human Rights recognizes both civil and political rights but also economic, social, and cultural rights.

In terms of crime rates, Oakland, like much of the nation, has gotten much safer since I was a kid. I was born in 1977, just before the huge prison-building boom spread like wildfire from California across the nation, an illusory promise of safety expressed in bricks and mortar, in concrete and wire. Yet despite the abrupt drop in crime, things seem much less safe now, not just in Oakland but across the country. All I seem to think about now is safety. Yes, this is undoubtedly in part because I not only no longer have the blissful ignorance of a kid, I now have kids of my own. But my kids seem much more anxious than I was at their age. I talk to other parents and they say the same thing: not only are they more concerned about safety than they can ever remember being, they also notice that their children are anxious about threats to their safety in ways they never remember being.

Some will say that humans do not aspire to safety; we aspire to greatness. Psychologist Abraham Maslow put safety near the bottom of his famous pyramid of needs, right after having enough food and warmth and sleep to literally stay alive—all the unglamorous foundational stuff humans require before getting to the cool, advanced stuff, like accomplishments, prestige, or enlightenment. In other words: safety is merely a prerequisite for the stuff we really long for and aspire to, stuff like having amazing relationships and doing meaningful work in the world.

But when I talk with people about how safe they feel, right in this moment, or in their life in general, the responses are visceral, powerful, clear. Parents full of anguish about their child's well-being every time that child leaves the house. Women who have been held down, hands clapped over their mouths to keep their screams from being heard, who fear going out alone after dark, or fear the reprisals if they speak out about it. People who fled violence in their home country, found shelter in America, and now must carry papers with them everywhere, in case of random interrogations by immigration officers. Queer kids who get tortured and hurt by straighter kids. Whether online or in real life, the general climate seems more dangerous, more toxic, more divided and vengeful and violent.

Not to mention the threat of losing one's home, or needing medical care but not being able to afford it, and the looming prospect of financial collapse. Terrorists. Toxins in our water, food, air. The climate: For two years in a row, wildfires engulfed entire towns just outside the Bay Area, keeping our kids home from school, as thick smoke blanketed Oakland. Each time I travel across country it feels like I am dodging another major calamity: a polar vortex, a hurricane, wildfires. The new normal.

A general sense of unease grips the country. We feel legitimately unsafe because the threats are many, and most of us are already stretched to our limits, coping as best we can, perilously close to the edge. I would say that right now, in America, we very much want to feel safe. I think I can legitimately claim that in America, safety has become a primary aspiration.

FROM ANXIETY TO AUTHORITARIANISM

Unfortunately, threats both real and imagined can also be used to manipulate us. It turns out that invoking safety—which inevitably means invoking *threats* to our safety—is an effective way to trigger automatic, irrational anxiety responses. The mere whiff of danger whips people up into a state of panic and sends us into an automatic "fight or flight" response, because our brains are finely tuned threat-detection devices. As humans evolved, those who recognized and avoided mortally dangerous things were the ones who survived to pass on their genes. We are literally wired to pay attention to any hint of danger—and those threat-detection-and-analysis processes in our brain happen mostly unconsciously and automatically, without the input of our rational brains. This makes us super susceptible to inflammatory rhetoric that magnifies uncertainties, risks, and threats.

"Politicians, journalists, advocacy groups, and marketers continue to blow dangers out of proportion for votes, ratings, donations, and profits," writes Barry Glassner, the sociologist whose 1999 bestseller *The Culture of Fear* has been reprinted and updated for the Donald Trump era.[5] When people in power trigger anxieties and then promise a plan for safety, many are likely to embrace that plan. No matter the consequences.

Against the drumbeat of constant news coverage about active shooters, terrorist threats, and jobs taken by foreigners, the stage was set for an authoritarian strongman who promised to bring everything back under control. *To protect our jobs, our wealth. To protect our way of life. To keep our homes and families safe. To make America great again.* People were desperate for safety and security, and the strongman offered it at bargain prices.

The rise of fascism often occurs when great expectations have been smashed to bits. It thrives under conditions of economic inequality, where the gulf between haves and have-nots is deep and wide. It was when the American Dream had shattered for so many that we were most susceptible to the rise of a strongman who promised to return us to bygone bucolic eras.

Connecting the dots between capitalism, inequality, and the politics of hatred, the economist Umair Haque writes:

> What do people do as hardship begins to bite—especially those who expected comfortable, easy lives? They become reactionary, lashing out violently. They seek safety in the arms of demagogues. . . . It's the once prosperous but now imploded middle which turns on the classes,

ethnicities, groups, below it. The people who expected and felt entitled to lives of safety and security and stability—who anticipated being at the top of a tidy little hierarchy, the boss of this or that, the chieftain of that or this, but now find themselves adrift and unmoored in a collapsing society, powerless. . . . They turn to those who promise them just that superiority, by turning on those below them. . . . supremacy and dominion over the weak, the despised, and the impure.[6]

Our generalized anxiety and economic insecurity in the United States coincides with a demographic shift: the browning of America—a near future in which white folks will no longer be the majority. It has already impacted every city across the country and is now impacting small towns and rural areas as well. For many who were previously the majority—white folks—this constitutes the ultimate threat, the dissolution of the long-standing social order, a kind of existential unraveling.

As john a. powell, legal scholar and author of *Racing to Justice*, notes: "When a person embraces the concept of supremacy, then equality is viewed as an attack. They believe this country belongs to whites. They believe that having people of color in positions of respect and power is un-American. There has been no greater example of a threat to their belief system than President Obama. It was not Obama's policies they objected to, but his humanity."[7] powell has written extensively about what he calls "othering"—systemic exclusion, and the rise of ethnic-nationalist and authoritarian politics.

Many of those who voted for Trump in 2016 did so because he conjured the image of a strongman who would protect them from threats, whether they were white voters fearing a loss of control over democracy in the wake of President Obama, or financially insecure voters feeling threatened by immigrants and globalization. Trump used people's fears to fuel marginalization and dehumanization. He promised to lock up or lock out all those he claims have caused the downfall of the nation. Fascism makes Us vs. Them—the politics of hatred—into national policy.

Jason Stanley, professor of philosophy at Yale University and author of *How Fascism Works*, explains: "The story is typically that a once-great society has been destroyed . . . and you make the dominant group feel angry and resentful about the loss of their status and power. . . . The goal is to make them feel like victims, to make them feel like they've lost something and that the thing they've lost has been taken from them by a specific enemy, usually some minority out-group or some opposing nation."[8]

The Us vs. Them story goes this way: "they" threaten "our" way of life. "Our" successes are dependent on "their" losses in a zero-sum game. "They" cannot be trusted because "they" always lie. "They" are always to blame; "they" are dangerous and must be contained. "They" are often described using language like *primitives, savages, apes, vermin, infestations,* and *animals.* And using the language of disease: *contagions, germs, pollutants, infections.*

Today one of the chief threats supposedly comes from Muslims, who are deemed threatening to the American way of life, and from our borders to the south: "They're bringing drugs. They're bringing crime. They're rapists." "We're not going to have a country" if things don't change, warns Donald Trump, ranting on about dangerous caravans of thousands of drug-dealing, murderous aliens closing in on our borders.

But the roots of Us vs. Them long pre-date the Trump administration, going way back to the beginning of our nation. Native Americans were called savages and heathens who threatened Christian values. The Us vs. Them narrative facilitated the demonization of indigenous peoples and their removal from what would become the United States. Black people were not seen as people but as wild beasts to be tamed, as property. The Japanese Americans in 1942 were called the "yellow peril." The media of the time called them "sneaky," "treacherous," even "lecherous."[9] Political cartoons characterized the "Japs" as monkeys and as men who lusted after white women—stereotypes long applied to men of African descent as well. With language like "fatherless" and "wolf packs," the social scientists who created the "superpredator" theory generated appeal for policies that targeted and dehumanized those youth, overwhelmingly boys of color. In the United States there has been a kind of musical chairs of oppression, where powerful white men set the tune and the last marginalized group standing is the first one scapegoated.

The rails upon which the train wreck of Trump's administration is riding were laid by bipartisan predecessors going back decades. In the 1960s, as crime rates were on the rise, President Lyndon Johnson articulated one possible way to achieve public safety: to wage a war on poverty that focused on increasing investment in communities still ravaged by decades of disinvestment and Jim Crow segregation. But interest in that strategy was short-lived. Richard Nixon campaigned and won election with a focus on "law and order." In so doing, he helped launch what would become the largest prison-building boom in human history. Year after year, politicians of all stripes, especially at the state and local levels, fought to demonstrate who could come up with the toughest "tough-on-crime" attitudes, the longest sentences. Decades later, despite the failure of this approach, the law and order politics of Bill Clinton and the "superpredator" rants of Hillary Clinton kept hammering the same notes.

Elsewhere, other similarly situated Western democracies chose to make deep investments in social welfare. Today they have much lower crime rates *and* lesser levels of inequality. They invested in a social safety net, while we invested in a punishment dragnet. They invested in care, while we invested in fear. If lawmakers in the US had taken the path of investment to address issues most salient in poor communities, rather than dehumanization, deprivation, and punishment, it would have benefited everyone. We might now be in an era of less harm and greater prosperity for all. Instead, America invested in systemic dehumanization, a choice that had the backing of Democrats and Republicans alike. Of all the bipartisan strategies of the past fifty years, this may be most responsible for the rise of fascism in the United States today.

FROM FEAR TO CARE

There are two ways to think about safety. There is a fear-based way and a care-based way. For the fear-based model, architects of anxiety cultivate and stoke the Us vs. Them mindset, based on a zero-sum mentality around the idea of scarcity: that there is not enough of the good stuff for everyone. This fundamental divisive and adversarial mindset extends beyond politics (Democrats vs. Republicans), race (white vs. people of color), and class (rich vs. poor) into most institutions. In housing we have landlords vs. tenants; in the law we have plaintiffs vs. defendants; in healthcare we have insurance companies vs. patients. When we set two sides against each other, rather than acknowledging they are components of one whole, the result is always less safety for both sides. Two-sided is always lopsided.

The fear-based model defines safety only in terms of being free from *crime* and *criminals*, which is limited, and limiting. This has resulted in a criminal legal system that holds close to seven million adult Americans in jail, in prison, on parole, or on probation.[10] With or without literal incarceration, millions of people are cast as "others" and "bad guys," including many children who have a hard time focusing in school, many people whose anxiety and depression pushes them to consider suicide, and many people who miss a paycheck, get evicted, and have to sleep in their car.

Over the past nearly 250 years, the architects of anxiety have leveraged the Us vs. Them mentality and the zero-sum mindset to select

groups of people to scapegoat, based on their race and ethnic backgrounds, their belief systems, their abilities, or sexual and gender identities. These architects then created and steadily expanded what I call
the "framework of fear," which employs four key elements: systematic
deprivation, extensive and expensive systematic suspicion, cruel punishment, and often-permanent isolation from the rest of society. According
to the architects of anxiety, this framework should keep us safe. In fact, it
has done just the opposite.

The framework of fear has led to the traumatization of not just the
individuals who have been targeted, dehumanized, and criminalized, but
the traumatization of entire communities, unfathomable devastation that
will be decades in the reckoning. Because trauma is as much a chief *cause*
of violence, as the *result* of violence, our current fear-based system par-
adoxically generates more harm than it prevents, in never-ending cycles
of trauma.

Perhaps most importantly, our democracy itself has been compro-
mised by the climate of scarcity, suspicion, and dehumanization that the
fear-based model of safety has propagated. In the last forty years, Americans' participation in associations and civic organizations has declined,
while trust in government and satisfaction with democracy have plum-
meted. That coincides with our economic inequality growing by leaps and
bounds as well as the explosion of our prison population. Those things
can't be disconnected. The fear-based framework threatens not just our
agency as individuals but also our democracy as a collective.

This moment presents the opportunity to take action toward a culture of caring and policies of caring. We need to shift our focus from
individual criminals and what qualifies as crimes, to what actually causes
most suffering and damage. The real threats to our safety are not coming
from a few bad apples; they simultaneously come from powerful massive
institutions and "-isms" (racism, capitalism) that we all have a hand in
upholding and from within our own families and communities.

The care-based approach asks how do we care for ourselves and each
other so that we all can be safe. A new care-based model of safety can
replace deprivation, suspicion, punishment, and isolation with resources,
relationships, accountability, and participation, what taken together I call
a "culture of care."

A culture of care prevents many harms from happening in the first
place, by investing in a social safety net (resources), by building our capacity to relate to one another across difference (relationships), and by increasing our sense of "skin in the game" with more vibrant engagement

on every level, within neighborhoods, and within our democracy and society (participation).

Care-based safety also means we address harms in ways that hold people accountable and bring about healing (accountability). It means we tackle all the harms going unaddressed by the current system: on the one end of the spectrum, the really huge harms perpetrated by huge institutions, over history, and on the other end of the spectrum, the interpersonal harms like domestic violence and sexual abuse.

In terms of paying for the shift from fear to care, where there's a will, there's a way. Much of the billions that we currently spend each year on the framework of fear, incarceration in particular, can be reallocated and used as investments in programs and services that keep us healthy and safe. A tax on the rich that merely matches the rate that was in place from 1913 until 1982 (70 percent for the highest tax bracket) also can be partially allocated to a social safety net that benefits everyone.[11]

Despite all the talk about "public safety," there is very little *public* in our safety system. We need holistic solutions to ensure our communities have the safety and security necessary to thrive. A care-based model of safety includes all the things that create and maintain stability and well-being on the level of the individual, the family, the community. The care-based approach gives all young people the opportunity to become responsible, engaged, and empathetic participants in their communities. Safety is not tied to our capacity to watch our neighbors, but rather based on our capacity to truly look out for one another. There is no doubt in my mind that we are safer when we act together than when we let ourselves be divided.

PART I

THE UNSAFE WORLD

WHO AND WHAT HARMS US

Oakland, 1977

I was a week old when my parents moved to Oakland and I sometimes say it was a week too late, because that's how much I love Oakland. My mom and dad had actually planned to arrive in Oakland prior to my being born. They had found a house they wanted to buy, but the fact that the windows were boarded up after having been shot out gave them pause. It turned out that the woman who owned the house had gone through a contentious divorce with her husband, and afterwards he'd returned in his anger and pain and shot through the windows. After some deliberation, my parents decided it would be a safe home for us. They took down the boarded-up, broken windows and put in new ones.

In the late 1970s, Oakland offered a working-class, mixed-race couple—my white mom, a schoolteacher, and my dad, a black shipyard worker—the chance to buy their own home. Leaving San Francisco because of already rising housing prices, the two of them could buy and own a home in Oakland, but not in nearby San Leandro, which put racially restrictive covenants into place in 1947 that limited property sales to "members of the Caucasian race"[1] and didn't begin integrating until the 1980s.[2]

In fact Oakland, which had birthed the Black Panther movement in 1966, was in some ways a bastion of black power in those years. The poet Ishmael Reed, who moved to the city just after us, in 1979, writes in his ode to Oakland, *Blues City*: "From the seventies through the nineties, there was a black mayor, a black symphony conductor, a black museum head, black members of the black city council, and, in Robert Maynard, the only black publisher of a major news daily."[3] According to Reed, this changed around 1999 with urban renewal plans, which aimed to bring ten thousand new residents to the downtown area (often called the 10K plan) . . . at the expense of many existing residents who found themselves priced out. After that, "the only reminder of the power that blacks once yielded might be the names of black leaders etched on downtown buildings, the post office, a courthouse, and the federal and state buildings, like monuments to now-forgotten pharaohs covered by desert sand."[4]

Historian Robert Self, in *American Babylon*, his political history of Oakland, extends the tradition of black influence back further, to the late 1940s: "Indeed, the generation of black activists before the Panthers developed strategies, alliances, and sources of power that profoundly shaped the political terrain."[5] In Self's analysis, postwar Oakland embodied the political tensions between urban black power politics and white suburban homeowner conservatism that continued over decades, up to this day. Aiming to attract businesses and investment, mostly-white, more suburban property owners relied on racial segregation, rising property values, and low taxation, which benefited suburban areas to the detriment of urban areas. This is why Self invokes "Babylon" in his title—the city in the Bible that crumbled under the weight of materialism, oppression, and corruption.

It was true that by the time I was a teenager, in the early 1990s, Babylon seemed to be falling. There weren't a ton of things for young people to be doing in Oakland. Most if not all of the places where young black people were having fun seemed to get shut down. For a while, people would meet up in the parking lot of the Eastmont Mall for "sideshows," where they flirted and mingled and showed off by doing donuts or figure eights in their cars.

Eastmont Mall had opened in 1970 on the site of a Chevrolet factory that had shut down. Turning it from a place of solid employment into a temple of consumerism at a time when black unemployment in Oakland was sky-high must have just seemed like a slap in the face to residents. In his 2016 book on the housing crisis, *Evicted*, Princeton sociology professor Matthew Desmond describes the same dynamics at work in Milwaukee and in cities across the country.

> Between 1979 and 1983, Milwaukee's manufacturing sector lost more jobs than during the Great Depression—about 56,000 of them. The city where virtually everyone had a job in the postwar years saw its

unemployment rate climb into the double digits. Those who found new work in the emerging service sector took a pay cut. As one historian noted, "Machinists in the old Allis-Chalmers plant earned at least $11.60 an hour; clerks in the shopping center that replaced much of that plant in 1987 earned $5.23." These economic transformations—which were happening in cities across America—devastated Milwaukee's black workers, half of whom held manufacturing jobs. When plants closed, they tended to close in the inner city, where black Milwaukeeans lived. The black poverty rate rose to 28 percent in 1980. By 1990, it had climbed to 42 percent.[6]

Though it was never wildly popular, Oakland's Eastmont Mall stayed above water through the 1980s, but became a desolate spot by the 1990s, following a huge drop in the disposable incomes of local residents. At one time the mall had a movie theater, but the movies always seemed to be at least a year old, and then that was closed down. Then the police shut down the sideshow in the Eastmont parking lot. They set up a police substation there instead.

For a brief period when I was a teen, a highlight of every summer was the "Festival at the Lake," alongside Lake Merritt, between Children's Fairyland and the boathouse. Lake Merritt, sometimes referred to as "the jewel of Oakland," is part of the heart and soul of the city. A "necklace of lights"—more than four thousand tiny bulbs strung between the posts of regular streetlights—glitter around the lake's 3.4-mile perimeter. It seemed like the weather always managed to be perfect during the festival, and I would feel like I was in the Fresh Prince's "Summertime" video. Apparently too many other young black people felt the same. After a few years, the festival was cancelled and signs were put up all around the lake: "No cruising." Oakland is a beautiful place but that beauty somehow seemed off limits to most black people, especially its youth.

The city's reputation for being riddled with crime, especially youth crime, especially crimes of black youth, plagued us. By the 1990s, youth crime rates were actually declining in Oakland, but increased news coverage—especially of criminal youth, the so-called "superpredators," the much-hyped tsunami of crime among urban black and brown youth that never came to pass—made it seem like the opposite was true. That was why events like the sideshow and the festival were shut down. Even as our crime rates dropped, the public perception of crime heightened and media coverage of crime kept increasing. In 1976 Oakland was the city with the highest juvenile arrest rate, but the following thirty years of records reveal a "massive, consistent drop" in crimes by youth, with felonies down 66 percent, homicides down 64 percent, rapes down 96 percent, property offenses down 81 percent, and misdemeanors down 93 percent by 2006.[7]

2010

Our loan was "underwater." About thirty years after my parents first moved to Oakland, my dad had helped me buy a house. On the application, we listed our race as African American and we could find only one lender that would lend to us. We took a subprime loan. We purchased the home in 2005 and by 2010, like so many other Americans, we found ourselves on the brink of losing our home.

I called our mortgage company repeatedly. I requested a loan modification and sent them all of the documents they asked for. It seemed that each time they finally got around to reviewing my application, they required new pay stubs and other documents. Nothing seemed to be working. As much as I love Oakland, I was tired and frustrated. I told my dad I was about to give up. He said, "You fight for other people, you better fight for our house." So I connected with organizers at Causa Justa::Just Cause. We held a "save our house party" and asked people to sign on to a letter urging Litton Loan Servicing, the company that serviced our home loan, to give us a loan modification. Through a little research, I found that Litton Loan Servicing was owned by Goldman Sachs. We decided to go to Goldman Sachs headquarters in the Bay Area and stage a protest.

Given it was the middle of a weekday, the protest wound up being just four people. The four of us stood on a remote corner of an immense plaza in front of what must have been a hundred-story skyscraper. The building seemed to extend endlessly into the sky, mocking our makeshift protest signs no matter how high we held them. People who worked in the financial district of downtown San Francisco passed on their way to lunch without looking up from their phones. Protests in San Francisco can grow massive and ours was less than tiny. This was a protest for *my* home, but even I felt discouraged. Organizers have a saying: "Organizing/direct action gets the goods." But our four-person picket just wasn't getting it. I decided to deliver our demand letter and then give up and grab some lunch.

Our demand letter asked that whoever oversaw Litton Loan Servicing within Goldman Sachs should pressure their subsidiary to give us a loan modification. We made the march across the plaza, signs in hand. We were greeted by a security guard who opened one of the large glass double doors just enough to hear what I had to say. He promised to make sure that the letter got to the "right people." By that, I was sure he meant the garbage collectors. Discouraged, my wife and I headed off to find lunch.

Although our protest was unsuccessful, Robbie, an organizer with Just Cause, had managed to get a direct line, maybe even the cellphone, for the vice president at Litton Loan Servicing. While we were staging our four-person protest, dozens of other people were flooding the vice president's office with calls. Incredibly, my cellphone rang as my wife and I were on our way to get something to eat. It was the vice president at Litton Loan Servicing. This was the first time anyone had ever *called me* from Litton Loan Servicing and it was the first time anyone had not feigned amnesia as they told me which documents were still missing from my application. He said they had received numerous letters and calls about our application. The vice president went on to say that we would have a loan modification contract by the close of business Tuesday. And sure enough, it arrived.

This was how I managed to avoid the fate that befell so many African American families. Other members of my family were not so fortunate. They lost their homes as a result of that same housing crisis. It caused the greatest loss of black wealth in decades.[8] There were identifiable people who knew the mortgages they bundled and sold were shams: their security overrated and their value inflated. These individuals committed fraud and helped precipitate the largest recession since the Great Depression. They were never really held accountable. Instead, many of them received multimillion-dollar bonuses. As the economy went into free fall, taxpayer dollars went to prop up their institutions and to pay for their executives' golden parachutes.

Losing your home is right up there among the top threats to any family's safety. I'd say it's a bigger threat than the majority of crime. In America we are unsafe at work, at school, even inside our own homes, and almost none of those harms count as "crime." The stories are all around us.

October 2000

At just six years old the child knew no one was supposed to find out about the whippings their mother gave out, or how their twelve-year-old cousin molested them, or, most of all, that they were not like the other boys. In subtle ways and obvious ways, they were told they weren't legitimate, weren't loveable, should be ashamed of themselves.

When they got a little older they lived with Grandma Dianne, who didn't seem to mind that they played with Barbies and dollhouses and coloring books instead of footballs and BB guns. But then their mother came back and things got worse again. Grandma Dianne had a bathtub, and they held their head underwater and opened their mouth and breathed it in, fighting to drown. *I will never make anyone happy.* It was only the first of many suicide attempts.

"For the next few weeks I tried to suffocate myself with pillows but the black hole in my chest hurts too much each time. I can't do it. I tied belts around my neck hoping that I will choke in my sleep. When I awake, I feel disappointed and silly. I untie the belt and start getting dressed for school."[9]

Yet they survived. Having been rejected by their family, having endured abuse and rape, and having done sex work to survive, they ultimately embraced a gender identity of their own creation and a new name—Lovemme Corazón. At the age of nineteen they wrote a memoir. "It was important to me to publish this memoir before I was dead. As trans women of color, we all hear about the murders and the mutilations and the abuse and I just knew that I was coming into this age range where that would be happening."[10] The book was titled *Trauma Queen.*

Discrimination and violence against transgender people, trans women of color most of all, is increasing. In 2017, advocates tracked at least twenty-nine deaths of transgender people in the United States due to fatal violence, the most ever recorded, up from twenty-three in 2016. Abuse, assault, and even murder at the hands of family or other intimates is common. Bri Golec was twenty-two when her father murdered her because of her gender identity.[11]

"Some of the cases involve clear antitransgender bias. In others, the victim's transgender status may have put them at risk in other ways, such as forcing them into unemployment, poverty, homelessness and/or survival sex work," notes the organization Human Rights Campaign.

Many trans folk face rejection and renunciation from their families and end up homeless as a result. More than one in ten trans people are evicted from their homes because of their gender identity, and one in five transgender people experience homelessness at some point during their life.[12] Keisha Jenkins was rejected by her family and took to the streets in Philadelphia as a sex worker, which many trans women do to survive. She was murdered in 2015, at the age of twenty-two.[13]

"Without money of my own, I had no doctors, no hormones, no surgeries. Without money of my own, I had no independence, no control over my life and my body. No one *person* forced me or my friends into the sex trade; we were groomed by an entire system that failed us and a society that refused to see us," writes trans author and television host

Janet Mock in her memoir, *Redefining Realness.* "No one cared about or accounted for us. We were disposable, and we knew that. So we used the resources we had—our bodies—to navigate this failed state, doing dirty, dangerous work that increased our risk of HIV/AIDS, criminalization, and violence."[14]

If that criminalization leads to incarceration, transgender people face deeply traumatic experiences. Being in a public restroom with people who feel you don't belong there is frightening and dangerous enough; being stuck within a prison population that feels you don't belong is horrific and sometimes lethal.

The violence that trans women in particular face is often not accounted for because society blames them for deception. According to Janet Mock: "As long as trans women are seen as less desirable, illegitimate, devalued women, then men will continue to frame their attraction to us as secret, shameful, and stigmatized, limiting their sexual interactions with trans women to pornography and prostitution. And if a trans woman believes that the only way she can share intimate space with a man is through secret hookups or transactions, she will be led to engage in risky sexual behaviors that make her more vulnerable to criminalization, disease, and violence; she will be led to coddle a man who takes out his frustrations about his sexuality on her with his fists; she will be led to question whether she's worthy enough to protect herself . . . she will be led to believe that she . . . must remain hidden."[15]

For the trans community, especially trans women of color, there's a long way to go to achieving safety.

June 1985

"I'm no one. I'm broken, moldy bread, throwaway trash, great leper."[16]

Peyton Goddard was ten years old when her special education teacher reported that Peyton had become unmanageable. In past years the San Diego Unified School District had provided an aide to support Peyton staying in the classroom, but new policies no longer provided aides for individual students.

Since age three, Peyton had been deemed unfit to attend regular classes with "normal" kids because of her inability to speak or control her physical movements or bodily functions. Her label was "autistic and severely mentally retarded." But Peyton's behavior changed radically for the worse over the course of 1984 and 1985: she was wetting herself, sleeping poorly, and, worst of all, lapsing into near total silence after a decade of speech therapy.

What Peyton didn't tell anyone until fifteen years later, when she was twenty-five years old, after a breakthrough communications strategy called facilitated communication (FC) finally enabled her to make herself understood, was that "my aunt asked me to not ever tell that her beloved son molested me." Two of her cousins had begun regularly abusing Peyton in 1984.

At age ten, Peyton was placed in a private developmental treatment facility called the Marshall Institute. Her mother was dismayed by the "detached and mechanical" nature of the program there: adults robotically repeating commands for rote mindless tasks and declaring Peyton "noncompliant."

"Years too late," writes Peyton's mother Dianne in the memoir she and Peyton created together in 2012, "I will realize that these private 'schools' are actually institutions—big boxes that for seven hours a day lock children in and parents out."

But Peyton's parents had almost exhausted the options available to them. Peyton remained in the class for second-lowest functioning children for four years, with children increasingly younger than herself and fifteen changes in teachers (most without valid certification); she was steadily "disintegrating," according to her mother. In the journal where her mother tracked Peyton's behaviors, the entry from July 1988 read: "Sleepy, lethargic, begs to go to bed, no stamina, spacey, out of it, headache, stomachache, no appetite . . . NO TALKING. Destructive . . . hurting self . . . aggression." Doctors placed her on antiseizure, mood-stabilizing and anti-anxiety medications, but nothing made much of a difference.

Until the FC, Peyton couldn't tell anyone about what was really happening to her at the Marshall Institute: how an employee named Dan repeatedly took her—and other girls—into a closet and molested them.

Peyton's next placement, beginning in 1989, was no better. She endured restraints, isolation, and further abuse. Years later the staff psychologist, Dr. Frank Dalbo, would be imprisoned for multiple life sentences for participating in a child pornography ring and molesting children.

Finally, on March 21, 1997, when Peyton was twenty-two, her life changed dramatically when FC technology finally enabled her to share her experiences. One of the first things she typed to her shocked parents were the words: "i am intlgent."[17]

Dr. Robert A. Friedman, who worked with Peyton and her parents for more than a decade to process and heal her—and their—trauma, wrote: "Imagine how frustrating it must have been for Peyton to hear and comprehend conversations around her and about her for decades with no way of letting people know she understood. Imagine how dehumanizing it must have been for people to treat her as 'retarded' and without meaningful thought because she had no way of letting the world know that her brain was in fact perceiving and understanding everything going on around her. Now imagine this little girl, who could barely communicate, being emotionally, physically and sexually abused by school personnel and caretakers that her parents trusted to keep her safe."[18]

People with intellectual disabilities are sexually assaulted at a rate seven times higher than those without disabilities, according to a 2018 NPR report based on unpublished Justice Department data. And that's probably conservative. People with intellectual disabilities are more likely to be assaulted during the daytime and by someone they know. For a woman without disabilities, 24 percent of the time the person who rapes her is a stranger, but for a woman with an intellectual disability, assault by a stranger occurs in fewer than 14 percent of cases.[19]

"Predators target people with intellectual disabilities because they know they are easily manipulated and will have difficulty testifying later," so few of the crimes are ever reported, let alone prosecuted or healed.[20] Survivors are often revictimized multiple times, as Peyton was.

She has since become an advocate for inclusion and neurodiversity, writing and presenting at universities and conferences because "children are dying in institutions and at the hands of parents who have lost sight of their child's value."[21]

Rather than setting them up to thrive, our society has created an environment where people with all kinds of disabilities face constant threats to their safety.

New Year's Eve, any year

She prepared herself mentally for the extra dose of harassment that always occurred on this night of the year. Any day of the year customers felt entitled to flirt, to remark about parts of her body, to say what kind of lover Latinx women like her were. But on New Year's Eve, the night nearly everyone was wasted and no one wanted to be alone, she was even more likely to be followed, cornered, and groped. It made her feel so dirty when she returned home that she didn't want her children to touch her. It was a degradation and humiliation that no amount of extra tips could make up for.

"It would be hard to design a context more conducive to being sexually harassed" than restaurant work, writes Ursula Buffay (a pseudonym—like most victims of harassment, she prefers to remain anonymous).[22] Employees are "a dime a dozen," easily hired and fired. Many employees are young, often working their first jobs, and unaware of their rights. Many are immigrants, who are especially vulnerable if their first language isn't English or their citizenship status is uncertain. Sexualized behavior is considered an accepted part of the culture, between lewd "kitchen talk" and the expectation that pleasing customers means being deferential and sexy, with some places even requiring employees to dress suggestively.

Ursula comments: "[Our] defining quality is incompetence/disposability. Women who work in restaurants are exponentially more likely to feel acutely disposable in any given context, I think because we so often start in semi-ornamental roles."[23]

Many of the jobs rely on tips. Federal law permits employers to pay tipped workers a subminimum wage of $2.13 per hour. The result is "an environment in which a majority female workforce must please and curry favor with customers to earn a living," according to a report by the organization my wife leads, Restaurant Opportunities Centers United (ROC). "Depending on customers' tips for wages discourages workers who might otherwise stand up for their rights and report unwanted sexual behaviors."[24] Women and gender-nonconforming staff experience the highest rates of harassment, "scary" and "unwanted" sexual behavior, but men in the industry also regularly experience it.

A female server told ROC: "The most disturbing experience I've had was with a guest that started with looks and glances that turned into remarks. Then he started to come into every shift that I worked and when I talked to my manager about it, they basically turned the other way, told me I was imagining it, that it wasn't really happening, or the customer is always right. Then the customer somehow got my number and I was getting text messages with sexual jokes. He would leave me messages at three or four in the morning and he was drunk and would be, like, "Where are you, why aren't you here?' And the culmination of all of this was one night, I was riding my bike home and he was following me. So I had to change my route and go to another place that wasn't mine because I didn't want him to know where I lived."[25]

"None of this is about sex, necessarily—it's all about power," says another woman who works as a bartender. "They're not necessarily getting off on it; they're showing us how small and insignificant we are and how our bodies aren't ours. Even our ear canals aren't ours."[26]

She continues: "I always found myself in these situations where I'd be like, 'This guy says things and it's disgusting and I don't like it, but is it going to make my life worse if I talk to somebody about it and they talk to him about it? Is that going to make my job harder, is that going to make me less safe, am I going to endure abuse of a different kind?' You're constantly weighing out these things. Not even what battle is worth fighting, but what battle is safe to fight?"[27]

The ROC report notes: "It is critical to contextualize the concept of 'living with' sexual harassment in the workplace as something different than *consent*. Our survey and focus group results show that most workers either ignore or put up with harassing behaviors because they fear they will be penalized through loss of income from tips, unfavorable shifts, public humiliation, or even job loss."[28]

Tragically, restaurant workers have to tolerate even more abuse from coworkers and managers than they do from customers. Many women, Ursula among them, find this even more challenging: "It's the harassment from bosses and superiors—the guys who decide whether you'll be waiting on three tables or ten tonight, who can choose to help you or chastise you if the hosts stick you with five two tops all at once and you get behind, the guys you see every fucking day—that really gets to you."[29]

Although there are a few cases of restaurant workers who came forward and won lawsuits against their employers—like the sixteen-year-old girl repeatedly raped by her manager at the Chipotle where she worked in Houston—the great majority of incidents don't get reported.[30] Reporting workplace assault can negatively impact later job prospects and have potential immigration consequences. Of the 23,570 charges made to the Equal Employment Opportunity Commission between 1997 and 2015, only 364 cases were litigated, according to research in the *Nation*.[31]

Anxiety, fear, and depression are common among workers. Because a restaurant job is often someone's first job, their whole working lives are colored by the experience. The trauma leads many women to expect and tolerate a lifetime of sexual harassment in other work environments. Given how vital it is to have a stable job in the United States—where your healthcare, your capacity to find a home, and increasingly your capacity to find your kids a decent school are all dependent on it—it's imperative that our workplaces are safe spaces.

CRIMES VS. HARMS

From among all the things that actually harm us, a mere sliver is addressed by our criminal legal system—a term I prefer over "criminal justice system," because calling it a "justice system" inaccurately links it to justice, as well as fairness, healing, and safety. Generally speaking, the criminal legal system works great at protecting you and keeping you safe if you are a rich white man. It protects your power, prestige, and property, while debunking, debasing, and diminishing those who would question your right to those privileges. If you're anyone else, it's a lot less likely to result in justice, let alone healing.

Much of what people go to prison for are actions that were not harmful to anyone. Meanwhile, there are so many actions that are actually harmful that we're not taking into account because the current criminal legal system can't or won't apply to them. In focusing so much on crimes—defined as what's against the law—we have increasingly lost sight of morality.

What about the pharmaceutical industry's denial of the addictive nature of opioids? The shamefully greedy behavior of massive corporations, making a handful of "banksters" and shareholders richer and richer at the expense of the other 99 percent of humans? What about predatory lenders who caused almost one million people to lose their homes? What about contaminating an entire city's water supply? There's a serious disconnect between actual harm and crimes. The worst perpetrators of harm, in terms of number of people hurt, tend to be mighty and complex institutions like corporations and governments; the very entities least likely to be held accountable within the current "justice" system.

The Enron Corporation was an American energy company whose executives hid billions of dollars of debt to inflate its value. In October 2001, this accounting fraud was revealed. The episode made it more likely that white-collar crime would be prosecuted. Yet high-status defendants generally can afford very talented, very expensive legal defense teams, and there are scant resources for white-collar crime enforcement. Even the Internal Revenue Service has had its budget significantly cut over the past decade. As I write, Trump's former campaign manager Paul Manafort has received a forty-seven-month sentence for crimes going back decades that include witness tampering, which carries a maximum penalty of ten years. Outraged, public defenders tweeted that their clients received more time for theft of a hundred dollars than Manafort had for his much more sinister crimes.

If they are even imposed, punishments for corporate crimes are typically fees that are absorbed as a cost of doing business and passed on to consumers, and many crimes, from investment fraud to insider trading and price fixing, are not even prosecuted. The very idea of a "loophole" in the law is foreign to ordinary people, but it is standard business practice for the rich and powerful. It means ultrarich companies like Amazon can pay zero federal taxes.

Belief systems that have to do with the allocation of power—such as capitalism and sexism and racism—are also the cause of immense harm. In fact, they probably bear the lion's share of the blame for suffering on this planet. But how do you hold a belief system accountable? Occasionally the criminal legal system can punish individual racists, sexists, or capitalists for harms they have caused (Bernie Madoff comes to mind).[32] Targeting and weeding out individuals doesn't change a toxic society-wide culture, whether we're talking about white supremacy, male supremacy, or the supremacy of profit over people.

At the same time, much of the harm that feels most devastating to us individually is intimate and interpersonal: every hurt that gets dealt, inside families, between friends, between parents and offspring, between lovers. We know that the prevalence of child abuse and domestic violence is far wider than what is reflected by reported offenses, let alone arrests or prosecutions. Harms that happen inside the home are largely invisible, occurring in a private sphere behind closed doors. Regardless of whether it happens at home or elsewhere, psychological and emotional abuse almost never gets "counted," yet causes tremendous damage. The more #MeToo stories we hear about harassment and abuse in the workplace, the more we understand how vulnerable women are—and how they risk retaliation, humiliation, and termination when they do come forward. Some of the most popular stories have been about celebrities, but we know that the reach of sexual harassment and abuse is at least as extensive in everyday occupations.

This is why I focus on "harms" rather than on "crimes." I'm not proposing that we do away with laws and the criminal legal system. I just don't think they're how we generate safety.

In their book *Beyond Criminology*, the British social scientists Paddy Hillyard and Steve Tombs call for a broader, more inclusive account of the causes of suffering and harm than the limited framework of "crime" can allow. Among their many critiques of "crime," they list a host of ways in which the concept maintains existing power dynamics:

> First, although the criminal law has the potential to capture some of the collective harmful events perpetuated in the suites and in corridors of state, it largely ignores these activities and focus on individual acts and behaviours on the streets. . . . Second, by its focus on the individual, the social structures which lead to harmful events—such as poverty, social

deprivation and the growing inequalities between rich and poor—can be ignored. Third, the crime control industry is now a powerful force in its own right; it has a vested interest in defining events as crime. Fourth, politicians use crime to mobilise support both for their own ends and to maintain electoral support for their parties.[33]

Shifting the focus away from crimes to harms means we address actions, policies, and behaviors that are most harmful. Shifting focus would mean we look at psychological harms, environmental damages, and social and economic suffering. Finally, it means that when it comes time to address harms and keep further harms from happening, we involve far more bodies than merely the law; the players include academics, policymakers, community leaders, historians and community members who are involved in arenas such as public health, epidemiology, urban planning, and social policy.

REAL HARMS: CAPITALISM

In a system where the primary directive is to promote profit, human well-being will always lose out. Inequality is not an accident, but a central defining feature of capitalism. Capital doesn't naturally trickle down like part of a watershed—as we were promised for much of the second half of the twentieth century. Instead what it naturally does is amass and concentrate in the hands of a few. Umair Haque does a great job of explaining the logic of wealth concentration in simple language:

> Mom-and-pop capitalism is a healthy and beautiful thing, an economy of a million little shops, bakeries, artisans—but it takes only a modest attachment to a profit motive. But thanks to the rise of massive, global speculation, only aggressive quarterly profit-maximization was allowed. CEO earnings were hitched to share prices, and your share price only went up if your earnings did, relentlessly, illogically, crazily, every single quarter, instead of stabilizing at a happy, gentle amount—and so the only way left, in the end, to achieve it, was to build titanic monopolies, which could squeeze people for every dime. Once the economy had Macy's, JC Penney, K-Mart, Toys-R-Us and Sears. Now it has Walmart. The story was repeated across every single industry.[34]

Part of that squeezing for every dime involves jobs, of course, which have been moved around as companies look for the least amount of friction with profit, whether that has meant reduced occupational health and safety standards, or reduced rights and wages for workers. Now, in the newest iterations of squeezing, we have automation and machine learning, along with increasing numbers of companies hiring for temporary, flexible, precarious jobs, instead of offering full-time, long-term employment with benefits. It is not so much that employers don't want stable employees as much as they don't want to reciprocate with stable hours and benefits. Why would they, if they can get away without doing so, increasing their all-important profit margins?

Meanwhile, the so-called "financialization" of the economy has meant that speculation—investment banks and hedge funds and others making money "placing bets with each other"[35]—has grown to be a huge part of the economy, dwarfing the real economy, where things that we actually need are invented and made and maintained, whether that means food, or the cure for cancer, or a new energy grid.

In 2008, all the house of cards speculation upon speculation led to a collapse, which is exactly what houses of cards inevitably do. And when that happened, it took down everyone. Except that the wealthy few at the top had the resources and connections to allow them to recover; and the rest of us did not, further undermining our already insecure positions. Almost three-quarters of the US population has under a thousand dollars in savings, and a third has zero.[36] This is why a single unexpected expense like a hospital visit or a car repair is all it takes for someone not to make rent. Then they're forced to make impossible choices: to stop refilling the prescription they depend on, or stop paying utilities, or to skip subway fare and risk getting caught. Even then, it's often not enough.

An economy that is geared toward speculation with a focus on short-term profits is like a hungry beast that must be fed. A wealthy few refuse to compromise the expansion of their profit, regardless of the impacts on natural resources and the planet, as well as on the majority of people's well-being and security. When the US government (among others) chose to spend its money propping up this system, it declared the need to make cuts elsewhere. Outside the United States, this gets called "austerity." Inside the US, some have referred to this framework as "Reaganomics," but its basic tenets have been enthusiastically endorsed by Democratic and Republican presidents alike. Healthcare, support in old age, the environment, renewable energy—the government decided the budgets for these items could be slashed. Let corporations make money providing them—a.k.a. "privatization."

That's where we are today in this stage of capitalism. Most resources are going to a tiny minority of people, while the majority can't get their basic needs met. Millions of Americans face a constant struggle to keep a roof over their heads. Four evictions are filed every minute.[37] Many Americans go without healthcare, given the absence of universal coverage in the US. As a result, the US ranks poorly on key indicators of health, such as infant mortality, and a hundred thousand Americans die each year from causes that were preventable with medical treatment.[38] This is really a violation of common decency and dignity, as well as a source of instability and insecurity for us as a society. There's a tendency to think of capitalism as inevitable, but like all human systems it was created by humans and there are other options.

And because wealth equals power, its concentration in the hands of a few means our democracy is getting replaced by oligarchy—the rule of the few. They make new laws and bankroll elected officials to protect their interests, while geting rid of all the laws and politicians who impinge on those interests. Pretty much everyone else is left suffering and plagued by anxiety about how much worse things can get.

REAL HARMS: WHITE SUPREMACY

There is no end to the harm done to people of color by the long prevailing belief system that holds that white people are superior to others and deserve more—more resources, more second chances, more of the credit, more starring roles, and on and on; more of all the good stuff. People of color, by contrast, get more of things like asthma, freeways through our neighborhoods, bad mortgages, and jail time.

"When over decades the police, courts, banks, buses, schools, and other parts of society regularly ignore, exploit, and harm non-White people, yet these incidents are largely denied, excused, or blamed on the victims, without being properly investigated, before disappearing from the accounts of history or the evening news or the general discourse: this is white supremacy. The humanity of certain people is made invisible," writes Native American Edgar Villanueva in his 2018 critique of philanthropy, *Decolonizing Wealth*.[39]

There are the explicit examples of racism that should be shocking but instead are unrelenting. If you are a parent of black children, your confidence in their safety is likely to be at an all-time low as videos and stories of police misconduct and violence emerge on what seems like a daily basis.

Antwon Rose was seventeen. Cameron Tillman was fourteen. Tamir Rice was twelve. Aiyana Jones was seven. "I see mothers bury their sons / I want my mom to never feel that pain / I am confused and afraid," Antwon had written in a poem that ended up being recited at his funeral.

White supremacy also manifests more subtly in behavior and attitudes, for example as white people believing that everything they've achieved is based on merit and hard work, as opposed to a system set up to make their success more likely, which leads to absurd ideas like "playing the race card" or "reverse racism," or defensiveness and woundedness when white privilege is mentioned—a phenomenon known as "white fragility," a term coined by the whiteness studies professor Robin DiAngelo.[40]

Most intractable of all is white supremacy that has been baked into institutions, culture, and policies, also known as structural racism, which has served to deprive people of color of resources over the entire history of the United States. These implicit forms of white supremacy are nefarious, making it hard to assign responsibility.

Even when we consider certain threats that appear to apply to everyone indiscriminately, such as nuclear war, natural disasters—people of color almost always bear more harm. Hurricane Katrina is an example. The lack of adequate evacuation plans and disaster relief caused the worst and most immediate hurt to low-income people, people with disabilities, and black people. According to Mimi Kim of Creative Interventions: "People with less power can be more vulnerable to violence because they are an easier target, because they are less likely to be protected, more likely to be blamed, and [have fewer] places to go to get help."[41]

The harm done is physical, economic, psychological. Physical: this includes police brutality and hate crimes, and the bias in medical care that has thousands of black women suffering, as legendary tennis player Serena Williams did during the birth of her daughter, because doctors don't listen to them or trust them to know their situation; and the diseases and chronic conditions caused by having highways, waste treatment facilities, and toxin-spewing factories disproportionately located in communities of color.[42] Economic: such as the disparity in wealth between white people and people of color, which doesn't correlate to education or income level; or the disproportionate impacts of job losses and mortgage crises upon people of color. Finally, psychological: the depression and trauma that come from all the other harms compounded, and from feeling the whole world, or at least the whole nation, considers you as less worthy.

Writing about the historic and intergenerational trauma that Native Americans experience, Edgar Villanueva writes: "Imagine that all your family and friends and community members regularly experienced traumatic events: upheaval, violence, rape, brainwashing, homelessness, forced marches, criminalization, denigration, and death, over hundreds of years." He goes on, and the next passage can be applied just as much to all people of color: "Imagine the trauma of this experience has been reinforced by government policies, economic systems and social norms that have systematically denied your people access to safety, mobility, resources, food, education, dignity, and positive reflections of themselves. Repeated and ongoing violation, exploitation, and deprivation have a deep, lasting traumatic impact not just at the individual level—but on whole populations, tribes and nations."[43]

REAL HARMS: PATRIARCHY

Like white supremacy, patriarchy is a system of domination, this one claiming the superiority of the father (the straight male) and granting him more of all the influential and desirable stuff: more political leadership and moral authority, and more rights to own resources and property. As a result, women must get less of the power and the resources. The patriarchy also disadvantages or outright harms anyone who does not conform to heterosexuality or gender norms.

Like white supremacy, patriarchy is baked into our culture. It is in the air we breathe. In the United States, boys are told: *be a man, grow some balls, don't be a pussy, stop crying, stop with the tears, pick yourself up, don't let nobody disrespect you, be cool, bros come before hoes, don't let your woman run your life, get laid.* I heard variations of these things growing up. Patriarchy imposes such strict norms and expectations on the male experience that men also suffer under it even as they experience the benefits of it. Men are socialized to not display most emotions, to be tough, to resolve conflict through fighting, to see women and all things feminine as less than, to take what they want, to see gender as binary, and to see people who are queer, gender nonconforming, homosexual as being less than and also perverse.

At one point, a friend invited me to join a men's reading group. The group was reading *The Will to Change: Men, Masculinity, and Love* by feminist author bell hooks. Her words undid something inside me: "Patriarchy demands of men that they become and remain emotional cripples. Since it is a system that denies men full access to their freedom of will, it is difficult for any man of any class to rebel against patriarchy."[44] Reading this book was the first time I felt free of the compulsion to adopt male bravado.

The harms caused by the patriarchal system are as far-reaching as those caused by white supremacy, going back generations and leaving a legacy of intergenerational trauma, while also causing fresh hurts on a daily basis. When our country was founded, women had no formal legal existence apart from their husbands. Women could not sign contracts or own wealth except under limited circumstances. They could not even be the guardians of their own children if their husbands died.[45] Patriarchy's impacts are different across races because of white supremacy, leading to particularly great harm to women of color and queer folks of color. Colonizers targeted "two-spirit" people and nonpatriarchal tribes with special intensity. Black women were the property of their white male owners, and the law actually sanctioned their rape by making the children of black women the property of white men. While many of those laws were eventually overturned, we still have patriarchal laws in place. As Senator Kamala Harris asked Brett Kavanaugh during his Supreme Court nomination hearings, pressing him on his stance on abortion rights: "Can you think of any laws that give government the power to make decisions about the male body?"[46]

There are numerous ways that male privilege and male supremacy show up in our institutions and personal lives, such as the persistent gap in pay between men and women who perform the exact same work. This is often stated as women earning an average of eighty cents per dollar that a man earns (which doesn't reflect much lower wages for black and Latina women) but may be as extreme as forty-nine cents, according to new research that compares earnings over a lifetime of employment.[47] Generally, women are more likely to occupy low-wage jobs, they face more barriers to getting hired or promoted, and when a given field becomes dominated by women, the pay in that field drops.[48] Trans women are often excluded from the formal economy altogether.[49]

Money matters when it comes to what women have to put up with in the workplace and with domestic violence. When women have economic power within a relationship, they are less likely to face violence in their homes. Research has found that "decreases in the wage gap reduce violence against women, consistent with a household bargaining model."[50] This helps us understand a key feature of domestic violence. It is not so much about anger as it is about domination and control. Men are so-cialized to believe that they should never be in a position subordinate to women.

As domestic violence counselor Michael Paymar describes in *Violent No More*, "Men are taught to suppress most of their emotions with the exception of anger, which then tends to build more anger and tends to lead toward violence" in their relationships with women in their homes and workplaces.[51] Our failure to address domestic violence as a public health crisis is an indication of the pervasive reach of patriarchy in modern society.

The year 2018 witnessed many women coming forward with allegations of sexual abuse and harassment by men in the workplace, events often referred to by the hashtag #MeToo. Although the #MeToo movement had already been around for years—and in founder Tarana Burke's original vision it focused on harassment and violence in homes and in communities, not just the workplace—#MeToo gained national attention after allegations of sexual misconduct by Hollywood producer Harvey Weinstein launched an industry-wide reckoning. Revelations about the number of people that helped him facilitate and cover for his abuse shows how engrained in the culture of Hollywood these acts were. The indicators were all around us and in plain sight for decades. As just one example, cultural critic John DeVore describes how Woody Allen's 1979 film *Manhattan*—about a forty-two-year-old man dating a seventeen-year-old girl—has been preserved by the Library of Congress's National Film Registry for its "cultural significance." If it's culturally significant, DeVore quips, it's because it is a "creepy message from the past that explains our awful present . . . the movie is about a society that doesn't protect young women."[52]

Although the most recent highly publicized #MeToo stories involved celebrities in media, government, and entertainment, it is clear that sexual misconduct is as extensive, if not more extensive, in less glamorous occupations. A related campaign called Time's Up (#TimesUp) was launched to move beyond sharing the stories and names involved in misconduct, toward creating workplaces that offer equity, dignity, and safety to all kinds of women.

My wife supports restaurant workers in getting fairer wages and better conditions. She took twenty waitresses to a conference organized by Michelle Obama called the United States of Women. At the beginning of the conference, when they were asked if they had been harassed on the job, almost all of the women said no. By the end of the conference, after doing a training, being in a safe space, and hearing the stories of other women, *all twenty women* revealed a story of being sexually harassed, assaulted, or raped on the job. Some of them were appalled that they had not previously recognized it as such. Many women have been brought up to be "polite" or "people-pleasing," or to believe that their bodies and their selves have value only when others take pleasure in them. This makes saying "no" to unwanted advances more complex and often more difficult. Not to mention the fact that women's livelihood in the restaurant industry is dependent on their tips.

Incidents of harassment, abuse, and outright violence against women, queer folk, and gender-nonconforming people are under-reported and under-prosecuted, which further reflects the scope of patriarchy's power.

REAL HARMS: VIOLENCE

I've noted the abrupt drop in violent crimes in the US over the past few decades. That's true, but it doesn't mean we don't still have a problem with violence in this country. America still has an extremely high rate of homicides and a fairly high rate of violent crime relative to most of the developed world. For example, US homicide rates in 2016 were about five times higher than in other high-income countries like Germany, Canada, and Japan.[53]

There's the threat of an "active shooter," some dangerous individual with a gun intending to kill multiple people in a confined public space. Between 2000 and 2008, there was one of these kinds of events every other month, or approximately five per year.[54] But from 2009 to 2012, the frequency of these horrifying events increased to sixteen per year, more than one per month. Of all those events between 2000 and 2012, 29 percent of them happened in schools.[55] Although school shootings receive a lot of media attention, we should be more alarmed by how many American children are dying from gun violence generally. A 2019 study in the *American Journal of Medicine* found that guns kill more kids than on-duty police and active military personnel combined.[56]

As for nonlethal violence, in 2014 more than seven hundred thousand children experienced maltreatment, a term that includes physical abuse, sexual abuse, educational neglect, medical neglect, emotional abuse and mistreatment—with those aged zero to three experiencing the highest rates.[57] The majority of children in the US, nearly 55 percent, have experienced some form of physical assault.[58] Experts say that any exposure to violence increases the chances that a young person will experience additional forms of violence and the probability of future victimization.[59]

According to the 2014 National Crime Victim Survey, at least three hundred thousand children are sexually abused each year in the US. Roughly one in ten boys and one in five girls experience sexual abuse before the age of eighteen.[60] Children who have developmental disabilities are sexually abused at nearly twice the rate of nondisabled children.[61] According to generationFIVE, which aims to end sexual abuse of children within five generations, "an estimated 60 million people have survived child sexual abuse and are living with its often-devastating consequences."[62]

On the other side of the age spectrum, there are threats to the safety of our elders. Elders and all those who are frail or sick have diminished capacity to fight or run when threatened with violence. Between one million and three million Americans aged sixty-five or older have been injured or exploited by someone on whom they rely for protection or care.[63] Women also face a heightened threat of violence. Nearly one in five, or almost twenty-three million women in the United States have been raped in their lifetime.[64] More than three-quarters of female victims of rape (78.7 percent) were first raped before they were twenty-five years old and 40 percent were raped before the age of eighteen.[65]

For everyone, vulnerability increases if a person is female, queer, disabled, darker-skinned, or recognizable as belonging to a religion or culture that gets targeted in hate crimes. Violence against the LGBTQ community, especially transgender people, has been rising.[66] We know that young people of color are at particular risk for brutality and harm at the hands of the police. Evidence of this takes the form not just of the videos shot by bystanders, with which we've become more and more familiar; there are also records of stop-and-frisks, car dashcam and bodycam video footage, police reports, and court records. All these reveal pervasive police intimidation and verbal and physical abuse that disproportionately is directed at people of color, especially young men of color.

Experts say most of the above statistics don't represent the true scope of the problem, because these are just *reported* cases. There are many instances of violence that don't get accounted for, let alone find healing, in the current system. Many of these occur in our homes, behind closed doors.

All the real harms described in the previous sections—including capitalism—cause much of the violence. In her book *Until We Reckon,*

Danielle Sered, who leads the organization Common Justice, working to support survivors of violence, writes: "Most violence is not just a matter of individual pathology—it is created. Poverty drives violence. Inequity drives violence. Lack of opportunity drives violence. Shame and isolation drive violence. And . . . violence drives violence."[67]

The greatest barrier to ending violence, writes Sered, is "the story we tell about violence that precludes the development and expansion of new strategies."[68]

REAL HARMS: TRAUMA

Having had the sense of safety stolen from us during a traumatic event causes trauma. All of the above forms of harm either directly constitute a traumatic event, as with violence, or are the root cause of traumatic events, like the loss of a home due to predatory lenders operating in our capitalist system. The trauma we are left with then manifests as physical disease, mental illness, substance abuse, broken families and communities, poverty, social instability, and crime.

It is a tragic irony that our current public safety model—the framework of fear—actually causes us harm and makes us less safe because of the role of trauma and cycles of trauma. Trauma is not just the consequence of harm, but also its cause. It is people who are traumatized who commit most violent crimes. Hurt people hurt people, goes the saying, or, "No one enters violence for the first time by committing it," as Sered has written.[69]

"[The behaviors of traumatized people] are not the result of moral failings or signs of lack of willpower or bad character—they are caused by actual changes in the brain," notes Bessel van der Kolk, one of the world's top clinicians and researchers of trauma.[70] Once it's been traumatized, the brain can easily be retriggered, reading normal circumstances as dangerous. Especially if we are repeatedly exposed to traumatic things, the activity patterns of our brain are shaped by this, thanks to neuroplasticity (the process described as "neurons that fire together, wire together"). We experience the same physical sensations of the past trauma in the present, and ordinary occurrences and conflicts are experienced through a lens of trauma. This makes it harder to see and imagine various possibilities: the only outcomes that seem possible are echoes of what happened to us when we were traumatized. Because of this, of how trauma limits imagination and cognitive functioning, trauma makes it more likely that people will repeat the same mistakes or patterns.

Trauma limits possibilities and the imagination because it locks the brain into certain assumptions about what is likely to happen. Even if the trauma is inherited, passed down your blood lineage, or even if it has been experienced by a group you belong to, perhaps professionally or socially—trauma can have this effect. All of that trauma builds up not just inside individuals, but in our neighborhoods, communities, and institutions, inside of our country. Unaddressed trauma at that scale is a recipe for long-term disaster.

THE ARCHITECTS OF ANXIETY

When we say things like the real harms are coming from multinational corporations and an economic system that privileges profit over living beings, as well as beliefs in the superiority of white people and straight men, it can sound as though the responsibility doesn't fall on individuals. That's not the case. There are indeed people we need to hold responsible. I've called them the "architects of anxiety": the fearmongers and the fear-profiters, people who manipulate our anxieties so that we buy what they want us to buy and vote the way they want us to vote. Another much vaster group consists of the fear foot soldiers—all those who buy into the rhetoric of scarcity and blame, and act upon it by furthering fear and hate. Finally, there are all of us who remain silent while the atmosphere of fear is stoked and maintained. Fear-bystanders: we also bear responsibility.

When elected officials and powerful corporate interests invoke our fears, we should consider what harms they are drawing attention away from, like sleight-of-hand magicians. In March 2019, Joe Balash, assistant secretary for land and minerals management, addressed fossil fuel industry leaders:

> One of the things that I have found absolutely thrilling in working for this administration is the president has a knack for keeping the attention of the media and the public focused somewhere else while we do all the work that needs to be done on behalf of the American people.[71]

What Balash calls the president's "knack" for capturing attention are Trump's "smoke and mirrors": his fervid descriptions of the threat posed by legions of dangerous hordes of immigrants storming our borders. When Balash refers to "the American people," what he actually means the extremely wealthy white men who benefit from unfettered drilling and production of fossil fuels.

Almost every time that powerful interests mention "bad guys" and outsiders who pose a threat to our families, our homes, and our way of life, we should pause and consider the implications, rather than allow a knee-jerk reaction based on our unconscious brain's hypervigilance to threats. With their smoke and mirrors, whom might the architects of anxiety be trying to protect, and whom are they blaming and scapegoating?

CHAPTER 2

THE FRAMEWORK OF FEAR

June 2018

The concrete floors and chain-link enclosures remind me of an animal shelter—the *pound*, as we used to say when I was growing up—where rows of stray dogs huddled in the corners of the cages: wary, whining, awaiting their fate. Except *these* cells are filled with children . . . hundreds of children. The smallest of them are just toddlers, under the age of five. Some of them are so young they haven't even learned to talk yet.

Some are lined up, maybe about to experience some of the mere two hours they are let out of their cages per day. Twenty-two hours of every day they are confined.[1] Others lie on the concrete floors, hardly covered by blankets that look like giant pieces of tin foil. One stares despondently, neck craned up at a TV that seems like it was hung for a giraffe to watch. They are not allowed to be touched, to be held, or to have the things that might bring them comfort. Worst of all, they are denied contact with the adults who love them. Most of the adults here in this place are guards, armed men. At eye level for one child are kneecaps covered in military-grade armor. Another child comes up as high as the waistband where a gun is holstered.

The similarity to the animal shelter may well be intentional: Donald Trump has referred to these children's families as "infestations" and as "animals." It's part of his communications strategy, which draws false links between undocumented residents and crime, to garner support among people who fear that immigrants threaten the American way of life.[2] The idea behind his zero-tolerance policy and the family separations was to deter migrant families from crossing the southwest border. Many of the families had been seeking asylum from violence in a Central American country. When the parents were taken and charged with the federal misdemeanor of entering the United States illegally, their children were "rendered unaccompanied" and put in these cages.

There is hysterical crying. There is a child wailing, interrupted only by her gasps for air. Other times her breathing and cries come together in one word: *Maaaamaaaa*. There is another child who calls repeatedly for Papa. *Papa. Papaaaaa!* There's a Spanish-speaking child saying "Can I go with my aunt? At least can I go with my aunt? I want her to come." She pleads with them; she knows her aunt's phone number by heart.

The footage of the children who are reunited with their parents, months later, is almost as chilling. Their parents weep and embrace them and rock them in their arms, but the children's faces are frozen, uncertain. One video shows a devastated mother whose toddler continues to crawl away from her as she tries to talk to him and pick him up.[3] Mental health experts had predicted this. This is the impact of trauma: disassociation, numbing, but also: trouble with speaking and eating, stomachaches, headaches, mood swings, tantrums. The brains and immune systems of these children have been indelibly altered by prolonged stress responses, the chemicals that flooded their little brains and didn't let up for months.

Reports of these detention centers filled us with outrage, horror, despair. Some of us traveled to protest outside of the facilities or in the halls of government. Others of us changed the channel and tried to forget the images, already overwhelmed enough with our own struggles.

When did we become a nation that would treat people, let alone children, as less than human? Unfortunately, the answer is: since the beginning of the country itself. Although Donald Trump has ramped up the policies, the practice of dehumanization and isolation didn't start under his administration.

January 25, 1996
"They are not just gangs of kids anymore. They are often the kinds of kids that are called 'superpredators.' No conscience, no empathy. We can talk about why they ended up that way but first we have to bring them to heel."[4] First Lady Hillary Clinton was addressing a crowd at a college in New Hampshire, campaigning for her husband's reelection and praising the "tough-on-crime" bill he'd signed two years prior. Indeed, she used the expression "bring them to heel," which is generally used to refer to dogs.

The "superpredator" turned out to be a myth, but it was a myth that would have terrible consequences, resulting in the caging and suffering of thousands of American children.

Neither Clinton coined the term. It came from a neoconservative Princeton professor named John DiIulio, describing a "new breed" of juvenile delinquent. Superpredators were "remorseless" and "fatherless"; they were "stone cold" and they had "absolutely no respect for human life and no sense of the future."[5] They sounded not quite human—they traveled in "wolf packs." The language invoked an instinctual response, evoking how, to keep safe from wild animals, humans have built fences, walls, and cages for thousands of years. And the new breed of predator sounded not-white as well: DiIulio published openly on the "black crime problem."[6]

DiIulio was joined by conservative political scientist James Wilson, creator of the "broken windows" theory of crime, which claimed that minor crimes such as graffiti and broken windows were forerunners of major crimes. His theory led to systematic roundups of people accused of petty crimes, and to ubiquitous stop-and-frisk policies. Wilson predicted that by the year 2000, there would be thirty-thousand more young muggers and thieves on the streets.[7] Not to be outdone, DiIulio predicted that "by the year 2010, there will be approximately 270,000 more juvenile super-predators on the streets than there were in 1990."[8] Neither theory went through the rigorous peer-review process that social science requires for theories to gain traction.[9]

Nevertheless, politicians and policymakers, including Mr. and Mrs. Clinton, believed them. Previously offered protection from the state for their vulnerability, youth in the justice system were now treated as predatory. By the end of the 1990s, all but three states had passed laws that mandated that youth would be tried in adult criminal court for certain crimes.[10] Sentences were expanded, in several thousands of instances resulting in sentences of life without parole. Many thousands of children were caged and subjected to solitary confinement, many are in cells to this day: according to 2015 data from the Department of Justice, "70,000 young people are held daily in state, county, private and federal juvenile residential facilities across the United States . . . the use of isolation, including solitary confinement, in these facilities is widespread."[11]

"Solitary exacerbates underlying mental illness and with kids can have a deeper effect on mental health and physical health. It's not surprising that kids would attempt suicide in solitary," commented Maria McFarland, deputy US program director of Human Rights Watch, upon releasing a 2014 report on the prosecution of children as adults in Florida.[12] In fact, the Department of Justice has found that more than 60 percent of children at juvenile facilities who committed suicide had a history of being held in isolation.[13] Approximately half of suicide victims were in solitary at the time of their death.[14] Others commit suicide after their release, as in the case of Kalief Browder, the sixteen-year-old boy who spent two years in isolation on Rikers Island after being accused of stealing a backpack, and who had unsuccessfully attempted suicide while incarcerated. Two years after his release, living at home with his mother, Kalief hanged himself.[15]

Describing the situation in a California youth prison located in Preston, researcher Selena Teji wrote:

> In 2003, after a string of suicides and horrendous use of force by staff on wards, the Prison Law Office filed a suit condemning the CYA [California Youth Authority] for unconstitutional and egregious conditions in the facilities, and demanding reform. National experts described Preston's lock-up units as "deplorable" and dungeon-like. Filthy, dank rooms covered with vermin, blood, and feces where youths were confined for 23-hours a day, with one hour spent shackled in a cage for exercise.[16]

The lasting trauma not only to those children, but also to their mothers and other loved ones, to their communities, is beyond calculation, and still unfolding.

The crime wave that was to be perpetrated by "superpredators" never materialized, and instead crime rates fell abruptly. In 2012, as part of the Supreme Court case *Miller v. Alabama*, a group of forty-six academics wrote to the court: "The fear of an impending generation of superpredators proved to be unfounded. Empirical research that has analyzed the increase in violent crime during the early- to mid-1990s and its subsequent decline demonstrates that the juvenile superpredator was a myth and the predictions of future youth violence were baseless."[17] Among those who filed the brief were DiIulio and Wilson.[18]

February 1942

"I was going to be four years old and have a party. But instead I was taken away with my family. Was I kicking and screaming? Was I stoic and mute? I don't remember. My mind could not contain the chaos, would not retain the memory."[19] The little boy had a beloved dog that would bark when he rang his tricycle bell. He begged to take the dog. It was not allowed. *Only What We Could Carry* was the rule.

The boy was one of 120,000 Japanese Americans, approximately half of them children, who were evacuated from their homes and incarcerated for the next four years, following President Franklin D. Roosevelt's Executive Order 9066, justified as a "military necessity" to protect against domestic espionage and sabotage, in the wake of Japan's attack on Pearl Harbor.[20] Only later did the truth come out: "Our government had in its possession proof that not one Japanese American, citizen or not, had engaged in espionage, not one had committed any act of sabotage."[21]

"I knew that we were so-called Japanese. I thought I was American too, but I found out I wasn't. I thought I was American the whole time," says Bill Shishima, who was eleven years old when he was incarcerated.[22]

First, Japanese Americans were registered and labeled, then transported via buses and trains to "assembly centers" (off-season or unused fairgrounds, racetracks, stockyards), where they were held, like animals, until they were moved to bleak, remote prison camps, surrounded by barbed wire and armed guards. In some cases, family members were separated and placed in different camps. The barracks were bare except for steel cots, a blanket, and an empty sack they filled with straw to make a mattress. They were just like the prisoner of war camps that housed German, Italian, and Japanese POWs.[23]

"I evolved from a robust child to a frequenter of infirmaries in the swampland of Arkansas, the windswept plain of Colorado, beset by infections, diseases, nightmares," wrote another survivor who was a child at the time.[24]

The long-term consequences of internment included psychological damage, increased risk of cardiovascular disease, premature death. And the trauma was not limited to those who were incarcerated: those "who had a parent interned felt the effects of that experience in numerous ways. They are sad and angry about the injustice and attribute a number of negative consequences in their own lives to their parents' internment. These include feelings of low self-esteem, the pressure to assimilate, an accelerated loss of the Japanese culture and language, and experiencing the unexpressed pain of their parents."[25] The children carry the legacy of their parents' incarceration. This is intergenerational trauma at work.

Mid-1920s, month unknown

There was a knock on the door. It was a federal agent saying the girl had to come with him. The girl was just five years old. Ignoring the protests of her parents, he took her to Stewart Indian School near Carson City, Nevada, more than two hundred miles away.

Her daughter Connie Reitman, a Pomo Indian, tells her mother's story. "So my grandmother and my grandfather didn't know where my mom was, and they didn't know how to get ahold of her."[26]

The federal government's compulsory attendance law of 1891 enabled federal officers to forcibly take Native American children from their homes and send them to off-reservation boarding schools.[27] The schools were based on a model of "assimilation through total immersion" developed by an army officer, Richard Pratt, with the Carlisle Industrial Indian School. His motto was "Kill the Indian, save the man." It was the final frontier in the settlers' war against the original inhabitants, after forced removals, violence, disease, and subjugation had failed to eradicate them: kidnapping their children from their communities and indoctrinating them with white, Christian culture.

"At the school, her hair was cut. She was not allowed to talk her language. There was a lot of hunger and abuse," Reitman says. Nine years after being taken, after contracting tuberculosis, the girl was allowed to return to her family on the reservation. "When my mother came home she was not really accepted—ever really accepted—back into the tribal community, because she'd been gone for so long."[28]

Children suffered and died at these schools, far from home, without touching, holding, or talking to the parents and siblings who missed them, without being able to hear them say, "We love you." Despite the damning evidence of an investigation in the 1920s that found that Native children were beaten, malnourished, and forced to do heavy labor (published in the 1928 Meriam Report), and yet another grim report in the 1960s, it wasn't until 1973 that the Indian Child Welfare Act gave Native American parents the legal right to deny their child's placement in the schools.[29]

Hollow Horn, a Native man from Cheyenne River, now approaching the age of seventy, was also taken. "They got us when we were young," he said. "I used to speak my native tongue when I went down there, and I can't even talk now. They beat it out of me. If you spoke your language, they held you down, put a bar of soap in your mouth." He said his boarding school experience broke him. He has been recovering from alcoholism for the last twenty-five years. "I've been in pain ever since. . . . Day in and day out, I go to bed with it," he said.[30]

The lasting trauma of being separated from their homes, families, and culture shows up in health-related, economic, and other life outcomes— Natives have the highest rates of diabetes, heart disease, and asthma among any racial/ethnic group in the US; the unemployment rate among Native Americans is 11 percent (almost double the national rate); and the suicide rate of Native youth is three and a half times higher than the national average.[31]

1823, month unknown

A seven-year-old boy stood on the auction block in Richmond, Virginia. His mother was in the crowd, begging her master not to sell her son. But the boy would fetch a good price. Slaveholders from the Deep South were more desperate for slaves since the abolition of the Atlantic slave trade in 1808, and since the cotton gin, invented in 1794, had allowed the production of cotton to really take off. The prices of enslaved African people had risen. In this period, one in every ten enslaved persons was relocated from the states of the Upper South to the Lower South. They were "sold down the river" into brutally hard labor in the Deep South with no means of staying connected to the families and communities they had known. Slightly over half of them experienced major family separations, meaning children were separated from their parents, or spouses were separated from each other.[32]

The little boy was just at the cusp of his years of highest output too, the ages from eight to fifteen years, according to popular wisdom among slaveholders. Children in these sought-after ages were often bought alone. On the auction blocks, enslaved people were lined up by height, making it even more likely that children would be separated from their parents.

The buyers examined the little boy as though he were livestock, pulling his mouth open to see his teeth, pinching his arms and legs to find out how muscular they were, walking him up and down to detect any lameness, making him bend and stoop. In the end, he was sold to another slave master in Mississippi. His mother followed him to the wharf where he was put on a ship. When the ship launched into the water, his mother was left standing on the wharf, crying. She never saw him again.

The boy's name was Joseph Norris. He was my grandfather's grandfather.

THE MYTH OF THE BAD GUY

These are unrelated yet connected stories. To scapegoat an entire group of people, making them the source of all evil, is to disregard their humanity. And as the United States grew from thirteen colonies to fifty states, this scapegoating made it is easier to justify taking the land and lives of indigenous people and the lives and labor of black people. There is a long tragic through-line, a trail of tears, a legacy of trauma, from stories like my family's to the immigrant families being demonized today. In the name of public safety—*to protect our jobs, our wealth, to protect our way of life, to keep our homes and families safe*—America has been engineering and expanding a model of systematic scapegoating for the past two hundred-plus years.

We recognize the "bad guys"—the *criminals*, the *wolf packs*, the *thugs*—from unending news broadcasts as well as fictional films and television shows that make it all very black and white. These stories magnify violent crimes and street crimes, especially homicides.

Research shows that fear of crime has stayed fairly constant over the past thirty years even as violent crime in America has actually declined precipitously since its height in 1990 to 1991.[33] For murder, arrests dropped from twenty thousand in 1980 to about twelve thousand in 2013. There were some spikes in the homicide rate in 2015 and 2016, yet even in 2016 it was lower than any year from 1965 to 2007.[34]

Yet the fear has persisted. In 1980, about 40 percent of those questioned in Gallup's annual crime survey responded that they were afraid to walk alone in their neighborhood at night; thirty-three years later, despite the dramatic drop in crime rates, it was 37 percent. When asked the question "Is there more crime in your area than there was a year ago, or less?," 37 percent of respondents in 1980 said "more." In 2013, even *more* people said, "there's more crime"—a full 41 percent.[35] In 2016, nearly two-thirds of Americans worried that they or someone in their family would be a victim of crime.[36]

People's feeling of safety does not match with declining crime rates. Sometimes when confronted with this mismatch, researchers point to the role of the media and social media in sensationalizing and publicizing violent crimes. But this is only part of the answer. It's possible the research reflects people's feelings about threats of *harm*, as opposed to crimes strictly defined—and their perception may be perfectly on point given rising inequality, patriarchy, and racism. Additionally, sometimes you don't *feel* safe even if all facts point to the reality of your *being* relatively safe, maybe because you've been hurt before and the trauma lingers and distorts reality, or because you're so encumbered by stress and anxiety that it skews your perception.

Sometimes it's easier to believe your worst enemy is outside prowling the streets, so you don't have to contemplate the enemy within or an incomprehensible- or intractable-seeming source of harm. A series of studies in 2010[37] found this to be true: people attribute exaggerated influence to enemies to compensate for the feeling that the threats to their well-being are less specific and out of their control. Somewhat perversely, the concept of having a specific, clearly definable enemy in mind—one that can be more effectively controlled or at least *understood* than diffuse, harder-to-predict hazards—allows people to believe in a sense of personal control.

This is especially true for those who have less control over their circumstances, and to be poor in America is to have less control over your circumstances. It means emergency room visits rather than meeting a doctor you know at a time you scheduled. It means being unable to escape the smoke from nearby wildfires by taking a weekend trip (something my family did) and instead making do with a donated mask. It means not being able to pay for a car and your car's registration and insurance and suffering increased anxiety each time the police drive by. The less agency you're able to exercise in your life, because of complex, intractable systems, the more likely you are to embrace the idea of an external enemy you can blame.

If we examine statistics on actual violent crimes, the "perpetrator" is only rarely some random "bad guy." Statistically it is likely to be someone we know. Not a "them," not an "other," not a stranger. I call this phenomenon the paradox of proximity: the one most likely to hurt you is someone close to you. For example, 45 percent of male victims of violent crimes knew the person that harmed them in some way, while fully 68 percent of female victims of violent crimes knew the person that harmed them in some way (2009 data).[38] In 2011, 54.3 percent of homicides were people killed by someone they knew (neighbor, friend, boyfriend, etc.), and 24.8 percent of victims were slain by family members. Of the female murder victims in 2011, 36.5 percent were murdered by their husbands or boyfriends.[39] For sexual abuse of children this is overwhelmingly the case: researchers have documented that as many as 90 percent of people who experience sexual abuse under the age of eighteen know the person who abused them. Of these, 34.2 percent were family members of the child, and 58.7 percent were acquaintances. Only 7 percent of people who committed child abuse were strangers to the child they abused.

Looking at acts of terrorism, more than half of those tried in ISIS cases since March 2013 (84 of 156 cases) were born in the US, which refutes the "foreign-born" propaganda used to justify the Muslim ban.[40] In fact, intelligence agencies are increasingly recognizing that white supremacist terrorists are responsible for the greatest number of acts of terrorism within the US. Politicians, by naming a clearly identified external enemy, give the illusion of a solution and control. If we just got rid of those others, we would be safe.

Further, as Danielle Sered notes, there are rarely hard and fast lines between the roles of "perpetrator" and "victim." "Nearly everyone who commits violence has survived it, and few have gotten support to heal. Although people's history of victimization never excuses the harm they cause, it does implicate our society for not having addressed their pain earlier. And just as people who commit violence are not exempt from victimization, many survivors of violence have complex lives, imperfect histories, and even criminal convictions. But just as it would be wrong to excuse people's actions simply because they were previously victimized, it is also wrong to ignore someone's victimization because the person previously broke a law or committed harm."[41]

In accepting the scapegoating of "bad guys," we have decreased our capacity to hold the architects of anxiety accountable for the most serious of harms.

UNPACKING THE FRAMEWORK OF FEAR

After fifteen years of working with families and communities who have been dehumanized and scapegoated, I have identified four key elements of America's current public safety paradigm, the framework of fear: deprivation, suspicion, punishment, and isolation.

DEPRIVATION   When a government seeks to reduce its spending—overall, or in certain arenas in order to allow for more spending in other arenas—it does the opposite of investment: disinvestment. Starting in the late 1960s, there has been a steady decrease in investment in America's social contract—the fundamental agreement that members of a society cooperate in order to achieve basic well-being for all. Instead of relying on the collective—including government—to ensure things like safe roads and bridges, good schools, reliable firefighters and medical professionals, and clean and safe drinking water and air, as well as support in our old age, we increasingly have to fend for ourselves. The programs that support these kinds of basic needs have been deprived of funding, privatized, commodified, and deregulated. This is deprivation at work in a broad context, operating across the board to destabilize all of us regardless of who we are, although decreased investment in the social contract especially hurts disadvantaged people of all colors, including rural white folks.

Then there is deprivation targeted at certain kinds of people: based on the color of someone's skin, on gender, on ethnic background, on a lack of ability, on habits or life experiences that disqualify them from receiving benefits. "Others" are much more likely to be denied services, access, and amenities. I think of Peyton Goddard being shut out of an education, despite her intelligence, until the discovery of the technology that allowed her to communicate.

Systematic deprivation along racial lines is often referred to as structural racism. Between 1983 and 2013, the wealth of the median black household declined 75 percent (from $6,800 to $1,700), and the median Latinx household declined 50 percent (from $4,000 to $2,000). At the same time, wealth for the median white household *increased* 14 percent, from $102,000 to $116,800. Today the median African American family has just 5 percent as much wealth as the median white family.[42]

I will use black lives as my example here, but the experiences of other people of color follow similar trajectories. Among black folks the deprivation—the systematic prevention of wealth-building—goes back to slavery and Jim Crow laws, which enforced de jure segregation in the South until the Civil Rights Act of 1964. In the 1930s and 1940s, New Deal programs like Social Security, the GI Bill, and landmark labor laws were explicitly denied to people of color or to the professions they were most likely to hold at that time, like domestic work and farmwork. In the wave of prosperity after World War II, white people left the cities for the suburbs, aided by low-cost mortgages ensured by the GI Bill and the National Housing Act. Their exodus was also supported by the construction of highway systems that were largely funded through the federal government—highways that further destroyed poor neighborhoods primarily inhabited by people of color.

Black people, meanwhile, were denied mortgages. The Federal Housing Authority's underwriting manuals explicitly instructed staff not to insure mortgages except to "racially homogenous" white neighborhoods, calling black folks "adverse influences" on property values. The term "redlining" comes from the residential security maps produced during the late 1930s by the Home Owners' Loan Corporation (HOLC), a federal agency. In HOLC's assessment of the credit risk of mortgages for different neighborhoods, it shaded "hazardous" areas—ones with a high percentage of nonwhite residents—with red. These were areas where it was nearly impossible to purchase or improve homes. These policies resulted in a full 98 percent of home loans going to white families between 1934 and 1962.[43]

Homeownership links to wealth in a number of ways: homeowners get a mortgage deduction, meaning they pay less income tax than if they were renting.[44] Homeowning communities tend to have better public services—everything from streetlights to garbage pickup to public schools. Homeowners can borrow from the equity in their home to start a business or send their children to college. Homeownership represents the largest part of a family's net worth, and rates of homeownership today are 74 percent for whites and 41 percent for blacks.[45]

Land and wealth have always been linked in this country. From the moment colonizers stepped on the shores of North America, the seizure of land and displacement of inconvenient nonwhite residents was ingrained in discriminatory public policy, as with the 1830 Indian Removal Act, which expelled hundreds of thousands of Natives from their ancestral homelands, and the 1848 Treaty of Guadalupe Hidalgo, by which the US annexed approximately 50 percent of Mexican territory and ignored the property rights of the existing residents.[46] Deprivation isn't just about disinvestment, it is also about the state-sanctioned capacity to take land when it is deemed valuable or ripe for "revitalization"—meaning gentrification, which profits private investors—with utter disregard for people who have lived there.

While explicit redlining may have been declared unconstitutional in the 1950s, systematic deprivation continues. De facto segregation still continues. For example, the federal low-income housing tax credit places housing for low-income families of color in neighborhoods that are far from job sites and near under-resourced schools.[47] Predatory lending by subprime loan marketers targeted black people and other people of color, which caused them to disproportionately suffer and lose their homes in the fallout of the 2008 mortgage crisis.

This history of deprivation correlates to neighborhoods with high concentrations of poverty and fewer amenities and opportunities: places with few or no opportunities to buy nutritious food, also known as food deserts; with overcrowded and underfunded housing and schools; with a lower tax base, fewer job opportunities, and therefore more crime. It is no secret that the most overpoliced neighborhoods and overincarcerated communities are often the most under-resourced. But not only is it not a secret, it is also not an accident. Poverty, lack of housing, lack of education and healthcare, unemployment, toxic and polluted natural resources, and other manifestations of economic deprivation serve to create a class of people for whom safety is never, ever guaranteed.

In a neighborhood with fewer amenities and opportunities, those conditions have a major influence on the lives of residents. This isn't to say that it's impossible to rise above the circumstances one grows up in—we all know examples of individuals who have—but there's no question that systematic deprivation limits the range of choices available for an individual starting out in such neighborhoods and makes it harder for anyone to thrive. This is why you hear the slogan "Nothing stops a bullet like a job" among leaders of antiviolence programs in cities.

Cultural deprivation compounds the economic deprivation. The same groups that are denied resources also tend to find it hard to find people who look like the group who are positive role models in films, television, and other forms of stories, and are simultaneously bombarded with negative, criminalized images of the group's people in the media. Cultural deprivation might take the form of being made uncomfortable or demeaned because of how you talk or dress or worship. You might be discouraged or even forbidden from speaking your own language, and your school curriculum will far less frequently reflect your heritage.

SUSPICION   Another key feature of the framework of fear is *suspicion*. As a nation, we invest heavily in police to patrol, and in border patrol officers to check papers. We maintain a general climate of mistrust and blame. The color-coded threat level system that Homeland Security instituted after 9/11 was abandoned once it became clear that we'd never again drop below yellow, which indicated "an elevated risk of terrorist attacks."

Suspicion shows up as metal detectors in public schools, mandatory drug testing, TSA security screening at airports, police stops and searches, patrols by private security personnel or watchdog groups and militias, and Immigration and Customs Enforcement raids. Thirty-eight percent of Americans—124 million people—were stopped by police at least once between 2011 and 2016.[48] These checkpoints rely heavily on *profiling*—leveraging stereotypes and prejudices that assume that certain kinds of people are more capable of doing us harm.

After the attacks of September 11, 2001, Muslim-owned businesses, Muslim student groups, individuals, and mosques became the targets of intense scrutiny and surveillance. A unit of the New York City Police Department created a list of twenty-eight "ancestries of interest" that included nearly every Muslim-majority country, as well as the category of "American Black Muslim."[49] Nationwide, not only were thousands of people harassed on account of appearing Middle Eastern or having Middle Eastern names; dozens of people were wrongfully detained in secret prisons on the basis of being suspected terrorists, and many were tortured.[50]

Members of the LGBTQ community are also targeted for searches, accusation, arrests, and humiliation at high rates. Almost a quarter of transgender people who had contact with the police—often on the basis of the so-called suspicious behavior that they refer to as "walking while trans"—reported harassment or misconduct.[51]

And then there's the profiling of people of color. As noted in *Born Suspect*, an NAACP report on racial profiling: "Throughout US history, law enforcement has used drug laws to target specific communities of color: in the 1870s, anti-opium laws were used against Chinese immigrants; in the early 1900s African American men were targeted by anti-cocaine laws in the South; and in the 1910s and 1920s, the first marijuana laws were used against Mexican migrants in the Southwest."[52]

Since 1999, stop and frisk, the New York Police Department practice of temporarily detaining, questioning, and searching civilians on the street—also employed in other cities under other names—was directed at black and Latinx people 90 percent of the time.[53] The practice was declared unconstitutional and racially discriminatory by a federal judge in New York in 2013, although this didn't stop Donald Trump from calling for stop and frisk to be instituted nationwide in September of 2016.[54]

In the fall of 2017, documents came forward that revealed the FBI had recently created a new domestic terror designation for "black identity extremists," a throwback to the COINTELPRO programs of the 1950s to 1970s that surveilled, infiltrated, discredited, and disrupted the civil rights movement, the American Indian Movement, and other domestic leaders and organizations that were deemed subversive.[55]

Profiling leaves the targeted individuals and communities feeling stigmatized, violated, humiliated, and oppressed. It breeds distrust of enforcement agencies. In April 2019, new research was released that showed that boys who were confronted by police officers were actually more likely to engage in "delinquent behaviors" afterwards. The younger the boys are when stopped for the first time, the more likely this was to happen, the study found, and the more frequently a boy was stopped, the more he went on to engage in delinquent behavior. In other words, if you treat someone like a criminal, he's more likely to act like one.[56]

One of the newest developments in suspicion are computer algorithms designed to "assess risk," which recommend to judges whether a person who's been arrested should be released. Writing about them in an op-ed for the *New York Times* in November 2018, Michelle Alexander, civil rights lawyer and author of *The New Jim Crow*, said these algorithms are "significantly influenced by pervasive bias in the criminal justice system. . . . Challenging these biased algorithms may be more difficult than challenging discrimination by the police, prosecutors and judges. Many algorithms are fiercely guarded corporate secrets."[57]

Suspicion shows up even on the level of families and parenting. If parents allow their seven-year-old child to walk home alone from the local playground, people dial 911. The police call in Child Protective Services, and sometimes arrest the parent on the charge of risk of injury to a minor. Although the "free-range parenting" trend has pushed back against that level of control, "what counts as 'free-range parenting' and what counts as 'neglect' are in the eye of the beholder—and race and class often figure heavily into such distinctions," as Indiana University sociology professor Jessica McCrory Calarco notes in the *Atlantic*[58]

Responding to Calarco's piece, Diane Redleaf, legal director of the National Center for Housing and Child Welfare in Chicago, wrote:

> Neglect laws currently are sweeping in millions of poor and minority families under amorphous standards. . . . 3.4 million children were subjected to highly intrusive investigations that left over 650,000 of them labeled "maltreated." But many of these maltreatment findings involved vague neglect claims. . . . In my Chicago law office, where we defended parents accused of neglect, dozens of these cases involved children in poor or minority families. . . . Some studies have shown that 53 percent of African American children have had a child-protection investigation. Millions of parents—including middle class parents—do fear the heavy hand of the state. They won't let their kids play outside anymore.[59]

Mass surveillance—meaning everything from security cameras on every corner to the invasive routine collection and review of our personal communications by the NSA, FBI, and CIA—is another aspect of the framework. And while that's disturbing enough, it's possibly even more unsettling that a climate of suspicion engages and encourages every one of us to spy on everyone else: *If you see something, say something. Please report any suspicious activity*. We keep an eye out and report behavior that feels threatening using Neighborhood Watch and the Nextdoor app. As a result, we are all suspects and we are all spies. We are quick to believe the worst of people, rather than looking for their best. A suspicious society leaves us being the catchers and the caught.

PUNISHMENT   A third feature of our current model is the focus on *punishment*. This is the core of the current safety paradigm: exacting harsh punishment upon those whom we believe have caused harm, to keep them from doing it again, and to deter others from doing likewise.

Jails and prisons inflict penalties for those harms that our laws and courts count as punishable crimes. As a result, nearly seven million adult Americans are in jail or prison, or are on parole or probation, while more than forty thousand young people are wasting away in juvenile detention.[60] We have state and federal prisons for criminally convicted adults who are generally serving more than a year for a felony. We have local jails for those serving shorter sentences and those awaiting trial. We have federal detention facilities for immigrants awaiting deportation. State hospitals house people with mental illness under civil commitment. And then we have an entire juvenile justice system devoted to the detention of children. For the last fifty years we have been caging people at levels never seen before in human history, with the US prison population growing by more than 700 percent between 1973 and 2017.[61]

In a system focused on punishment, we spend more of our public money on police, and on "militarizing" them, meaning we outfit them with armored personnel carriers, riot gear, tear gas, sonic and ultrasonic weapons, assault rifles, submachine guns, flash-bang grenades, grenade launchers, sniper rifles, and SWAT teams. The 1033 program transferred $5.1 billion in excess military equipment from the US Department of Defense to more than eight thousand local law enforcement agencies, including school-based police officers.[62]

In a punishment society, wanting to be perceived as "tough on crime," elected officials—including judges and district attorneys—are incentivized to show high conviction rates. As a result, legislators define crimes more broadly (too broadly) and expand criminal liability, often by reducing or eliminating intent requirements for many crimes. For example, burglary once required violent entry, but then in many states became any entry into a room, even if the door had been open, so what would have once been called "theft," a lesser charge, becomes "burglary." The designation of "violent crime"—no longer necessarily correlating to what people think of as violent (as in the burglary/theft example, or in other examples, such as embezzlement or possession of marijuana, or aiding an attempted suicide, in certain states)—carries severe consequences.[63] So while it's true there has been some progress in reducing sentences, this has been connected mostly to the "nons"—nonviolent, nonserious, and nonsexual crimes—and shouldn't be misconstrued as significantly reducing incarceration. As Fordham law professor John Pfaff writes in *Locked In*, "The primary driver of incarceration is prosecutorial toughness when it comes to charging people."[64]

Generally, over the past several decades legislators have made sentences more severe, as with mandatory minimums for drug and weapons possession—often by deeming these crimes "violent"—leaving the overall architecture of mass incarceration intact. Prosecutors use the combination of more severe definitions of crimes and the possibility of more severe sentences to induce defendants to take the plea, even if they aren't guilty. Judges and prosecutors, many of whom are also elected, are in lockstep. As a result, more people go to prison more quickly and for longer periods with lower-quality judicial processes.

And in a punishment society, not just crimes but all social ills are treated with penalization. Immigrants are rounded up and caged. Schools use police, arrests, and expulsions to address classroom discipline issues, while punishment is also the answer to the decimation of mental health services for poor people, which has resulted in our nation's jails being the primary "service provider" for people with mental health issues. Chemical dependence, substance use, and drug abuse are systematically met with criminalization rather than much-needed treatment. Homeless people are also often considered criminals. One in three cities has anti-homeless legislation on the books, outlawing camping, loitering, and sleeping in vehicles.[65] Homeless people are often issued citations for loitering and trespassing, and the inability to pay the fines associated with such citations can result in arrest and incarceration.

Because our solution to almost everything is "lock them up," we have to build more jails. The US has 1,719 state prisons, 109 federal prisons, 1,772 juvenile correctional facilities, 3,163 local jails, and 80 Indian country jails, as well as military prisons, immigration detention facilities, and prisons in its territories.[66]

ISOLATION   The final element of our current system is *isolation*. This begins when we think of the nation, our neighborhoods, and our homes as fortresses, building fences and walls around them. We do our best to stay out of neighborhoods that have a reputation for being violent and dangerous. We lecture our children on staying away from the kinds of people we believe could hurt them. We isolate ourselves from "others"—often people of certain races, religions, or occupations—believing that they pose a danger to us. As john a. powell has said: "Segregation is a formal way of saying, 'How do I deny my connection with you in the physical space?'"[67] Internationally, America's refusal to enter into or honor standards and human rights agreements intended to promote global security and prosperity sets America on its own against the world.

Isolating yourself is one of the three instinctual responses to fear and powerlessness: it's the "flight" in *fight, flight, or freeze*. Many of us who have been through a rough time understand the impulse to withdraw, to become antisocial, like a turtle retracting into its shell—even if it's the exact opposite of what's healthiest and safest for us to do. There are a number of studies that show that Americans as a people are retracting into our shells, in what's being called an "epidemic" of loneliness. Over half of adults in America report feeling lonely: that no one knows them well, that they lack meaningful relationships, that they are isolated from others.[68] Sociologists say it's most common for people to have zero confidants—someone with whom they can discuss important things— down from three confidants for most Americans in 1985.[69] I can't help think our epidemic of isolation is partially a result of the atmosphere that the architects of anxiety have created, with their incessant rants about threats and criminals and terrorists.

We're also isolating a huge number of people by force. Incarceration equals isolation. Every time a person is removed from society and imprisoned, for any length of time, it's a form of isolation. Then there's the fact that facilities in which we lock people up are usually located in remote places. Visitation is limited. It is very difficult to know what is really going on behind the barbed wire fences and impenetrable walls. There is zero—or very close to zero—transparency or accountability. Solitary confinement, under any of its aliases—*lockup, 23 and 1, dark room, seclusion, segregation, exclusion, room confinement, special management*—is the most extreme form of isolation used in our system. The United Nations Special Rapporteur on Torture condemned the use of solitary confinement as tantamount to torture in 2011.[70]

Those who survive the ordeal and get out of the prison system still find themselves excluded in any number of ways upon reentering the world. Many return home with trauma stemming from the separation from their families, homes, and communities. Far too many people suffer post-traumatic stress from the violence they witnessed and often endured while incarcerated. Other challenges may be less traumatic but equally devastating in terms of a person's lifelong prospects. People returning from even short-term stays in prisons can face difficulties finding employment and places to live, and securing necessary medications, to name just a few basic needs.

In twelve states across the US, the right to vote—that most fundamental right of a citizen in America—is forever denied to those who have had a felony conviction, cutting them off from participation in our democracy.[71] As of 2016, 6.1 million incarcerated and formerly incarcerated Americans were legally denied the right to vote.[72]

Additionally, many people coming out of prison are barred from all sorts of occupations. There are forty thousand laws restricting formerly incarcerated people from obtaining employment. Entire occupations, from accounting to haircutting to firefighting, are off-limits.[73] In California, people in prison are paid one dollar per hour to fight raging wildfires but are denied access to this occupation after getting out.[74]

This means that the isolating effects of the criminal legal system are enduring. Even the language that we use to describe people who spent time in the system creates a kind of indelible stigma, terms like: *inmate, juvenile delinquent, offender, criminal, felon, ex-convict.* Can you imagine if your identity were forever fixed, based on your worst mistake or your weakest moment? As my former law school professor Bryan Stevenson writes in his book *Just Mercy*, "Each of us is more than the worst thing we've ever done."[75] But the current paradigm denies this reality, and reduces many people to their worst mistake.

Family separations are another form of isolation. Family separation is not a new phenomenon in the United States. It has just been brought into stark relief by the Trump administration. As the stories of scapegoated people at the start of this chapter illustrate, family separations go back to our very beginnings and keep recurring like a nightmare. Sometimes the architects of anxiety justify family separations as a matter of national security, and other times they're a result of rigid social norms (think of Lovemme's and other trans folks' rejection by their families) or a result of the lack of support to help families stay together (think of Peyton's story and the frequent institutionalization of people with mental illness, people with substance abuse issues, or people with disabilities). In the context of incarceration, people often think of the destruction of families as unfortunate fallout, an unforeseen consequence. Over two decades of working with families whose loved ones are incarcerated, however, I have realized that those consequences were not just foreseen but intentional. When we look further back in history, at slavery and at the Indian boarding schools, this becomes crystal clear:

the intention behind family separation was to weaken certain communities—largely those of people of color—in order to strengthen certain other communities—largely white ones.

FIGHTING THE FRAMEWORK

The framework of fear cannot lead to possibility and growth. It is antigrowth and antisocial. It's engineered to keep certain people down as opposed to lifting them up, when they most need support.

Because the framework of fear involves so many institutions in the public and private sectors—courts and enforcement agencies like the police and Immigration and Customs Enforcement, as well as prisons (both publicly and privately operated) and other parts of government, along with schools, banks, real estate developers and investors, and the media, among others—it can seem intractable. How can we possibly dismantle such a many-headed hydra? A positive aspect of this is that it gives us so many intervention opportunities. There are many separate institutions and sectors we can target in order to ensure a safer and ultimately more prosperous society. When we shift the focus from crimes to harms, as I've described, we also can involve many more sectors. Rather than limiting the issue of safety to police, lawyers, judges, and prison guards, the responsibility extends to include every sector and all of us as individuals.

It's helpful to remember that, intractable though they may seem, society-wide systems and cultures are composed of individual choices that humans made along the way. That means we can make different choices now to achieve different outcomes. john powell believes the systematic exclusion that occurs with "othering" can be combated with "belonging," or strategic inclusion: the expansion of the concept of "we" in lieu of an Us vs. Them view. Another inspiration for change is the indigenous worldview, which calls for balance and wholeness, rather than division and dehumanization.

THE SUM OF US

If there's no such thing as a Bad Guy *out there somewhere*, then it's clear why our fear-based system of dehumanization is failing to keep us safe: we can't get to lasting safety by insulating ourselves from mythical external threats with border walls; we can't get to real safety by expelling or confining certain kinds of people, like the mythical "superpredator." The paradox of proximity means that the real threats are not coming from a few "bad apples"; they come simultaneously from powerful massive institutions that we all have a hand in upholding, and they come from within our own communities and families. We can't run from ourselves. The answer to safety is always closer rather than farther away. Only together can we create safety.

To achieve real safety we are going to have to transcend the hyperactive threat-detection wiring in our brains. On an individual level it is not always possible, realistic, or even desirable to interrupt the fight-or-flight response in the face of danger, yet as a society we have an opportunity to take a step back and use our powers of reason and compassion to move from fear-based reaction to care-based action. On the scale of societies, it is the difference between civilization and barbarism.

In order to truly be safe, we are going to have to transcend the mythical divisions of Us vs. Them. We will have to bridge the divides and build relationships. There is no Them, there's only *We*. And that We, the fabric of American society, is always evolving and expanding. Rather than hold on to a fixed notion of who We the People are, we have to embrace what john powell calls "a bigger We."

We desperately need a new approach to public safety. We won't stop harms and violence altogether, but we can manage them in care-based ways that reflect a shared faith in a common future. In a comprehensive new model of public safety, we must move from punishment to accountability, from deprivation to resources, from suspicion to relationships, and from isolation to participation.

PART II

A VISION OF SAFETY

CHAPTER 3

ADDRESSING HARMS

Moving from Punishment to Accountability

June 28, 2010

In a civil trial brought by one of his victims, Jon Burge is convicted of two counts of obstruction of justice and one count of perjury for having previously lied under oath when he denied having tortured people. He is sentenced to four and a half years in federal prison, of which he will go on to serve three and a half. It doesn't in any way feel like justice has been served. To those whom he harmed, it feels more like salt in the wound.

For almost twenty years, from 1972 to 1991, Burge, a former police commander in Chicago, and his crew of midnight-shift detectives tortured at least 120 and as many as 200 young men into false confessions.[1] Most of them were black; some were Latinx. His victims were suffocated with plastic bags, stomped on, and held down against radiators until their skin burned. They had soda poured up their noses and were beaten with pistols. Their genitals were shocked with electricity and loaded guns were placed inside their mouths and pointed at their heads during rounds of Russian roulette. Burge called the electric shock device "the nigger box."[2]

"They went home every night to be with their wives and their kids. They went home every night to teach their sons how to read, how to ride a bike, or how to drive a car. They went home every night to their families. They set the table and ate dinner. They got on the telephone to talk to friends as much as they wanted to. They were with their mothers before their mothers got sick and passed away. . . . The City of Chicago cut 21 years of my life. They can't give me the time I wanted to teach my son how to ride a bike or how to tie his shoe. They can't give me anything that I missed out on. No, justice has not been served," said Ronald Kitchen, arrested in 1988 and tortured by Burge and his associates into a false confession that landed him twenty-one years in prison, thirty of them on death row.[3]

How many times did the justice system fail these young men? Let me count the ways, or at least give you some highlights.

The first allegations against Burge and his men were made in 1972. A request for an investigation into torture allegations was made by the medical director of Cook County Jail in 1982, yet the then-state's attorney (later mayor) Richard Daley took no action. In 1984 the police department's disciplinary agency, the Office of Professional Standards (OPS), filed a report about the use of electric shock on persons in custody. No action was taken. Between 1981 and 1988, fifty-five people were tortured in order to obtain confessions, and although the state's attorney's office was aware of this, the coerced and false evidence was still used in hearings and trials to send the victims to prison.[4]

In 1989, one of the victims, Andrew Wilson, sued Jon Burge and several other officers for civil rights violations, including torture. Burge was represented by private lawyers, paid for by the city government. The trial ended when the jury was unable to reach a unanimous verdict. Burge was acquitted of the charges in a second trial. In 1990, the OPS filed a report, recommending Burge be fired and citing fifty cases of torture and abuse that were "systematic" and "methodical" and "included psychological techniques and planned torture."[5] No action was taken. In 1992, OPS released the reports to the public. The mayor and the police superintendent attacked the credibility of the OPS reports and took no action, while the city's police union hosted a fundraiser to pay for his defense, which some three thousand people attended.[6] In 1993, finally, Burge was fired. He continued to receive his monthly police pension until his death in 2018.[7]

Between 1993 and 1995, further investigations were undertaken, findings were hidden, Andrew Wilson's case was retried and the judge approved a $1.1 million award, which the City of Chicago unsuccessfully appealed. Further cases came forward. Burge kept pleading the Fifth. Half of the claims were deemed credible, but because the statute of limitations for police abuse of suspects had by now been exceeded, no indictments were made.

Attorney Flint Taylor, part of the People's Law Office, which represented many of Burge's torture victims, described it as an "unremitting official cover-up that has implicated a series of police superintendents, numerous prosecutors, more than 30 police detectives and supervisors, and, most notably, Richard M. Daley."[8]

Meanwhile, young men served time in jail and lived with recurring nightmares, depression, anxiety, and other trauma for the next three decades. Mark Clements was just sixteen years old when he was brutalized by Burge, and served twenty-eight years for the confession police elicited from him.[9] Anthony Holmes, tortured by Burge and his associates in 1973, served his full thirty-three-and-a-half-year sentence before being exonerated.[10] As many as twenty survivors of the torture ring remain incarcerated today.[11]

How do you possibly begin appropriately addressing the harms from a case like this, one in which almost an entire city government is implicated, over decades?

May 6, 2015

The City of Chicago signed into law legislation for $5.5 million in reparations to the victims of Burge's racist and sadistic practices.

Under the legislation, each torture-ring survivor received nearly $100,000, defined explicitly as reparations. Checks went out in January 2016. All survivors and their families are eligible for free college tuition. The ordinance includes a formal apology from the current mayor.

In his apology, Mayor Rahm Emanuel said: "Jon Burge's actions are a disgrace—to Chicago, to the hard-working men and women of the police department, and most importantly to those he was sworn to protect. . . . Today, we stand together as a city to try and right those wrongs, and to bring this dark chapter of Chicago's history to a close." A permanent official public memorial recognizing the victims is also to be erected in the city.

The ordinance also includes a mandate to teach the broader public about racial injustice through a public school curriculum. Starting in the 2017–18 school year, the Chicago public school system introduced a new required text in eighth and tenth grade. It is titled *Reparations Won: A Case Study in Police Torture, Racism, and the Movement for Justice in Chicago*.

A range of social services is available to survivors of the torture ring as part of the reparations. Under the motto "Sorry is not enough," the

Chicago Torture Justice Center offers a public health clinic with private therapy rooms, treatment for physical traumas, and case managers to coordinate access to public services. This is America's first official trauma center for the victims of its own police forces.

The ordinance and reparations package was the idea of community activists and lawyers who felt betrayed by the justice system's response to the atrocities. Between 2012 and 2015 they organized meetings, petitions, marches, teach-ins, and a Twitter campaign to pressure Mayor Emanuel. They met with city officials, and they were energized by the rise of the Black Lives Matter movement. And finally, after decades of trying to get justice, they pushed the ordinance before the city council, and made history.[12]

"Police accountability" is a term that has come to mean that police officers should follow the law enforcement directive to control crime and maintain order. But the real question is, Which order, imposed by whom? The order of the day is a society in which many go without. Police intervene on behalf of bosses when people press for a living wage that the law doesn't yet require. They intervene on behalf of businesses when people are loitering, sweeping those people away. As with the criminal legal system, the police are more likely to protect you and keep you safe if you are a rich white man or corporation. They protect power, prestige, and property.

America's police need to be accountable to America's people. This example from Chicago is a good first step toward making it so.

FROM PUNISHMENT TO ACCOUNTABILITY

What do we do with those who cause harm? I am not so naive as to believe that we can have a world without any violence or harm. Sometimes we fail. We fail to live to the best standards for ourselves, or we fail to escape the patterns of abuse that wrecked our childhoods. However, if we don't figure out a different way to treat each other when we make mistakes, then no one is truly safe. We need a transformation of our current culture such that we can handle conflict, violence, and harm in more effective ways.

The important questions are: *What can accountability and consequences look like beyond courts and prisons? How can we provide satisfactory experiences for those who were harmed? How can justice truly be served?*

Punishment teaches that those who have the power can force others to do what they want them to do. Punishment involves control over someone, by fear or coercion, denying their fundamental dignity and rights. It is done *to* someone. Accountability, by contrast, occurs *with* someone. Even if someone makes a mistake, that person is still worthy of basic respect and humane treatment. When respect and basic dignity are present, accountability takes on qualities of a partnership, where those who made mistakes engage as agents in their own transformation, rather than having things done to them or for them. The sense of being in partnership with those who hold you accountable for your mistakes has been demonstrated to create more impactful and sustainable transformation. Punishment cuts people off from society and from participation, from the opportunity to thrive in the future. Accountability is about creating a future in which people change their lives as a result of learning from their mistakes, and the whole fabric of society is stronger for it.

Accountability consists of two parts: acknowledgment and consequences. Both parts involve dialogue with your community. Acknowledgment means you take responsibility for what was done (looking to the past). Consequences are the actions you take to make the present and future right (looking forward). Appropriate consequences are determined by dialogue with those you have a relationship with; they are the actions you must undertake to repair the relationship in a way that's satisfactory to everyone impacted.

We can hold people accountable only when they are in some kind of real relationship with us—we have to share a community. Another word for accountable is *answerable*. You can't answer if there's no one on the other end. You need a relationship in order to answer, to be answerable, to be accountable. Establishing community, maintaining community, feeling a sense of community is a prerequisite for accountability. If you have harmed someone, you have harmed the relationships, destroyed the fabric of community, so you need to honor the relationships—that is the full meaning of accountability. It's not just admitting: "I did this"—it's also about acknowledging the real impacts on the person(s) you harmed and all the fallout of your action within your shared community, so that you can make amends.

The anthropologist Max Gluckman, who observed the judicial process among the Barotse of Rhodesia (now Zimbabwe) in the 1940s, made the point that traditional societies, being smaller and more closely knit, often have "multiplex" relationships, meaning members interact in multiple arenas and are connected in a number of ways.[13] For example, imagine if your landlord were a distant relative, also ran the shop where you got your car serviced, and served as a firefighter in your neighborhood. Gluckman contrasted this with modern societies, where many people tend to only have one connection to each other: just a landlord, or just a relative, or just a mechanic or firefighter. When you rely on each other for more types of interactions and services, you're more motivated to resolve conflicts. There's more of a sense of collective responsibility.

Even without the multiplex relationships of traditional societies, a strong social contract—in which people and government share both the responsibility for and the benefits from things like parks, public transportation, and healthcare—creates more sense of collective responsibility. Government disinvestment weakens the sense of collective responsibility; a social safety net will help us hold each other accountable.

Many traditional societies have long had justice systems where, when someone transgresses or causes harm, the response is to heal the relationships that have been hurt. According to Chief Justice Robert Yazzie of the Navajo Nation: "Western adjudication is a search for what happened and who did it; Navajo peace-making is about the effect of what happened. Who got hurt? What do they feel about it? What can be done to repair the harm?"[14] In New Zealand/Aotearoa, prior to European contact, the Maori had a well-developed system that prioritized the stability, harmony, and integrity of relationships and kinship groups, with an exchange of goods and services usually considered adequate compensation when hostility occurred and relationships were disturbed.[15] The goal of their process is peacemaking and the restoration of balance.

The idea of restoration of balance is key to overcoming the adversarial nature of Us vs. Them, expressed in the realm of crime as "good guys" vs. "bad guys," perpetrator vs. victim, innocent vs. guilty. To restore balance is not about having one side win and one side lose: it's about creating the conditions for well-being as everyone moves forward.

RESTORATION

Relationships, accountability, and healing are the principles at the foundation of the movement for restorative justice. Restorative justice is based on holding people accountable, because they are held in community. Restorative justice is influenced by the principles of healing and peacemaking; in fact, a key component of restorative justice is to view violence prevention as a public health issue.

Where the criminal legal system focuses on whether a law was broken and how to make someone pay for breaking the law, restorative justice emphasizes the root causes of harms. Rather than asking: "What law was broken, who broke it, and how should they be punished?" restorative justice asks, "Who was harmed? What do they need? Whose responsibility is it to meet those needs?"

Restorative justice places the needs of the survivor at the center. It avoids terms like "victim," "perpetrator," and "offender," because of the way in which those labels can stick to a person forever and deny them the ability to evolve, to heal, to change.

Restorative justice asks: How can everyone in a given community—family members, friends, neighbors, coworkers, bystanders, and community members—get actively involved in making amends, ending violence, and righting relationships? Where are the elders and trusted members of the community who will intervene for the good of the whole? Who will be willing to step in and say, "If we do not deal with the unresolved conflict, it will divide the community into factions, leaving us fractured and less resilient?" School counselors and teachers, social workers, housing advocates, medical providers, faith leaders, and many others join forces to address why a harm was committed, how to repair the harm, and how to prevent other harms from being committed in the future.

Restorative interventions involve dialogues and discussion circles with trained facilitation that support people who have done harm in recognizing the impacts of what they've done and acknowledging their accountability. Sometimes the survivor and the person who harmed them participate in separate circles, as a safe way to offer for survivors to participate. Together they reach agreements and make a plan for appropriate consequences and reparations, which may include: stopping the harmful behaviors, listening to the person who was harmed and acknowledging the impacts of the harm, apologizing for the harm, making appropriate reparations, and agreeing to not repeat the harmful behavior with anyone, ever again. Sanctions and further consequences for failing to carry out their agreements and commitments are also part of the plan.

For survivors, healing can take time and may not happen immediately, but the coming together of community to discuss root causes and responsibilities always succeeds in the sense that it inherently refuses dehumanization and curtails cycles of trauma. Restorative justice builds our capacity for holding each other accountable and holding ourselves accountable, for the next time that harm occurs, on whatever scale it does. Through the act of repairing harm done to people and relationships, we learn to develop community, manage conflict, build relationships, and increase social capital.

Sometimes people object to the term "restorative," pointing out that there is no idealized state to restore things to. In other words, the United States has never been a fair, safe, or just society for many people, given its roots in the genocide of Native people and slavery, and the lack of equal rights for women and gender-nonconforming and queer people, among other injustices and forms of discrimination that continue through the present day. But that's not what I believe "restoration" means with regards to addressing harms and crimes.

What do I mean by *restorative*? On the first level: what is restored is individual humanity. Dignity. Agency. It is about healing from dehumanization.

The second level of restoration is interpersonal. When harm is done—especially if violent crime is committed—relationships are harmed. Because of what I've called the paradox of proximity, the one most likely to hurt you is someone close to you. So the relationship must also be repaired and restored.

The third level of restoration involves healing whole communities. The framework of fear has targeted entire races of people and types of people. In the same way that the ecosystem of a wetland must be restored after being destroyed, the integrity and safety of these communities must be restored.

Finally, there is the implication on the national level, of healing our bitter divides and restoring the fabric of democracy and the dream of America as a place of liberty and opportunity, where everyone is welcome regardless of religion or background.

HARDCORE ACCOUNTABILITY

But is it tough enough? We have to address this question head-on if we are going to transform the model of public safety in America, because when we are harmed, desires for revenge rooted deep inside us are activated. When my home was broken into, it felt like an invasion. Even though my daughters were unhurt, it awakened the most primal parts of me, and a desire for revenge shot through me. These are the natural and unconscious responses to a threat of harm, and they arise automatically when we consider how to keep ourselves safe.

The desire for retribution and vengeance is natural, in the sense that it is hardwired into us as a species. It's human nature. When we experience vengeance, the same "reward" parts of our brains activate that are stimulated with cocaine and nicotine use. Evolutionary biology explains how vengeance was beneficial to our species (and other animals as well): "Revenge's ability to punish aggressors, its ability to deter would-be aggressors, and its ability to discourage cheaters made it adaptive in our ancestral environment," writes Michael McCullough, author of the book *Beyond Revenge*.[16]

So yes, it's human nature to desire revenge against the one who has harmed us. Yet just because we're individually wired to demand something that was advantageous to us when we lived in primitive societies doesn't mean that as a society we can't evolve and transcend that wiring. Evolutionary biologists have likewise traced how forgiveness was also advantageous to our primitive ancestors, in that it supported cooperation, which also contributed to survival. What makes revenge as opposed to forgiveness more or less advantageous in today's world is social context.

As McCullough notes: "When people live in places where crime and disorder are high, policing is poor, governments are weak, and life is dangerous, they will tend to use revenge as a problem-solving strategy . . . we'll see more forgiveness in places where people are highly dependent on complex networks of cooperative relationships, policing is reliable, the system of justice is efficient and trustworthy, and social institutions are up to the task of helping truly contrite offenders make amends with the people they've harmed."[17]

We do not live in that context as yet. Still, we have the power to create a social context in which revenge makes less sense. What's required for that is a society in which sufficient resources are available to individuals and communities, and the value of relationships is recognized and supported as of utmost importance.

OK, so in the meantime, is restorative justice tough enough? There's a perception that alternatives to criminal justice like restorative justice are "soft" and "weak"—that they "let folks off easy." The reality is that facing the full impacts of the pain you have caused is anything but being let off easy. Yes, it is a different kind of "toughness" than the horror and misery of prison, but it is hardcore. All we have to do is reflect on how deeply uncomfortable it is for us to be confronted by a loved one for even a relatively minor transgression, like not listening or becoming impatient. If you're like me, like most of us, staying present in that moment and taking responsibility feels like a herculean task.

Sending people to remote prisons and into isolation is often described as being "tough on crime." In reality, this is the opposite of hardcore accountability. Prisons and cages just remove you, cutting you out of the fabric of community.

But to have to stay, to be forced by your entire community to hear the pain, trauma, horror, fear, and grief you caused, that is hardcore. Real accountability comes when a person has to face what they have done, when they have to own up to it, and work to make it right. To be forced to acknowledge that you have heard it, let it in, and allowed yourself to feel what that felt like is tough. To know that until you have come clean and made amends not only to the person(s) you directly harmed, but also to your entire community, is hardcore.

Restorative justice causes a real reckoning with the harm an individual has caused. Studies have found that people who go through restorative justice processes are much less likely to break the law again than those who have gone through the courts and prison. The restorative justice approach has been proven effective at reducing rates of repeated offenses: in a recent study of a hundred felony cases, youth who went through restorative justice processes were 44 percent less likely to commit further crimes than those who went through the juvenile justice system. At the same time, survivors also reported a higher level of satisfaction: 91 percent in the same study said they would recommend the restorative process to a friend.[18]

So how does restorative justice work in various settings? Here's an overview of how it's implemented with harm that happens in our homes, in the workplace, and in schools, and on the national and international level.

HOME

Harm that occurs within the home or the family has a special set of challenges. The person doing the harm is almost always someone the victim knows, and often, knows well. Survivors often don't want to talk about it, and members of the family or community can refuse to see it or acknowledge it. Given the multiple relationships, and often close bonds, that people have with one another, it is difficult for family members and community members to know what to do. Its prevalence and its presence within our most intimate spaces make us feel powerless to stop it.

Traditionally, violence in the home was considered a private affair. Calling the authorities could be fraught with danger. The police tend to rely on threats of punishment, which tend to make the abusive person angry and likely to mete out more violence, if the police leave without removing them. For decades, many police departments had policies that specifically discouraged arrest in domestic violence cases.[19]

Sexual assault of domestic partners is one of the most under-reported harms that happen in homes. Only a fraction of abuses that do get reported are prosecuted, and only in a fraction of those cases is someone found guilty. Far more harm is happening than is being punished, let alone healed. Survivors of sexual assault know that the current approach, which can mean facing interrogation and possibly blaming and shaming in court and perhaps also in media coverage, is likely to be uncomfortable at best and traumatic at worst. All of this leads to even fewer survivors coming forward.

Mary Koss, a professor of public health who has focused her research on sexual violence, comments: "Many victims say, 'I want to tell my story to him, to the person who did this to me, and I want my family and friends to be sitting there so they can understand I am a legitimate victim.'"[20] While some survivors may want their cases to end up in court, others are dissuaded by the fact that judges and lawyers continue to blame victims and that conviction rates remain stubbornly low. They would rather hear the person who violated them acknowledge the harm than navigate a criminal system that seems stacked against them.

If someone is arrested and convicted, which has occurred more often since the passage of the Violence Against Women Act in 1994 (the law is currently up for reauthorization as I write, and it is being opposed by Republicans), they are unlikely to have learned any new skills for dealing with conflict or how to be a better spouse, partner, or family member. The criminal legal system often serves just to deepen divides and normalize violence. When violence happens in a home, within a partnership or family, it destroys trust, safety, and health. Yet the traditional lock-'em-up response usually just increases everyone's sense of powerlessness and promotes dissolution of trust, safety, and health, rather than their restoration. Of course sexual assault should continue to be a crime that is denounced and prosecuted. Yet survivors should have an array of options available that allow them to pursue the path that best suits their circumstances and need.

Further complicating matters, sometimes people who experience violence and harm at home want to remain there. This is often true when the harms are done to children. Some people want their abusive loved one to stay home and get treatment, therapy, and support. In other instances, it is necessary for the safety of others that people who have caused harm are removed from the home, but they should still be able to play a role in the community. The criminal legal system has little to no flexibility in accommodating these different cases.

According to the project generationFIVE, which aims to end the sexual abuse of children within five generations, putting people in jail and prison has proven to be unsuccessful in preventing child abuse, changing behavior, or making restitution to those impacted by child sexual abuse. When the person who has been sexually abusive is able to take accountability for their actions and to make meaningful reparations, greater healing is possible for everyone involved.[21]

The project generationFIVE also calls for accountability of bystanders who did not manage to protect children. Protective action by bystanders can include "setting limits with, confronting, and challenging those who exercise power in abusive ways" as well as offering to listen to those who were impacted by the abuse, and acknowledging their own collusion in the abuse. Community accountability recognizes that generally there are a number of ways that others in the community (and even within the family) ignore, minimize, or even encourage violence.

Moving from punishment to hardcore accountability asks how family members, friends, neighbors, coworkers, and community members can get actively involved in ending violence when their own loved ones are experiencing violence. Often, when asked to get involved in a conflict, people say things like, "I don't want to take sides," or "I love you all too much to get involved." In restorative justice, rather than stepping *away* from people in a conflict, we are asked to step *in*.

#METOO AND THE WORKPLACE

Sexual harassment and misconduct in the workplace share some of the same complicating factors of violence and harm committed in homes. Given the power dynamics, survivors often don't feel secure coming forward, and members of the workplace or community can refuse to see it or acknowledge it. This means that community and bystander accountability has to be part of the solution, as it is with harms happening in homes.

Recent events have indicated how widespread harm is in the workplace, particularly harm to women, and how far we still have to go to achieve safe workplaces. As allegations came forward against dozens of powerful men in 2018, some apologies were made and some of those who caused harm stepped down from their positions, but little was done to address the underlying power dynamics. As the reaction of half the country to the brave and credible testimony of Dr. Christine Blasey Ford revealed during the Brett Kavanaugh Supreme Court confirmation battle, we have a long way to go, baby. Tarana Burke reflected: "Where's the self-reflection and accountability? Perhaps if we saw some evidence of that, then we can have a more robust conversation about the road to redemption."[22]

This moment in time presents us with an incredible opportunity to implement a form of justice that offers healing and that transforms the broader culture such that powerful people no longer feel free to commit sexual misconduct, as they have clearly felt until now. Those who have committed harm, particularly the powerful, publicly visible ones with many followers and fans, should use their platforms to model accountability and transformation, rather than denial and defensiveness. They should behave in ways that demonstrate not only their commitment to changing their own behavior but also their commitment to challenging the belief systems around power, namely patriarchy and white supremacy. We know violence isn't just about violence: it is also about power. One of the campaigns my wife leads is for One Fair Wage. It calls for an end to the subminimum wage for tipped workers, which currently means many tipped workers endure sexual harassment so they can earn enough to feed themselves and their families. Restaurateurs committed to healing can step forward and pay one fair wage as part of their consequences—and because it's the right thing to do—and lobby their colleagues in the industry to follow their lead.

Consequences cannot make the original harm go away, but there's the possibility that it can lead to healing and behavioral change across society.

SCHOOLS

Many settings are conducive to restorative justice, and schools are among them. We know that zero-tolerance policies, suspensions, and expulsions are all associated with low achievement, poor attendance, and juvenile crime. Restorative justice, which has become a popular alternative to out-of-school suspensions, typically features a meeting of the person involved, students, parents, teachers, administrators, and a counselor or psychologist. The goal is to get students who cause harm to take responsibility for their behaviors and acknowledge they caused suffering to others. It works because it's empowering. Rather than imposing a harsh set of punishments determined by the system, restorative justice enables students to create the consequences they deem appropriate and hold each other accountable. Young people have a strong sense of fairness and justice and how to make things right. Schools that have adopted restorative justice and accountability processes are seeing decreases in suspension and expulsion rates and disciplinary referrals. Restorative justice calls in the community to help resolve conflict, and many students benefit from that process. When you adopt restorative justice, you call students in and give them an opportunity to learn from their mistakes. When you suspend or expel, they are pushed out of school, and no such opportunity exists.

One model, Positive Behavioral Intervention and Support (PBIS), is a nationally recognized framework for shifting away from a punitive school culture. The model developed from individual behavioral support for children with severe disabilities. George Sugai, a professor of educational psychology and expert on PBIS, asserts that supports and rewards systems for individual behavior cannot be successful unless the entire school is transformed, including, for example, policies around hiring, training, and teambuilding among school staff; the system of collecting data, such as test scores and attendance, on students; and classroom management strategies. The social culture is as important as the instructional culture, and the relationships and the interactions that students have with each other is as important as the relationships and interactions that occur between adults and students.[23]

In PBIS, students and school staff collaborate to create the expectations of how to treat each other and how to behave, such as through a set of rules developed and agreed upon by staff and students requiring that the school be safe and that staff and students act respectfully and responsibly toward one another. These rules specify minor and major disciplinary infractions, as well as the associated interventions or consequences, in a process that is sensitive to the cultures expressed in the school's student body and community. There's a shift from assimilation to empowerment. Nationwide data on schools that have implemented PBIS indicate a reduction in disciplinary events that averages 50 percent.[24]

One of the caveats around restorative interventions in schools is that relationships are the prerequisite for accountability. This means that if students have poor relationships with one another and with teachers and administrators, restorative processes will be less effective. We need relationship-centered schools and social and emotional learning programs, which teach self-awareness and ways of coping with one's own emotions in order to practice empathy, compassion, and awareness of the experience of others. Rather than use student performance on standardized tests as the default form of school accountability for evaluating and rewarding or punishing, we should use the personal growth of all stakeholders and the overall quality of community as our metric for schools.

CORPORATE ACCOUNTABILITY

The criminal legal response to corporate crimes needs to be stronger, with expanded resources devoted to prosecuting white-collar and corporate crimes; however, resolution of such prosecutions would not necessarily involve a prison sentence. True accountability is more likely to occur through restorative, community-based justice in which corporate actors have to participate in community accountability sessions, where they must come to terms with the harm they have caused and make amends.

When consumers organize to protest the behavior of corporations through boycotts or shareholder activism (such as when people purchase shares in a company for the sole purpose of speaking out and voting against bad policies or behaviors as members of corporate boards), it can be quite powerful. But consumers are only one part of the community of a corporation. The communities involved in growing, mining, and producing the materials for products are another part of a corporation's community, as are the workers all along the supply chains of products and the provision of services. Collectively, all these people are stakeholders, and they all should have a say when it comes to holding corporations accountable and have a place at the corporate board table. More power than that wielded by shareholders is held, of course, by owners of corporations, so the movement promoting collective ownership is the most powerful way to keep corporations accountable. In places where workers don't have ownership shares, they hold employers accountable by participating in unions. Unionization and bargaining need to be made easier through policies of default unionization, unless a majority of workers vote otherwise.

Finally, government at all levels should be the community that holds corporations accountable, rather than serving as a tool of corporate power. Efforts to diminish and ultimately end corporate control of government, by establishing public funding of campaigns and limiting corporate donations, are top priorities.

NEIGHBORHOODS AND NATION

Restorative interventions can be effectively implemented at various scales. For elected officials, for example, accountability is always to the communities that form their constituencies. Consequences for harms they cause might include community service to support people they've harmed, or being removed from their positions if the harm is too great. The example of Chicago, which opened this chapter, is instructive.

But even on the federal government level there are examples of restorative justice. Truth and reconciliation committees have been implemented in many places around the world. As their name implies, the committees are tasked with investigating, uncovering, and revealing the truth about wrongdoings on the national level, then cocreating efforts to address the damage. These include reparations to survivors that provide financial or other kinds of supports, as in Chicago. Official apologies, public memorials, and monuments are also often involved.

One of the first such commissions, the National Commission on the Disappearance of Persons, was created in Argentina in 1983. It produced a report entitled *Nunca Más* (Never Again), which documented the widespread human rights abuses of the military dictatorship that ruled Argentina from 1976 to 1983. It documented 8,961 *desaparecidos*—victims of disappearance. In this case, the report led to a war crimes trial in civilian court.[25]

Most famous is probably the South African Truth and Reconciliation Committee, formed in 1995, which brought survivors and perpetrators of apartheid-era violence together in an attempt to heal and move forward with Nelson Mandela's vision of a rainbow nation. Chile also created a Commission for Truth and Reconciliation, and later a Commission on Political Imprisonment and Torture following the reign of Augusto Pinochet, during which approximately three thousand people went missing or died. In 2006, Canada launched a Truth and Reconciliation Commission after the last of its Indian boarding schools closed in 1996. Government officials had kidnapped some 150,000 Native children from their families in order to assimilate them.[26]

Rarely has the United States government made amends for the kinds of actions I described in the first chapter—the forced relocations, family separations, and forced labor among entire populations, including Native Americans, African Americans, and immigrants. If anything, after decades the government might issue an apology, but this has not gone anywhere near accountability for the scale of harm rendered. The one exception on the national level is the case of Japanese Americans who were incarcerated during World War II.

In 1988, President Reagan signed the Civil Liberties Act to provide reparations to the 120,000 Japanese Americans who had been incarcerated during World War II. The legislation offered a formal apology and paid $20,000 to each of the survivors.[27] As with the legislation in Chicago, the bill was the result of over a decade's worth of campaigning by activists in the Japanese American community, including the Japanese American Citizens League, which formally resolved to pursue reparations at its 1970 convention. The Japanese American Citizens League first sponsored legislation to create a federal investigative commission, which was approved under President Carter. The findings of the 1982 commission report justified reparations and prompted the 1988 legislation.[28] Of all the atrocities I recount in stories of America's historical scapegoats and forced family separations, this is the only one that has been federally acknowledged with reparations.

But the time of reckoning is coming. Between author Ta-Nehisi Coates's landmark article "The Case for Reparations" in 2014 and the official platform of Movement for Black Lives, which includes a demand for reparations to African Americans, consensus is growing.[29] Reparations are due not just for slavery, but for decades of Jim Crow injustice and the systematic dehumanization, deprivation, and criminalization carried out through the framework of fear.

In nearly every city across America, there is a history of violence against black people and other people of color. A new president should create incentives for every city's police department to embark on a process of truth and reconciliation. This would help build real community/police dialogue. By doing so, government officials might identify officers who are unwilling to take part in such an examination and thereby begin to identify and remove officers with ties to white supremacist groups and or officers sympathetic to the ideology.

People in power rarely want to be held accountable; few of us do, but people in positions of power have more means, helpers, and enablers to avoid it. Overcoming trauma in this country will require holding powerful institutions and people accountable. Full accountability means we take responsibility for our history as well as our present.

RESTORE OAKLAND

A new vision for community healing and accountability is what my organization is modeling with Restore Oakland, a place that will demonstrate what investment in communities, resources, and relationships makes possible.

A true justice system has to be based on two things: One, it should ensure that people who have caused harm can make amends for the harm they have caused. Their consequences should be commensurate with the harm they have caused, while taking into account their membership in their own families and the human family. Two, it should provide an opportunity for people to do better moving forward, and to engage fully in society. If people make amends but still find themselves without meaningful work, they are more likely to risk committing economic-driven crimes again.

Restore Oakland is both a building and a scalable model of future possibility. A partnership between the Ella Baker Center, the Restaurant Opportunities Centers United, and other community-based organizations, Restore Oakland is an advocacy and training center where Bay Area residents can heal together and create the future together.

It will house a restorative justice center where the organizations Community Works and Restorative Justice for Oakland Youth will hold accountability circles. Their work helps ensure that people are held in community while being held accountable. We will welcome everyday people looking to address harms and violence in their communities. We plan to offer a program that will train and certify people as facilitators for accountability processes and healing circles. The more people are trained in these skills, the more we build capacity for solving conflicts and addressing harms within community, and are no longer reliant on the framework of fear.

The first floor of the Restore Oakland building will house a restaurant run by formerly incarcerated people and others who have been locked out of opportunity. It will include worker training programs for people to access career ladder jobs in the restaurant industry. Finally, it will be a place where people can come together to exert their collective agency in order to bring these solutions to scale.

Restore Oakland encapsulates all the constituent elements of the care-based safety model: resources, relationships, accountability, and participation.

CHAPTER 4

PREVENTING HARMS

Moving from Deprivation to Resources, from Suspicion to Relationships, and from Isolation to Participation

2005, Richmond, California

Bad accounting and mismanagement had led to a debilitating $35 million budget crisis that resulted in layoffs of three hundred city employees—nearly a third of the city's workforce. Services were curtailed and community centers and the library were shut down. The same year, some members of the city council requested the declaration of a state of emergency, which would mean the city, which they called a "war zone," would go into lockdown mode.[1] Two years later, Richmond received the unhappy distinction of being the ninth most dangerous city in America, its murder rate eleven times that of New York City's.

Violence and financial difficulties created an intertwined downward spiral. "Richmond was like a toxic zip code; developers would tell me they just couldn't get the financing. You know, redlining is still alive and well. But when violent crime goes down and the city gets safer, all of a sudden the investors say: 'This place is a good deal!' Violence prevention and economic development and investment really go hand in hand," says Bill Lindsay, city manager of Richmond.[2]

Richmond is located directly across the bay from San Francisco, on a peninsula, making it a natural spot for a major shipping port; for the western terminus of the railroad, which arrived in 1900; and for industry, like the Standard Oil refinery that was built in 1901. During World

War II, Richmond became one of the largest shipbuilding centers in the US, drawing tens of thousands of workers, many from the economically depressed South and Southwest. New systems were developed to care for those workers and their families, like the Kaiser Permanente HMO and daycare facilities that were designed to support Rosie the Riveter-type newly working women. But the care and investments that went into supporting wartime communities would give way to a cycle of poverty, violence, and suffering.

When the war ended, the shipyards closed. Some other industries took up residence, primarily in warehousing and chemicals, but the population steadily declined, even as many African American residents stayed, joined more recently by growing numbers of Latinx people. Slowly, the street corner replaced the shipyards and factory floors as the workplace for many of the city's young people. By the 1980s, war had returned, in a different form. The crisscrossing rail lines that had once brought workers to Richmond now created the Iron Triangle—the epicenter of violence, much of it related to sales of crack cocaine. The grandsons of war heroes and shipbuilders who fought for democracy now fought to control drug sales.

In the wake of the budget crisis, Lindsay, formerly the city manager of Orinda, California, took over in Richmond "ready for a challenge," as he puts it. He saw the potential in Richmond and encouraged the city's employees to think differently: "They were fearful. They wouldn't even apply common sense, out of fear they'd make a mistake. Fear was like a ball and chain, holding the city back from succeeding. You know, going back to what Roosevelt said when he came into the office dealing with the Great Depression: the most important thing we need to do is to *try something*."[3]

2007

DeVone Boggan didn't hail from Richmond or Oakland, or even California. He was from Michigan. But when he was seventeen, his mom, calling him "incorrigible" (DeVone himself admits to being a "knucklehead") sent him to live with his father, Daniel Boggan Jr., who was then the city manager of Berkeley. Daniel Boggan was of that generation of black men who, if they were to succeed, had to be "the first." He was the first African American city manager in Jackson, Michigan, and then in Portland, Oregon. He would later become the first African American chief operations officer of the National Collegiate Athletic Association. DeVone Boggan was deeply influenced by his father's persistence and success.[4]

DeVone graduated from UC Berkeley and Golden Gate Law School. Once he identified his passion for mentoring—remembering the life-changing intervention of a mentor he'd had back in Michigan when he first got in trouble for teenage antics—he found his way to the Mentoring Center in Oakland, which provides training and technical assistance to mentoring programs all over the country, and ultimately became its director.

The City of Richmond, in utter despair over its out-of-control violence and murder rate, after shelling out millions for ineffective and punitive anticrime programs, had hired a number of consultants to make recommendations, and it invited DeVone to submit his as well. His idea was creation of a brand-new agency, an Office of Neighborhood Safety. The ONS would not adopt a law-enforcement approach but would focus instead on accountability, by empowering the agency of residents, by providing resources and opportunities in strategic ways, and by leveraging relationships within the community—accountability, resources, agency (participation), and relationships.

Richmond's city manager, Lindsay, gave him the green light, inspired by the public health model focused on prevention and intervention, in hopes that less "treatment" (law enforcement) would be necessary. "It was different than what other cities were doing, but it made intuitive sense," says Lindsay. "And it was based on data." Analysis of the city's violent crimes had shown that approximately 70 percent of the homicides and gun-related violence were committed by fewer than thirty individuals, and more than half the killings occurred within an area of central Richmond less than five square miles in size. The strategy was to focus efforts in that area, track down those individuals, and engage them in the spirit of partnership.

In 2007 DeVone Boggan set up the ONS program, which diverged sharply from the status quo "lock 'em up" solutions. Between 2007 and 2014, murder rates dropped by 77 percent—in the words of many, a miracle. DeVone succeeded where most everyone thought he would fail, with scant resources, but with a huge heart, ingenuity, and determination.

When I met with DeVone in 2018 to interview him, he was sporting an ONS sweatshirt and a fedora. The hat is apparently his trademark, and it suited him. We sat in the lobby of his office to talk. As people came and went, he interrupted to greet each of them by name, usually with a long-distance fist bump. DeVone seemed to me like a pioneering coach who figured out the basic math behind the game before anyone else did and thus succeeded where everyone else thought he would fail.

Determination was key. "People did not like me. People didn't think I knew what I was doing. I'll be honest, I had my own confidence to deal with. I didn't know much about gun violence," he admitted to me.

Six days into the job, DeVone had his first city council meeting. He remembered the public comments: "Speaker one: 'This dude been here six days and he ain't done shit. We still got gun violence.' Speaker two: 'Why did we hire this house nigga, when we got all these field niggers in Richmond that can do the job?'" When the meeting was finally over, DeVone made a beeline for the door, depleted, only to be told by someone who would become a future city council member: "Don't unpack, nigga. We gon' have you out of here in thirty days."

Undeterred, DeVone created a team of people known as neighborhood change agents for street outreach and case management. The primary qualification? That they had been formerly incarcerated, preferably on gun charges. "I insisted," DeVone told me. "I said, I want them to be full-time, fully vested city employees. I wanted them to have the same benefits that I had as the director." The city bureaucracy seemed eternal and unrelenting, but DeVone got approval, and by April 2007 had hired a team of four, "three of whom are still with us today," defying all expectations. They were best suited for the job, for developing real relationships with those most at risk of violence—just so long as it was clear to community members that they had absolutely nothing to do with the police.

"I told them: Your job is to gain people's trust. You'll never be able to influence or direct or guide anyone that doesn't trust you," DeVone recalls. "They looked at me like, *nigga please*. We gon' show you who we are."

The neighborhood change agents spent hours talking to people, attending family gatherings, playing dominos and basketball, so they could connect with the thirty-plus people in Richmond whom the police had identified as most likely to do harm or come to harm. They built a rapport with those individuals until trust was established, and then offered them a voluntary "peacemaker fellowship." At first, ONS gave these "fellows" social services referrals and life-skills training to find jobs and earn degrees. Later, and more controversially, it offered them a monthly cash stipend and supervised trips outside Richmond.

"'You're paying people to not shoot each other?' the reporters asked me, incredulous," Bill Lindsay recalled. "But it was working, so I defended it." In fact, the money for the stipends comes from foundations and donors, while the city pays for the ONS staff and operations. But it's still highly controversial. A 2016 article in the *Guardian* newspaper commented: "Resistance to the ONS method may also reflect a more broadly American stigma against handouts. While the use of tangible incentives such as cash stipends and travel are very much in line with prevailing capitalist values, the very act of giving them away for free—especially to those who may still operate outside of society's lawful boundaries—would seem to conflict with a deep-seated ethos in our culture that opportunity must extend from merit."[5]

DeVone said it's all pretty much common sense to him: "I don't think there's anything original about this fellowship. It's made up of the things that healthy people have. In my family we have individual goals and family goals. I've been doing that with my kids since they were young. So I decided these fellows would make individual life maps and the elements of their life map will be things they need to be proficient in: personal safety, stable housing, educational pursuits, employment pursuits, behavioral health, and medical health—support with substance abuse issues, financial management, spirituality, recreation, parenting, conflict resolution, those kinds of things. And they're not going to develop it themselves; they develop it with a life coach."

He added: "Our theory of change is simple. I want them to desire to live." In fact, of the sixty-eight fellows who had participated at the time of our interview, sixty-four were still alive. It's impossible to say how many murders and acts of violence were prevented, but the reduction in homicides has endured over time. In the five years following adoption of the program in 2010, the average number of homicides in the city has been eighteen per year, compared to forty-one homicides per year average in the five previous years.[6] The positive economic impacts of the reduction in violence in those first five years were valued at $500 million, making the $1.9 million costs of the program (total for 2010 to 2014) a worthwhile investment.[7] It's evidence that federal and state resources should be directed to community-based violence interruption strategies that more than pay for themselves.

DeVone's strategy to reduce gun violence doesn't focus on guns. It focuses on people. Like most Americans, even a majority of NRA members, I think DeVone and I would agree that having comprehensive background checks and gun registration is common sense.[8] Like most Americans, we would agree that there are certain kinds of military-grade weapons that should be banned. These kinds of weapons don't serve the purpose of hunting or protecting one's home from a burglar. Commonsense policies could absolutely reduce the number of lives lost to gun violence. And yet changing the laws would not have had a great impact on the violence in

Richmond. In fact, California gun laws are already some of the toughest in the nation and the state banned assault weapons in 1989, a restriction that was expanded further in 2016.[9] In Richmond, however, a lot of the killings were committed using illegally obtained weapons. Focusing on the people behind the acts has the potential for the greatest transformation. DeVone's interventions end the cycle of violence itself, rather than just address its lethality.

The strategy is now widely called "the Richmond model," and is being adopted and considered by other cities, like Toledo, Ohio, and Washington, DC. DeVone has gone on to create a national organization called Advance Peace dedicated to investing in the development, health, and well-being of America's cities, in order to end gun violence.

The story of *The Little Engine That Could* is a quintessentially American tale of the power of persistence and optimism in overcoming all the odds. There's an echo of it in the real-life story of Billy Beane, who, as manager of the Oakland Athletics baseball team, revolutionized the sport by leveraging statistics in a way no one had before, leading his team to become competitive with much wealthier teams—a feat made famous by Michael Lewis's book *Moneyball* and the film starring Brad Pitt that was based on it. These are the comparisons that sprang to mind when I met with DeVone Boggan and Bill Lindsay to hear about what they achieved in Richmond.

What took root in Richmond isn't an exact blueprint for a new care-based model of safety, yet it illustrates several of the key ingredients. The moral of the story here is that we need to focus on the powerful combination of *resources, relationships*, and *participation*. The further lesson is that thinking outside the box, beyond dehumanization and criminalization, can lead to much more effective solutions. Also, like *The Little Engine That Could* and *Moneyball*, it exemplifies the spirit that will be required to implement a culture of caring across the country.

FROM DEPRIVATION TO RESOURCES

Given the harm done by an economic system that privileges profits and the rights of corporations over the well-being of the great majority of people, it is clear that we need a bold overhaul of the system. Where our spending—our resources—go reflects our priorities. Rather than investing further in the framework of fear, in the criminal dragnet, we need to invest in the social safety net. That's one of the major lessons of the Richmond model. When we devote resources to programs that make the most vulnerable people in our society healthier, more educated, and more engaged in meaningful pursuits, we make all of America safer. In the next part of the book, the "Reimagined Realities" chapters, I'll delve into many concrete examples of the opportunities we have for investing resources in a culture of care.

One major shift overall is taking a public health response to all the issues that are really health issues, such as substance abuse, depression, and other forms of mental illness. This includes supplementing or altogether replacing security personnel and police with trained counselors and crisis prevention teams, what I call robust first responders, in all kinds of public settings. These professionals, trained to handle mental health issues, substance abuse issues, issues that come with adolescence, and conflict resolution in general, would be the first point of contact in myriad situations that police now struggle to handle appropriately. In allocating more resources to them, we would need fewer resources for policing. New York University sociologist Patrick Sharkey has similarly called for "community guardians," a concept that shifts the emphasis away from aggressive and militarized policing and toward a community-building stance.[10] His vision entails convening and involving neighbors, government agencies, and service providers alongside police to share information about violence and harm that is happening and to collaborate on ways to create public safety.

California provides one of the best cautionary tales about what happens when resources for a culture of care get appropriated for the framework of fear. In the 1950s and 1960s, California governors Earl Warren and Pat Brown invested in care: in massive public infrastructure programs, including construction of the aqueduct that moves water from the wet northern regions of the state to the hotter agricultural regions in the south and the development of the nation's best public college system and public schools that were among the best in the country. Then, in 1978, California voters passed Proposition 13, which essentially locked in the tax on a property to the year the property was purchased, no matter how much the property increases in value.[11] Both residential and commercial properties are reassessed only when sold, resulting in a situation in which some businesses pay property taxes based on assessments that haven't changed in forty years.[12] When someone inherits a residential property, they inherit its low tax bills, too, and can turn a huge profit by renting the place out for skyrocketing rates. An example in real-life numbers: investment magnate Warren Buffett paid property taxes of $14,410, or 2.9 percent, on his $500,000 home in Omaha, Nebraska, but on his $4 million home in California, he paid only $2,264, or 0.056 percent (this was in 2003).[13]

Needless to say, Proposition 13 decimated California's tax base. Californians who attended the public school system that came after Prop. 13 were robbed of their educations as class sizes increased and teachers were laid off, and funding for the arts and libraries and computer labs were slashed.

In her book *Golden Gulag*, professor Ruth Wilson Gilmore describes how at around this time a little-known union called the California Correctional Peace Officers Association (CCPOA) began to make big promises on prisons. The CCPOA had a presentation that it took to rural towns across the state. It promised to bring roads and sewer connections by building prisons. It promised a funding source that would help revitalize local areas. Its pitch was wildly successful. From 1980 to 2000, California built twenty-three new prisons and just one new university. From the state's general fund revenue in 1970, corrections received 3.7 percent, while nearly 14 percent was allocated for the state university systems; in 2014, corrections received nearly 9 percent and the state university system received 5.2 percent of funds.[14]

The prisons were financed through state-funded lease revenue bonds. Such bonds had historically been used to fund hospitals and tolled highways, which provide some return. Prisons do not provide a return. As the power of the CCPOA grew, it began to redirect its union dues back toward policies that would benefit it, lobbying for longer sentences. Longer sentences meant more prisoners which meant more union jobs, which meant more dues for lobbying for longer sentences, in a self-serving cycle.

By the mid-2000s, the state had been sued for overcrowded prisons, and California's coffers were more than empty: the state was in debt. Even the prison guard union began to have second thoughts about the system. The year 2008 was a turning point: a "tough-on-crime" ballot initiative called Proposition 6, which would have put more youth and adults in prisons, was resoundingly defeated—by 70 percent, the largest margin of any ballot initiative that year. Because of concerns for its workers' safety amid prison overcrowding, the CCPOA itself not only remained neutral on the bill but went so far as to deploy Minorities in Law Enforcement, a nonprofit arm associated with the CCPOA, to oppose the proposition.[15]

Since then the tides have continued turning, and there has been progress in California to undo some of the worst excesses of this prison building boom. There is an initiative on the 2020 ballot in California called Schools and Communities First which would undo Prop. 13 and restore the tax base in California. California corporations should pay their fair share to ensure the future health of the state. The generation of homeowners who benefited most are well into retirement now, while many younger Californians and newcomers want the affordable housing, strong public education, and other services, such as assistance to families and infrastructure maintenance, that restoration would support. It would go a long way toward shifting California from a broke, unequal, and punitive economy toward a more caring economy where social services and schools support families and their children.

A shift from deprivation to availability of resources means we can and should utilize direct government investment, rather than rely on the market, as we have been—especially when universal access and more equitable outcomes are a priority. To build an inclusive economy that is the foundation for safety and well-being, the government should directly ensure universal access to those goods and services that are essential for human dignity, including housing, healthcare, higher education, childcare, eldercare, and pensions, as well as basic financial services and internet access. Government resources are especially necessary when our goals have long time horizons and hard-to-measure outcomes, or require national (and international) coordination to achieve, such as addressing the issue of climate change.

What resources? For starters, there's the $80 billion to $1.2 trillion that we spend annually on incarceration, most of which should be reallocated.[16] Mathematician David Roodman estimates "the societal benefit of decarceration at $92,000 per person-year of averted confinement."[17] There's the "$100 billion to $150 billion [we spent] on failed or unworthy homeland-security programs" in the fifteen years following 9/11, according to a 2016 article in the *Atlantic*.[18] A tax on the rich that merely matches the rate that was in place from 1913 until 1982—70 percent for the highest tax bracket—or, even better, the 90 percent top tax rate we had in place from 1944 to 1963, would go a long way to providing the resources we need.[19] For example, Senator Elizabeth Warren proposes a tax on wealth (as opposed to income) of 2 percent for net worth above $50 million and 3 percent for those with more than $1 billion, which could generate $2.75 trillion in revenue over a decade.[20] A higher estate tax, a higher capital gains tax rate, a tax on financial transactions . . . there are a lot of places to go to get the resources we need.

In March 2019, Congresswoman Alexandria Ocasio-Cortez tweeted: "Cost of the GOP Tax Scam for the rich: ~$1.8-2.3 Trillion. Cost of forgiving all student loans in America: ~$1.5 Trillion. Clearly where there's a will, there's a way. When people say that there isn't 'enough' to do these things, what they mean is they don't *want* to do them."[21] Several days later she asked: "Why is there more money for a fake crisis than a real one?"[22] Exactly. We have plenty of money for what we need to do.

We must start reallocating resources for safety now—since we can't start yesterday—because we know that the principle of compound interest holds true in community investments as it does in the world of finance. The earlier investments are made in a community's history, and in a child's life, the greater the dividends and rewards for everyone in our society.

FROM SUSPICION TO RELATIONSHIPS

When people talk about the Richmond model, they tend to focus on the stipends that were given to the young men who participated in the fellowship. They often overlook the importance of the relationships that were built. DeVone didn't just see people who were believed to be responsible for violence. He saw people with the same needs as his own children. He saw people who could be his family members.

"The first thing that came to mind for me is: I have two children. It [the program in Richmond] couldn't be anything less than what they have access to. So what do they have access to? First thing is daily contact and engagement every single day of their life with healthy people, multiple times a day."[23]

Accordingly, DeVone made sure each fellowship participant had daily contact with one of the change agents. He took these young men on trips outside of the Bay Area, then outside of the state, and then outside of the country. With each trip, he stretched their sense of possibility in the world and in their own neighborhood. With each successive trip, young men from rival neighborhoods were brought in closer proximity. As he expanded their horizons, he built a foundation for peace in all of Richmond.

Richmond illustrates the role of relationships in keeping us safe. Whether the relationship is between parent and child, teacher and student, or neighbor and neighbor, rather than turning *on* each other, we must turn *to* each other, as one of my mentors, Van Jones, has said. When we turn on each other, the cycle of trauma and violence just continues.

Lovemme Corazón, whose story I shared previously, decided to enroll in a psychology program, saying: "As a survivor, I grew up with the idea that abusive love is love. I think community is a very imperative tool to unlearn that. . . . Communal care to me is very much about developing personal relationships with people. You know, when you're sad or you need support you call your friend or your family. Communal care is opening that up and instead of having one or two people, having . . . this network of really close friends who all check in with each other. Especially as marginalized folks, [it] is very important."[24]

Safety is not tied to our capacity to watch our neighbors, but rather based on our capacity to truly look out for one another. This is what the social reformer Jane Jacobs, author of *The Death and Life of Great American Cities*, recognized as she looked out of the window of her Manhattan apartment: "The first thing to understand is that the public peace of cities is not kept primarily by the police, necessary as the police are. It is kept primarily by an intricate, almost unconscious, network of voluntary controls and standards among the people themselves, and enforced by the people themselves."[25] This is exactly what the neighborhood change agents in Richmond were tasked with doing.

As DeVone says: "The fellows will tell you: once a fellow, always a fellow."

Shifting the focus away from suspicion and toward trust and relationships helps to address one of the core failures of the framework of fear: there is no "them," there's only "us." I know that right now, in the middle of this extremely politically and morally divided moment in our nation's history, this perspective seems naive. Yet this is not only a fundamental truth of humanity—reflected in sciences such as ecology, physics, and biochemistry, where our actual physical interrelatedness is proven at every level of complexity—it's the reality of the complicated identities of perpetrator, bystander, and victim/survivor. We all embody all identities at some point. The paradox of proximity means that harm will most likely be caused by someone we know, and this is most true when we look at domestic violence and abuse of children. There are no permanent "bad guys." We all harm each other, just in different degrees.

The farther apart we become as a society, a nation, a neighborhood, and a family, the greater the opportunity there is for hurt and harm to occur. When we come together, hard though it may be, we increase the likelihood of resolving conflict. When we separate, there is no such opportunity.

After the 2012 murder of Trayvon Martin by neighborhood watch captain George Zimmerman, we at the Ella Baker Center developed an event called Night Out for Safety and Liberation (NOSL). It's a remix of a community event that's been going on nationwide for the last thirty years, known as National Night Out, which is hosted by police precincts and sponsored by the National Association of Town Watch with the intention of promoting the role of law enforcement in creating community safety. At traditional block parties and barbeques, police enlist residents in the effort, for example by having residents become the "eyes and ears of the police." I don't believe that we make neighborhoods safer by encouraging people to spy on each other and report back to the police. That sounds more like a George Orwell novel to me. Focusing on policing as the primary path to public safety causes harm to many innocent people, especially people of color, and does not lead to safer, stronger, or healthier communities.

"One day a year of hosting a block party and trying to reach our community by putting up a bouncy castle for our children doesn't make up for the other 364 days of the year when that's not happening—when we see ongoing murders by the police in our community, and see the effect of mass incarceration on our families," says Cindy Martinez, who hosts, with her organization Enlace (now called Freedom to Thrive), NOSL in the South Bronx.[26]

The point of our NOSL event is to reimagine safety from a broader perspective, a more holistic one. We want people to get to know others in their community and build relationships and compassion. We believe community residents can do much more than be the eyes and ears of law enforcement. Residents also have hearts, hands, and minds. By leveraging all of our skills and capacities, we have a much better chance of creating safe neighborhoods. We believe that this is what leads to greater safety, not suspicion of one another. My favorite poster associated with NOSL says, "I don't watch my neighbors. I see them. We make our community safer together."

FROM ISOLATION TO PARTICIPATION

There is individual participation and collective participation. Participation for an individual entails having access—in the literal, physical sense of being free to move, as well as access provided via social connections and a sense of possibility. It's related to being free, autonomous, and empowered. Sometimes it gets expressed as *agency*, the ability to be the protagonist of your own story. You can see all the choices, and beyond that dream up previously unthinkable new choices, unlimited by past experiences or deprivation, or any of the other factors that can get in the way. And having seen the various choices, you are free to make your own. The flip side, of course, is that agency involves being accountable for your choices: that is what it is to be the protagonist. You cannot lay the blame at others' feet.

Agency is the antidote to trauma, according to the trauma expert Bessel van der Kolk. He defines agency as "the feeling of being in charge of your life: knowing where you stand, knowing that you have a say in what happens to you, knowing that you have some ability to shape your circumstances."[27] Given the magnitude of trauma caused by the framework of fear, it's clear that participation needs to be part of healing harms as well as preventing harms from happening. Individual agency leads people to form associations that generate public discourse and hold the government and other powerful institutions and people to account.

What agency is for the individual, democracy is for the nation. It is We the People, being the protagonists of the American story, dreaming up new choices, taking collective action, and holding ourselves accountable for those choices. Real democracy expands access to power, choice, and decision-making for everyone. The promise of democracy is *e pluribus unum*. Out of many one. We are supposed to be one whole, one interconnected people: America. Strengthening the muscle of collective action is imperative so we can hold large institutions and powerful individuals accountable.

Almost two decades ago, sociologist Robert Putnam tracked the steadily declining level of participation in America's civic life in his seminal book *Bowling Alone*. He attributed the shift to various factors, including the popularity of television, and "the so-called 'slum clearance' policies of the 1950s and 1960s [that] replaced physical capital, but destroyed social capital, by disrupting existing community ties."[28] I'd add that people need to have fair wages and work hours in order to be able to participate in social and civic activities: how are you going to make it to extracurricular activities when you're doing three jobs to make ends meet?

Putnam argued that people's voluntary membership and engagement—whether in a political campaign, a union, a book club, or a bowling league—generates trust and social cohesion. It is a way of creating multiplex relationships in a complex society. Your coworker becomes your book club buddy or childcare co-op member. Putnam presented evidence for how robust civic participation and collective action correlates with reduced violent crime, greater health, higher standardized test scores, and increased prosperity.

According to some sociologists, civic engagement increased after 9/11, especially among young people, who showed up in record numbers for President Obama's 2008 campaign and mobilized for Occupy.[29] Yet a 2014 poll found that only 1 percent of Americans are really politically active, measured as participation in activities that included: writing or calling an elected official, attending a community meeting, volunteering in the community, attending political rallies, and donating money to a political campaign or community organization. They found that people with higher incomes and college degrees were much more likely to participate in at least one of the civic activities.[30]

A University of Maryland study on the link between inequality, trust, and civic engagement determined that "where inequality is higher, the poor may feel powerless. They will perceive that their views are not represented in the political system and they will opt out of civic engagement. . . . Wealthy, more highly educated people take a greater role in civic life. . . . They are more likely to be interested in politics, to know whom to contact, and perhaps most critically, to know how to make their voices known."[31]

Although political engagement goes beyond voting, being denied the right to vote obviously limits your sense of agency. We know that many formerly incarcerated people are denied a voice in elections, and the disenfranchisement rate for African Americans was four times higher than for the non-African American population.[32] The Union of Concerned Scientists found that when people aren't allowed to vote it makes it harder for them to protect their health and safety. This creates what they described as a "vicious cycle," in which already disadvantaged communities are made worse off because of felony disenfranchisement and other barriers to voting.[33]

People of all backgrounds feel disillusioned with government. They feel like it doesn't work for them. Trust in our democracy is dropping to record lows at the very time that we most need to have everyone participating. Events like election tampering, voter suppression, and gerrymandering—adjusting the boundaries of voting districts to give your party the advantage—seem to be happening more and more frequently, further undermining people's trust and willingness to participate. A 2018 survey found that only 40 percent of Americans were satisfied with American democracy right now, and almost half of those aged eighteen to forty believe that "democracy serves the elite" (48 percent of those aged eighteen to twenty-nine; 46 percent of those aged thirty to forty).[34]

Now more than ever we need to engage with each other and with our democracy. We need to build our tolerance for constructive disagreement so that we feel safe participating. We need to make our voice heard in support of the kinds of government spending and programs that will support our well-being and safety.

All of us can also participate in public safety by playing the role of community guardians. This is different from the "if you see something, say something" culture of suspicion that has people acting as the eyes and ears of the police. In fact, when we expand the role that ordinary people play as first responders, that will help reduce the violence and brutality by police, who are currently responding in all kinds of instances where other responses are more appropriate. Currently there is too expansive a view of the role police should play—they essentially are expected to act as social worker, mental health provider, school discipline officer, vice principal, etc.—while there is simultaneously too narrow a view of how community members can engage and take a role in creating safety.

We know what the impact is of members in the community and neighbors who engage, who listen to each other across differences and become involved in helping each other out, and who help solve domestic challenges and share with each other. Research by sociologist Patrick Sharkey illustrated the connection between community engagement and crime reduction:

> It was hard work by residents, organized into community groups and block clubs, that transformed urban neighborhoods. . . . In a given city with 100,000 people, we found that every new organization formed to confront violence and build stronger neighborhoods led to about a 1 percent drop in violent crime and murder. On the basis of these results, which provide the strongest evidence to date of the causal impact of local nonprofits, we concluded that the explosion of community organizations that took place in the 1990s likely played a substantial role in explaining the decline in violence.[35]

There are countless stories of the community elders who, now retired, spend their time talking with everyone in the neighborhood, knowing everyone's business, and facilitating and resolving conflict situations, who serve as informal violence prevention powerhouses, reducing both gun violence and the role of police. These forms of community engagement and strengthened relationships are the foundation of efforts to hold each other to account when we cause harm, and help each other heal from that harm.

Everyone has a right to participate. When we take part in things, when we engage, when we have a sense of choice in the matter, we feel a greater sense of worth, dignity, purpose. All this goes a long way to creating social cohesion, trust, relationships, and accountability and, therefore, a greater sense of safety.

PART III

REIMAGINED
REALITIES

CHAPTER 5

ALLEN AND DURRELL

February 2004

I had just gotten out of law school. I was preparing to take the bar and would later find out that I passed . . . trouble was, I didn't want to be a lawyer. Thankfully, I was hired not as an attorney but as a community organizer—the same kind of work President Obama had done on the South Side of Chicago, as he describes in his memoir *Dreams from My Father*, which had just been reprinted that same year. Unfortunately, I didn't have a great deal of organizing experience. I did have one skill, though: the ability to listen, which is required of all community organizers.

My supervisor, Lenore Anderson, was also an attorney, but a real one. She had finished law school two years before me. Lenore was supporting a small group of families with loved ones inside the notorious CYA youth prisons. CYA stood for California Youth Authority, but others ominously said that the other meaning of CYA—"cover your ass"—was more appropriate, given the rates of sexual abuse of young people within the system.

Our mission was to build a statewide network of families with loved ones in the CYA prison system. The idea was that if enough families came together and collaborated, they could change the system.

You know those sports team movies where a coach or a player has to recruit teammates to form an underdog team that no one believes in, but that will, against all odds, somehow win the championship? That was us: a handful of mothers and grandmothers sitting around a table, a group that decided to call itself Families for Books Not Bars. And me.

There were huge obstacles to overcome. The families were isolated from one another geographically, and even if they did see each other while visiting a prison, they were forbidden by the prison guards from interacting. Then there was the paralyzing shame associated with having a loved one in the justice system. Sometimes the loved one had to be reminded that everyone deserves to be treated with dignity, even when they have made terrible mistakes.

I heard the stories of so many families that they started to blend together. The children and grandchildren of these families were locked in remote youth prisons across California, suffering unspeakable abuses. When they were allowed to visit, family members found those children bruised and abused. There was an utter lack of programming, nothing remotely qualifying as rehabilitation, only traumatization. Over and over I heard how young people were being isolated for twenty-three hours a day, for days and weeks, and sometimes months on end. Sometimes, I heard about a child who died in prison.

The first time I met Allen I was nervous, anxious, worried, and beginning to question whether I was cut out for my new job. Neither law school nor organizing training could have prepared me for this moment. What do you say to someone who's just endured a horrific loss? Making matters worse, I was going to meet Allen at his place of work, a ritzy hotel called the St. Francis. It was just blocks from our small and windowless nonprofit office space in downtown San Francisco.

The walk over felt too quick. It was a windy day; I felt it on my back as if it were pushing me forward. The hotel's giant opulent hallways and soaring ceilings reminded me that I had left school like yesterday. At the end of one of those long hallways was my destination: the shoeshine stand. I managed to put one foot in front of the other over ornate carpet designs until I arrived.

I had worried it would be even more difficult to talk to him while he was at work, but it turned out to be a relief. When I got there, Allen was already chatting with the man whose shoes he was caring for. (I would learn quickly that Allen did "shoe care"—he did not "shine shoes.") All I had to do was listen. Tacked to the stand was a photo of Allen and a young man: proud father smiling from ear to ear, arm around his son. His hands moving effortlessly, Allen talked about his son's love of baseball. He talked about what went on inside the CYA prison system. He would talk to anyone who would listen about the need for answers and for change. This is how I learned the details of Durrell Feaster's story.

January 19, 2004

It was a holiday: Martin Luther King Jr. Day. Your average eighteen-year-old boy would spend the day hanging out with friends or holed up playing video games, or maybe sports. Maybe he'd screw around a little, drink some beers, or smoke some weed, take his dad's car out for a joyride, make out with his current crush. When I was eighteen, I'm fairly certain that I spent MLK Day sleeping in. I would impress myself by how long I could sleep in on a weekend or holiday. I think my record was about 1 p.m.

In many ways, Durrell Feaster was your average eighteen-year-old. He was upbeat. He loved baseball. He had a thing for Reese's Peanut Butter Cups. He had been corresponding with college admission officials about starting school in the fall. After completing a course in installing sprinkler systems, and enjoying the work, he had begun dreaming of launching a landscaping business after college, maybe even going into the business with his dad. In the photo I've seen of Durrell, he looks like a biracial James Dean, his head tilted back, a slight challenge in his gaze, that classic cool look of youthful immortality.

But on Monday, January 19, 2004, Durrell took his own life. He managed to hang himself with his bedsheets, from the top bunk of his bunk bed. He was found too late to be revived, and the coroner declared the cause of death to be asphyxiation due to hanging.

It was about four years prior to that when things had begun to unravel for Durrell. His parents divorced, and he wound up living with his dad, Allen. Allen was a great dad, twenty years sober, taking great pride in his job providing shoe care at the prestigious St. Francis. Entire baseball teams would stay at the hotel. Once Allen brought home Boston Red Sox ace pitcher Pedro Martinez's autograph for his baseball-crazy son. Father and son considered themselves each other's best friends.

But even without your parents divorcing, being a fourteen-year-old boy has its own challenges, as your voice cracks and deepens, hair and acne sprout on your face, and your hormones go berserk. Durrell had ADHD on top of that. He started skipping class, skipping school altogether. Struggling to raise his teenage son alone, Allen sought assistance from the police to help with the truancy. Allen had survived a tough youth himself, having been born in the Bronx in 1954, with violence, abuse, and alcohol all present in his early life. He credited the Air Force with saving his life, and hoped for something similar when he turned to the police for help with Durrell.[1]

But instead of providing resources for support or guidance, the police sent Durrell to a group home six hours from his dad. It's a common enough intervention strategy, removing a kid from his home and placing him in a boot camp, treatment center, or group home—to be yelled at by drill sergeant-like supervisors and to do group therapy with delinquent peers. It's most often not an effective strategy. Even if there's positive behavior change *inside* this kind of place, everything changes when the kids get back into "the real world." Rates of recidivism, of getting tangled up in the criminal legal system again (or again and again) tend to be high.

Allen, who did not have a car, was unable to visit his son due to the distance and the cost of the trip. Miserable, Durrell ran away from the group home with another kid who stole a car in order to get back to his family. Durrell rode in the stolen vehicle with him. For this offense, fifteen-year-old Durrell was charged with grand theft auto and was placed in California's youth prison system at the Preston Youth Correctional Facility. This time Durrell was two hours from his father, but still inaccessible, as there was no public transportation that would get Allen even close.

Preston was located in Ione, California, off of Highway 104 in the Sierra Nevada foothills. Originally known as the Preston School of Industry when it opened in 1894, it's best known for its towering red brick "castle" . . . and for its reputation for more than a *century* of atrocious living conditions and extreme brutality by staff, and malnourishment and overwork of the youth imprisoned there.[2] A series of reports in the 1980s condemned it for rampant sexual abuse, violent assaults, gang activity, suicide attempts, and appalling isolation cells, which were described like dungeons: "filthy, dank rooms coved with vermin, blood, and feces where youths were confined for 23-hours a day, with one hour spent shackled in a cage for exercise."[3]

Durrell Feaster was one of those who spent the greater part of his days at Preston in solitary confinement—twenty-three hours a day.

With only a month left to serve of his three-year sentence, Durrell and his cellmate, seventeen-year-old Deon Whitfield, were found hanging by their bedsheets, side by side. They were in cell number 27 in the Ironwood unit, where cells measure about six feet by eight feet, like dank closets, just a slat in the metal door for a window.

Allegedly it was suicide. Allen did not believe that his son took his own life. Three days earlier, on January 16, he had spoken on the phone with Durrell, who was happy about his upcoming release and optimistic about his future.

"They killed my son," Allen said. "They treated him like an animal. He was not a hardcore criminal. He was a child. They killed his joy."

Things did not have to unfold like this, for Durrell or for so many youngsters like him.

It's not difficult to imagine a different outcome for him and for Allen. There are at least three turning points in his story that could have led to a happier ending for father and son, and their community. While this hypothetical reflection on alternate realities won't help Durrell, it can be valuable as we set about creating a new model of public safety and accountability. After all, part of what makes us uniquely human is our capacity to be self-reflective about our past and present, and imagine a different kind of future.

The first turning point for Durrell was in school. Like so many children today, Durrell had been diagnosed with ADHD. He had stopped showing up for classes and then for school altogether. What would have held his interest in school? I don't believe there's any student so hopeless or apathetic that they can't be engaged in learning: it's just a matter of figuring out what will hold their interest. We know for a fact that Durrell wasn't apathetic; we know that before he died, Durrell discovered a passion for landscape design. Is it beyond the realm of imagining that Durrell's school could have offered ways for him to learn about gardening and design?

Recognizing the problems with the standardized "factory model of education"—a result of schooling intended originally to train factory workers during the industrial era—more affluent schools have devoted more and more resources to personalized and project-based learning. Underinvestment in public schools, however, meant fewer innovations in learning and education. A 2019 report revealed that "nonwhite school districts receive $23 billion less than white districts, despite serving the same number of students."[4] Most public schools constantly have to do more with fewer and fewer resources, resulting in the decimation of arts, physical education, libraries, and other "nonessentials," even as they struggle to attract and retain good teachers.

At the same time, however, many of these schools are investing in security systems—everything from metal detectors to security cameras to
armed guards—with negligible or even counterproductive effects. Through
the federal 1033 program, school police agencies around the country obtained surplus military equipment, such as powerful rifles, grenade launchers, and armored vehicles. At least twenty-two districts in eight states used
1033 before President Obama implemented restrictions on the program in
2015, but President Trump rescinded the restrictions in mid-2017, clearing
the way for schools to once again obtain military equipment.

So why not take that money and invest it instead in, for example, ex-
periential learning programs, including landscaping and gardening, which
would provide the kind of hands-on, project-based learning and problem-
solving experiences that many believe will best prepare our children for
the future?

We even have models for schools where this is already happening.
One example is Orchard Gardens, a public school in Roxbury, Massachusetts. At the pilot school's opening in 2003, the community had high
expectations. The building was clad in panels the deep yellow color of a
school bus, with pops of red around the windows and doors. Inside were
art studios, a dance studio, even a theater with cushy seats. But the vision
of a *Fame*-type school of arts never came to pass. There was so much violence that students were prohibited from wearing backpacks, out of fear
that they would hide weapons in them. The school ranked in the bottom
five of all public schools in the state of Massachusetts.[5] In 2009, Boston
Public Schools superintendent Carol Johnson announced that Orchard
Gardens would be one of fourteen Boston "turnaround schools" and was
slated for massive overhauls and reinvention due to its low test scores
and the unrelenting turnover of principals.[6]

In 2010, Andrew Bott ignored the advice of his colleagues, who called
the school a "career killer," and became the school's sixth principal in
seven years. He fired the security guards and took the funding ear-
marked for security and used it for arts programs instead. The results
in both safety and school scores were remarkable. Within the next four
years, the school had one of the fastest student improvement rates of
any school in the state, ranking in the top 10 percent as measured by
growth in mathematics and English language arts of all schools in Massachusetts, while the percentage of students reading at grade level increased 250 percent.[7]

If Durrell had gone to such a school, he might have felt engaged
enough to stay in class and graduate and go on to make his dream a real-

ity. As it was, he lost interest and started skipping school, and it was up to Allen to hold the line.

One of the challenging things about adolescence is that at the precise time kids most need mentorship from adults (often parents) who care about them, they usually don't want to hear anything those grown-ups have to say. During the time when they're experimenting with becoming independent and self-sufficient, their relationships with their parents are often at their most fragile. Until recently, the prevailing mentality was that because most of the human brain has been formed by age six, older kids and teens were "a lost cause"—that it was "too late for them"—resulting in experts and policy mostly focusing on early childhood. But adolescent brain science has revealed that our brains are still developing until we reach the age of 25.[8] Teenage brains are much more changeable than we once thought.

Because of this, schools can play an important role at a formative time. Unfortunately, especially in under-resourced schools, most teenagers have next to no relationships with adults. They are much more likely to find a police officer than a guidance counselor. A recent study by Californians for Justice (CFJ), a student-led organization working to improve public schools, found that one out of five students did not have a single teacher or staff member make eye contact or greet them by name. Nearly 50 percent of students were never asked how they were doing by a teacher or staff member at school.[9] Based on those findings, CFJ is leading an initiative of "relationship-centered schools." Instead of asking how we improve test scores, they ask: How do we build relationships as the foundation for student achievement? Even when he had zero interest in listening to his dad, if Durrell had had just one positive relationship with a teacher or counselor at school, things might have gone differently for him.

Adolescents are also hardwired to break the rules at the very time when the consequences for actions quickly grow in severity, especially in the context of zero-tolerance schools. Zero-tolerance policies grew out of the war on drugs in the 1990s and became more aggressive in the wake of school shootings like the one at Columbine High School in Colorado. The idea is that if a student is acting up and doesn't stop when asked to do so, then the student needs to be removed from the classroom. When a student misbehaves repeatedly, the typical response is to kick them out, either temporarily (suspension) or permanently (expulsion).

Both my sister and mother are teachers, so I am not unsympathetic to the idea that for the good of the rest of the students and their learning, the disruptive one has to be removed from the class. There are between fifteen and thirty or more other kids in a classroom, depending on the school district. The logic of zero tolerance is that, from a greater good perspective, the needs of the majority should be prioritized.

Yet, zero-tolerance policies have been proven to cause more harm than good. The majority of students who have been arrested on school grounds have been accused of minor nonviolent infractions, like possessing marijuana or spraying graffiti; however, there are many instances in which such policies resulted in children being suspended or expelled and sent through the criminal legal system for completely harmless actions, like talking on cellphones or watching a fight between other students. A twelve-year-old girl was arrested after doodling on her desk.[10] A seven-year-old boy was suspended for taking bites out of a Pop-Tart until it was gun-shaped.[11] A ten-year-old boy was suspended for playing with an imaginary bow and arrow, even though no one was harmed.[12]

"We've become reliant on distancing as a way to manage conflict. That's what a suspension is—I can't manage you, so I move you away," says Barbara McClung, the director of behavioral health initiatives for Oakland Unified School District.[13]

Zero-tolerance policies in school discipline were supposed to reduce bias and level the playing field by having standard predetermined consequences for misbehavior, but studies, including a landmark report from the American Psychological Association, have proven that disabled children, African American children, and Latinx children are being disciplined more severely and expelled or suspended at disproportionately higher rates. More than 70 percent of students involved in school-related arrests are black or Latinx.[14]

The measures that schools have implemented include controlling access to school buildings by locking or monitoring doors during school hours, installing security cameras and metal detectors, requiring staff to wear ID badges, using random dog sniffs to check for drugs, and stationing security guards or police officers on school grounds.

Research has shown that instead of effectively preventing threats, fighting, and perceptions of violence and disorder, the presence of metal detectors, security cameras, or armed guards in schools is counterproductive, decreasing students' sense of safety, and often increasing fear and mistrust. In some schools, attendance has worsened when metal detectors were employed. Many people argue the hours students lose standing in line for metal detectors would be much better spent studying or engaging in the classroom.

Security or law enforcement personnel who work on school campuses do not generally receive any specialized training tailored to the policing of youth. This lack of training results in the over-usage of punitive measures like arrests, thereby deterring vulnerable students from receiving support resources. Suspended and expelled children often wind up home alone or out on the street, falling behind academically. This winds up being the first stop on the so-called "school-to-prison pipeline" for many children, resulting in arrest records and low academic achievement, and high drop-out rates. Those arrested face the stigma of having criminal records, which have a lifelong effect on chances of getting a job, financial aid, or a home. An arrest doubles the likelihood that a student will drop out or be pushed out of school. Moreover, just coming into contact with police as a youth is linked to involvement with the criminal justice system as an adult.

What would it take to create school environments that were capable of supporting children through adolescence? Is it possible to imagine a school environment that would have been supportive of Durrell without detracting from other students' experiences, and even enhancing their experiences? One thing we could do is recognize that part of being an adolescent is breaking rules. It is as normal as a toddler dropping their food on the ground to see what happens. Why can't we create middle and high school environments where certain rules are set up with the *intention* that they be broken, in order to stimulate and engage young people?

These more humane and engaging kinds of school environments were not in place. So when Durrell ignored his attempts at discipline, Allen sought an intervention. He knew that Durrell might be removed from home if he continued to miss school. Truancy is a crime that impacts both children and their parents, who can be fined, arrested, or imprisoned, or have their custody revoked because of their child's repeated unexcused absences. Allen called the police out of utter desperation. As an African American, Allen had to be familiar with the reputation of police as it relates to the treatment of young African American men. Yet he held out hope that, much like the armed forces had created an opportunity for him to become more disciplined and successful, the police might help his son. Ultimately, by calling the police, Allen set in motion precisely what he feared: his child being removed from the home and entangled in the juvenile justice system.

The juvenile justice system doesn't do a good job of supporting parents partly because it sees the parents as part of the problem rather than part of the solution. The background assumption of the juvenile justice system is *parens patriae*—Latin for "we can take your kids." The state can step in and assume responsibility for a child when it deems this necessary. The problem is that the United States has a long and flawed track record when it comes to the use of this power, a record particularly troubling when it comes to children of color. Since the inception of the juvenile justice and foster care systems, youth of color have been treated badly, unnecessarily separated from their parents and disproportionately subjected to harsh and cruel treatment.[15] Unfortunately, these trends continue into the present day.

Who has a much better track record of helping children thrive? Parents and grandparents, whenever they themselves have sufficient resources to thrive. As they announce every time you travel on an airplane, it is hard to take care of your child's oxygen mask if your own mask isn't in place. The oxygen mask for the grown-ups can be interpreted as having basic needs fulfilled, in the form of dignified steady work, decent housing, healthcare, clean air and water and food—the fundamental tenets of human existence.

Beyond that, for more challenging circumstances, the oxygen mask may be represented by so-called "intensive in-home therapy."[16] These interventions typically include the support of a psychologist who provides counseling sessions in the home and in the family's community over a period of three to five months. Despite the "intensive" part, these programs have actually proven less costly and more effective than youth detention and incarceration. Costs average between $6,000 to $9,500 per youth, compared with a typical stay in a juvenile corrections facility, at $66,000 to $88,000; meanwhile, arrest rates for young people who received this type of service were 25 to 70 percent lower.[17] Allen could have benefited greatly from the support of a trained social worker providing him with advice and resources for Durrell.

Every parent needs help. I love my daughters. But on my worst days, the challenges of work and life can mean that I don't show it the best way I could. If I were out of work or sick, or had a job but couldn't afford rising rents, the stresses of those situations would compound quickly, making it that much harder to be the parent I want to be. Surviving in the United States is becoming increasingly difficult. Rather than punishing parents, especially poor parents, we should be investing in ways to support them. As Bessel van der Kolk explains:

> We can assume that parents do the best they can, but all parents need
> help to nurture their kids. Nearly every industrialized nation, with the

exception of the United States, recognizes this and provides some form of guaranteed support to families. . . . Quality early-childhood programs that involve parents and promote basic skills in disadvantaged children more than pay for themselves in improved outcomes.[18]

Government systems intended to serve youth should be designed not to supplant parents but to supplement and support them. Making such support universal, guaranteed, and unconditional (rather than based on elaborate applications or assessments) would help to eliminate the perception that families whose kids are struggling are less capable and less deserving. The US differs from most developed countries in failing to offer universal child benefits, also known as "child allowances," which are paid to every family with children whether the parents work or not, and can be used for whatever the family deems necessary: food, rent, childcare, lessons, etc. The evidence says that not only are parents less stressed and more able to engage in parenting as a result of government allowances, but over a lifetime, a child whose parents received supports got higher test scores and higher earnings, and was healthier. A 2018 report in the *Cornell Policy Review* concluded:

> The United States already recognizes the value of assisting its citizens with childcare via the child tax exemption and Child Tax Credit. . . . The United States currently uses a patchwork system of subsidies to help cover the costs of childcare that is administered through the federal tax system. The Child Tax Credit offers a refund of $1,000 per child per year, and the Child Tax Exemption offers $4,000 per child per year. . . . While these programs have been helpful to middle-income families, they have systematically omitted low-income families, and their once-yearly payment schedule is not designed to address the growing epidemic of family income instability throughout the year. By replacing these two tax-based programs with a universal child allowance, the United States would provide an income floor for all families with children and formally recognize the notion that the well-being of future generations is worth a significant social investment.[19]

It's hard to imagine how different Allen's and Durrell's story might have turned out had they received an allowance of $250 to $300 per month. But that didn't come to pass.

Even though nothing changed at two intervention points—Durrell didn't get support at school and Allen got no support at home—there was still an opportunity for a different outcome when Durrell was caught in the act of stealing a car to get back home.

What if instead of being sent to a remote youth prison as punishment, Durrell and the car's owner had sat down together and talked? A plan might have been developed so that Durrell could make amends and pay the owner back for any damage, loss of income, and other negative outcomes associated with the crime. It wouldn't have been an easy conversation for Durrell, facing that person's anger and disappointment, and being confronted directly with his own shame and responsibility. But Durrell would have learned a lot from it, and it might have been the encounter that made him take responsibility for the rest of his life. This would have been the path of restorative justice. Durrell would have been held accountable, while still being held in community. Upon completing the program, Durrell could have connected to an earn-while-you-learn program, essentially an apprenticeship under a professional that would have him gaining qualifications and building skills while earning around $15 per hour.[20]

Sending young people to remote youth prisons is often described as being "tough on crime." In reality, this is the opposite of hardcore accountability. Real accountability comes when a person has to face what they have done, when they have to own up to it, and have to work to make it right. Accountability should be a cornerstone of our system. Yet far too often youth (and adults) are never faced with the person(s) they have harmed (except possibly in a courtroom), and an enormous opportunity for learning, growth, and transformation is lost.

Even though it is not possible to turn back the clock for Durrell and Allen, we do have potential moving forward to support families like them and hopefully turn a new page in the history of our system.

After hearing the story of Durrell's death, I asked Allen if he would join the work we were doing. He was all in. He became a founding member of Families for Books Not Bars. Allen was not alone. Over a span of just a couple of years, five different young people had lost their lives in California youth prisons. Five different families not only mourned their deaths but also wanted answers. These families demanded answers. How many would have to die inside these youth prisons before things would change?

Kids who were fortunate enough to make it out of the youth prisons alive often turned right around and went back in. Three out of four young people coming out of the system were being rearrested within two years.[21] The state was spending $150,000 per year per young person on this failing system.[22]

Faced with these facts, the families didn't say, "We want to change things a little bit." No—they wanted to close the youth prisons down, once and for all. Privately, I had my doubts that we could accomplish that goal. Close all the youth prisons? But mothers and grandmothers like Lanita Mitchell, Lourdes Duarte, Ruth Whitmore, and Joyce Cook insisted: *Yes, we can, and we will. Our children and grandchildren are not safe inside of these institutions. There's a different way to do this.*

It is not the case, as often is claimed, that most families abandon loved ones who are locked up. Most struggle to stay connected and to find out whether their child is even safe. Families frequently incur significant expenses when they visit their children, given that many youth corrections facilities are located in remote rural regions. Indeed, when I began working with families of incarcerated children in California, I found that none of the stereotypes held true. "These are youths neglected by parents, whose parents deny any responsibility for them"—that's a common one. Or, "The families that were supposed to raise these kids into law-abiding citizens have failed." The parents and families I met dispelled all the myths. The overwhelming majority of them care deeply about their children. They are hardworking individuals with deep ties to and concern for their communities.

The families I worked with were driving 250 miles on average just to visit their kids, only to be subjected to intimidating searches by armed guards and dogs upon arrival. The treatment these grandmothers, mothers, and other family members received from guards and administrators often ran on a spectrum from rude to verbally abusive. Frequently, they were told their children and grandchildren would never amount to anything. Families were denied visits because they were wearing the wrong color pants—really—or an underwire bra, or because their child was on lockdown. In a 2010 survey conducted by Justice for Families, a national network of families with loved ones in the criminal legal system, 86 percent of family members surveyed said that they would like to be more involved in their children's treatment while they are confined in a correctional facility or other residential placement. Seventy percent of families responded that they were not able to reach their children by phone as often as they would have liked while they were in these facilities.[23]

Families who share the fate of enduring the incarceration of loved ones ought to be able to support each other with everything from legal resources, to carpooling for visits, to having a knowing shoulder to cry on. An obvious place they could make such connections is where they visit or wait to visit their incarcerated children. Yet families involved with the CYA were routinely told that they could not talk to each other while standing in visiting lines.

So most families struggle desperately to support their loved ones, yet are met with obstacles and barriers at every turn. As a result, every step further into the US juvenile justice system drives a child like Durrell further from the very support he most needs from his family and community.

Families for Books Not Bars began by doing what was prohibited at the youth prisons: talking to one another. We talked about the conditions inside. We wrote letters and we strategized about what could be done to immediately address some of the worst conditions inside. We held vigils for young people outside of the youth prisons where young people were losing their lives. Every time we returned, our numbers were greater, and our black T-shirts—emblazoned with "Close CYA Youth Prisons" on the front and "Open Youth Opportunities" on the back—became more ubiquitous.

What started as a handful of families grew to a couple of dozen and then a couple hundred and then over a thousand families across the state. Our allies—the Prison Law Office (which sued the CYA over conditions inside the youth prisons), the Youth Justice Coalition (a membership-based organization of young people who had been through the criminal legal system), the Center for Juvenile and Criminal Justice and the Youth Law Center (advocacy organizations), among others—were instrumental in turning the tide. Those same legislators who first laughed at us and slammed doors on us started to listen. They saw that families did care about their kids. They saw the multiple paths that had led young people into the youth prison system and began to be disabused of the perception that these young people were the "superpredator" boogeymen described in the news. They also saw the cost and wondered why the state would continue to spend so many resources on such a failing system.

Legislators initially said we would never close a single youth prison. By 2012, when we suspended the campaign, we had closed five of eight youth prisons across the state and helped reduce the youth prison population in California by over 80 percent, with no increase in youth crime. Our victory had ongoing ripple effects across the country. In recent years, the governors of Virginia, Wisconsin, Connecticut, and New Jersey have ordered the closure of all youth prisons, replacing them with community-based rehabilitation programs, while in California, Governor Newsom has moved oversight of youth prisons from the agency that oversees adult prisons to the state's Health and Human Services Agency.[24] In April 2019, leaders representing dozens of juvenile justice organizations launched a national campaign—which has revived our Families for Books Not Bars campaign—to close all youth prisons across the country.[25]

Our victory demonstrated the importance of relationships and collective agency in overcoming dehumanization and isolation. These families coming together in the context of a campaign to close youth prisons was a visible example of how, as Bessel van der Kolk says, "traumatized human beings recover in the context of relationships."

When I visited Allen again in 2018 to fill in more details of Durrell's story, he reminisced about the Families for Books Not Bars campaigns: "I wouldn't trade anything for those days when we were working so hard to expose the system and speak up for the parents and the kids and what they were going through inside those institutions. Looking back, I just appreciate the conviction of all the folks involved in our campaign to shut down youth prisons."[26] Even after we suspended our campaign to close youth prisons, Allen devoted his off hours to publishing opinion pieces in newspapers and testifying before the state senate (three times) for general reform in the CYA (renamed the Division of Juvenile Justice in 2005).[27]

"I'm a fighter. I gave all I could to the Families for Books Not Bars movement, and I feel the same will help me beat the situation I'm in now."

His new situation in 2018 was daunting. The latest round of chemotherapy to fight his pancreatic cancer had left him exhausted, with his voice hoarse and his hands trembling.

The cancer was discovered during a routine medical checkup. In a follow-up biopsy the doctors discovered multiple tumors and gave him a devastating diagnosis of inoperable stage IV metastatic pancreatic cancer. One of the most deadly, most aggressive fast-growing cancers, pancreatic cancer is often found only in later stages because of the location, hidden behind the major large organs. Many people show no symptoms, as was the case with Allen.

When Allen and his new wife, Terry—the love of his life, his "queen"— heard the shocking news from the oncologist, they slumped to the floor, crying and reaching for each other's hands. They were determined to fight it, and Allen immediately started chemotherapy. The harsh treatments caused Allen intense pain, swollen hands and feet, debilitating stomach flu-like symptoms, exhaustion, and major weight loss. He had to give up his beloved shoe care business at the St. Francis.

The couple struggled to pay for their health insurance policy with Kaiser Permanente, along with the hundreds of dollars each week for doctor and pharmacy copayments. At the time of my visit, they had recently launched a crowdfunding campaign with GoFundMe because Kaiser refused to cover immunotherapy treatments and other proven breakthrough integrative treatments that were the best chance of saving Allen's life. The immediate out-of-pocket costs they faced came to $15,000 just to qualify for the treatment, and for the required doctor visits, tests, consultation fees, hospital stays, medications, and travel costs.

I supported the campaign personally and shared it as widely as I could. Allen passed away October 26, 2018, at the age of sixty-four.

Since Allen's death I've been more attuned to the number of fundraising requests I receive to support people's medical costs. How many people are crowdfunding their healthcare? I looked it up and found that one in three GoFundMe campaigns are for medical costs—250,000 campaigns per year—and they raise some $650 million per year.[28] And GoFundMe is only one of the crowdfunding platforms available. It actually made me cry, thinking about how, despite the fact that one in three Americans live near the poverty line, they're still giving to their families and friends, and even strangers. Two words came to mind: *failed state*. Typically, we as Americans use that term to refer to other countries, but for me stats like this one are indicators that we should look in the mirror. Jennifer Siebel Newsom calls the American Dream "the great American lie" in her documentary of the same name. This statistic is a sign of our failure as a country to take care of one another and to keep each other safe from harm.

This should be unacceptable.

Between 33 and 80 percent of cancer survivors exhaust their savings to pay for treatment. Up to 34 percent borrow money from friends and family to make payments. Bankruptcy goes up 260 percent compared to similarly situated households, and the bankruptcies are associated with a higher mortality among survivors.[29] So if the cancer doesn't kill you, the debt might.

To his credit, President Obama made healthcare coverage his signature domestic priority. But I think it's time to admit that the Affordable

Care Act (ACA) was more like rearranging the deck chairs on the *Titanic*. Attempts to repeal the ACA have further undermined its effectiveness. As of the end of 2018, 13.7 percent of Americans still have no health insurance.[30] That is not as many people as had been the case before implementation of the ACA, but it is still tens of millions. And even people *with* coverage struggle to pay their medical bills in our system. According to a 2015 survey, 20 percent of Americans with insurance reported problems paying their medical bills.[31]

The ACA sought to change healthcare while prioritizing the well-being of insurance companies. But that's a conflict of interest. The idea that the market can solve healthcare is wrong, and too often has fatal consequences. Economists have long noted that markets and healthcare are a mismatch. "Consumers"—i.e., people—undervalue the regular care that would keep them healthy. Or they simply can't prioritize it, given the other compelling demands in their lives (where the social contract has further failed them). If you are a single parent, working long hours, finding time to take yourself to the doctor regularly often falls off the radar. Then when disaster strikes and you become seriously ill, you are in no position to then comparison shop for the best coverage and care. At that point, you just get the bill.

In fact, as an African American man who smoked cigarettes during his lifetime, Allen was at higher risk for pancreatic cancer, and any real healthcare system would have mandated regular screenings for it. Had it been caught earlier, Allen might have survived, and never run up those medical bills that he did.

Advocates of privatized health insurance contend that it spurs innovation and helps to advance medical research, which ensures the best care possible. If you are among the 1 percent of people who can afford $750,000 that may make some sense. If you are among the 99 percent of us who can't, then it doesn't. So, direct public provision of health insurance is essential. Providing universal healthcare not only allows for universal access to care, but actually lowers total healthcare costs and keeps us more secure as a society. When people go to the doctor as part of regular check-ups, it prevents more costly emergency room visits. When the government pays for insurers to provide care, it can influence those providers. The government can help ensure that doctors and hospitals provide care at a reasonable cost.

The last time I saw Allen, his selfless spirit still radiated through his pain. "I don't dwell on my situation. I keep fighting, I don't give up. My prayers are with the folks at the Ella Baker Center who are continuing the work and fighting against a system that destroys our youth," he told me. For Allen's memorial, Terry wrote: "Allen could fly. But that was never enough for him—he wanted us all to fly with him. So he lifted up everyone he touched with his magnificent, warm smile and encouragement. . . . His spirit soars on, flying above us, forever pulling us up."

Here is a summary of my recommendations:

- We need a federal program of child benefit payments that provides universal, guaranteed, and unconditional support for parents. The models for this program might be Kindergeld in Germany, the family tax benefit in Australia, or the family allowance in Sweden. We should replace the current child tax exemption and child tax credit with monthly allowances that reflect our societal commitment to providing security for the next generation.

- In times of crisis, we need to provide parents and other caregivers with intensive in-home therapy that includes support from social workers and counseling sessions with a psychologist. These alternative interventions cost approximately one-tenth of a typical stay in a youth prison.

- We need to improve teacher-to-student ratios and counselor-to-student ratios in all of our schools, which will improve safety in our schools along with student achievement.

- Our public schools need to provide hands-on, project-based, and personalized learning opportunities—programs that engage different kinds of learners and kids with different interests and needs. These serve as the best preparation for the evolving future of work that the current century-old factory model of education doesn't support.

- Especially for adolescent years, our schools should experiment with rules made to be broken and adapted, as learning experiences for youth, rather than zero tolerance policies which criminalize students without giving them the breathing room they need to mature.

- We must stop criminally charging youth for incidents that merit school discipline.

- We should be developing relationship-centered schools that ensure that children have meaningful connections with adults other than parents and families.

- Families with loved ones behind bars need networks of support for sharing their emotions, strategies, and resources. Instead of keeping these families apart, we should be facilitating their connections, in order to share burdens (like travel and communications) and support each other.

- We must close all youth prisons and replace them with community safety centers that house restorative justice programs, earn-while-you-learn work opportunities, and wraparound services. The goal of these institutions should be to support youth and their families, not to punish them; to help them find new paths rather than put them on the path to adult prison.

- Youth under the age of twenty-one should never be tried in adult courts.

- Government (public) provision of universal healthcare is essential. All people should be ensured access to quality healthcare. The system should focus on affordable prevention—more effective for patients, and usually less expensive—as opposed to emergency treatment.

CHAPTER 6

MARLENA AND JAMES

June 2013

In 2013, I became the executive director of the Ella Baker Center for Human Rights in Oakland. Ella Baker (1903–1986) was a hero from the civil rights movement who fought to end racial segregation in the United States. She helped organize young people to fight against "whites only" facilities that were prevalent throughout the South. She fought to realize black people's right to vote and for the ability of their children to attend desegregated schools.

The Ella Baker Center has been around since 1996. For most of our history, we fought the worst "dumb-on-crime" ideas, which at the time were described as "tough-on-crime" ideas. We held up signs that said "books not bars" and "jobs not jails," but admittedly, most of our limited resources were spent on fighting *against* prisons, rather than building out the alternatives. We were mostly focused on the "not jails" and "not bars" part, because that was the best we could do. Today, the Ella Baker Center works to move resources away from the nation's prison system and toward investment in education, employment, and healthcare. We're focusing on shifting resources from punishment approaches to public-health responses to what are largely public-health issues.

It was shortly after taking the helm of the Ella Baker Center that I heard Marlena Henderson and her family's story, which, perhaps better than any other, illustrates the urgency of focusing on health and healing.

In 2013, Marlena's worst nightmare came true. One beautiful day in June, she walked into her East Bay house to find her home phone ringing off the hook. She had been at a yoga retreat and was feeling relaxed and renewed. That lasted until she picked up the phone. It was her aunt calling. Marlena knew just from her aunt's tone of voice what had happened, she didn't even need to hear the words: "Get your kids and get out of your house. You are not safe. There's been a terrible tragedy. Go *now.*" Marlena called out to her two young sons and rushed them into the car.

It was the call that she had always anticipated, and the one she hoped she would never receive. Her parents had been murdered. And they had been murdered by their own son, Marlena's brother James.

Marlena and James grew up in East San Jose, in one of the most diverse sections of the city. Their father was African American, from the poorest of the poor part of Mobile, Alabama. Their mother was white, born in San Luis Obispo, California. The couple met in California: Dad worked for the city of San Jose in the engineering department, and Mom worked in tech at IBM, NASA, Sun Microsystems, and other notable Silicon Valley companies. Being a mixed-race couple, they found most of San Jose inaccessible to them as would-be homeowners. Yet it was a good place for Marlena and James, who attended their local public school.

"We had teachers who looked like us and could relate to us," Marlena told me. "My brother was an extremely intelligent kid, but he could not sit at a desk. He was impulsive. People weren't being diagnosed with ADHD at that time. My brother was what we called 'hyper.' But the Latina and African American teachers in East San Jose were really good with James and were able to hold space for him."[1]

James thrived outdoors. He played soccer and baseball. On weekends the family often went camping or hiking, or to the beach. Their neighborhood had a strong sense of community: families took turns caring for each other's children. James was happy and relatively well adjusted.

Things began to change when they left East San Jose. Following better employment opportunities, the parents moved the family to Aptos, California. There, Marlena and James were usually the only children of color in their classes. James had a difficult time in public school so his parents sent him to a small private school in Santa Cruz, where he received a great deal of attention and guidance. However, that school only went through fifth grade. He was then enrolled at the local public school, which wasn't such a good fit for him. It was in junior high that James started getting kicked out of school. In addition to being incredibly impulsive, he had started smoking weed. Soon there were repeated suspensions, then

expulsions. As a young teenager, he started getting locked up for possession of marijuana ("meaning a joint or two," specifies Marlena) and petty
theft. Eventually, James was taken away from his family and put in the
CYA youth prison system.

In that moment, James's life took a sharp turn downhill. It was as
though he were caught in a revolving door between freedom and incarceration. For periods of time, he was living with his family, going to school,
working, and enjoying time with his girlfriend, then he would be hit with
a petty theft or marijuana possession charge, and he was right back in the
system. He was no longer able to hold jobs or maintain consistent relationships. Spending so much time on the inside made it difficult for him
to retain friendships. Marlena imagines that the stigma associated with
incarceration also caused James a lot of shame, and possibly contributed
to his insecurity and inability to develop appropriate social skills.

"Prisons are by definition confined spaces and therefore were not a
good place for James," says Marlena. She believes that being there worsened his mental health condition. She is pretty sure that he was beaten
up. Perhaps even raped. "I can only imagine that what was done to him
inside the youth prisons made matters much worse," Marlena tells me.
"Every time he came home from a facility, he was a little bit worse—
more impulsive, more anxious, less connected, less social, more angry."
Marlena found herself bracing for his return and the stress on the family
that came with it. The experience of being the primary support for formerly incarcerated loved ones after their release is shared by two-thirds
of families, who must fill the gaps left by diminishing resources for reentry services.[2]

As James evolved out of the juvenile system and into the adult correctional system, the family spent many weekends and holidays making the
long multi-hour road trips to his prison. Marlena describes:

The routine became familiar. Awake before sunrise. Make the long
drive in silent trepidation. Arrive several hours before visiting hours actually begin in case there were delays. There were always delays. Long
delays. Bring several changes of clothes, in case the guards would not
let you in wearing that color, that style, that fit, that particular zipper or
button that they believed could be converted into a weapon, or whatever
else may have been banned on that particular day. It seemed random.

Marlena recalls mothers and grandmothers at the facilities crying because they had driven over five hours one way and were told (for one

reason or another) that they could not visit their loved one that day. She recalls a sign on the window of one California prison that read, "No visiting Mexicans today. All Mexicans on lockdown." Sometimes James was behind glass and they took turns talking to him on the phone. If they were lucky, they could talk to him in the visiting room and buy popcorn from the vending machines. They spent many Christmases in prisons, eating popcorn from the machine, talking to James with armed guards standing by, making sure they didn't kiss or embrace him.

Later, James was sentenced to several years at California's first supermax prison, Pelican Bay State Prison, which has been ranked as one of the worst prisons in America. No phone calls are allowed, and on the rare occasion a visitor is permitted, there can be no physical contact.[3] Pelican Bay's solitary unit, or security housing unit (SHU) as they call it, is particularly notorious. "More than 500 Pelican Bay prisoners have lived in the SHU in excess of a decade, nearly 80 have been there for more than two decades, and one prisoner recently marked his 40th year in solitary," reported *Mother Jones* magazine in 2013.[4]

James spent nearly a decade moving between solitary confinement and mental health wards. None of that helped to rehabilitate him, or gave him any skills that could help him to live successfully on the outside. He was constantly sentenced and released. Each time he deteriorated a little more. "Prior to Pelican Bay, even though he had all of these issues, he was often able to demonstrate himself as a loving, concerned, compassionate person. But after that it was as though his mind had permanently changed," Marlena says. When I hear this, I am reminded of Bessel van der Kolk's words: "[The behaviors of traumatized people] are not the result of moral failings or signs of lack of willpower or bad character—they are caused by actual changes in the brain."[5]

"From that point, things took a nosedive. He became unpredictable, unable to care for himself, unable to live by himself or with anybody else because of his extreme behaviors. My parents tried many times to let him live with them, but he would destroy their house by smashing things, breaking things, burning things, stealing things, and using various drugs." The more unpredictable he became, the more Marlena began to fear for her own safety and the safety of her children when he was around. Eventually, one day, he killed their parents' cat.

After the incident with the cat, the parents checked James into a locked mental health facility, but he managed to escape, and they were never able to get him to go back. His violent behaviors and threats escalated. He began threatening to kill their parents and acting out in other extremely disturbing ways. That's when Marlena first called the local sheriff's office to get help. She had watched and witnessed his behaviors most of his life, she knew the patterns, she feared what would come next. She knew he would eventually try to kill one or all of them. The threats were real and the patterns were clear.

Yet she was told, "There is nothing we can do unless he commits a crime."

James went on to murder his seventy-one-year-old father and his sixty-eight-year-old mother.

By the time the first responders arrived, Marlena's parents were both dead. James was apprehended hiding in a neighbor's yard. At that point, law enforcement got involved. But of course, at that point, it was way too late.

When Marlena and I meet so she can tell me the whole story, almost five years have passed since the murders. "This is the first time I've gotten through the story without crying," she says.

One part of the story ended with the murders of their parents, but Marlena's trauma has continued.

When I spoke with Marlena in 2018, her brother's fate had yet to be determined. "It's been almost five years and I'm just starting to figure out how the process works, because the stories change, the dates change, attorneys change, the judges change, everything changes all the time and these cases just kind of get lost," she tells me. "They keep delaying. There are really only two options, because of the amount of evidence. There's the option that he is found insane and goes to a mental institution, or there's the option that he is found guilty without insanity and goes to prison. There's no other option, so I don't understand why it's taking so long."

As a single mom, Marlena had relied heavily on her parents to help her raise her boys. Forced to constantly reschedule work and childcare for court dates, she is now on her own with all of it. Until the trial, and potentially even after, Marlena has to cope with uncertainty and fears for her safety and the safety of her sons. She ends her story with the sobering conclusion she has come to: "Initially I thought it would be better for James to be found insane. I had thought that would be better because conditions in prisons are horrendous—no place for a human being. I thought going into a mental asylum would be better conditions. However, from what I understand—I'm still a little fuzzy—if James is found insane, he could potentially get out. Because I know him so well and know how his mind works, I am convinced that if he got out, my life and my children's lives would be in danger. I know he would come after us because we're the next closest people and that's just how his mind and his life is at this point."

I don't agree with the death penalty or life without the possibility of parole, but it's hard to argue with her on this. I think about how I would feel if one of my siblings murdered my parents. I would have a difficult time seeing the person I once knew. This points to the fact that even a culture of care will probably still need prisons, but they will be our last resort rather than our first option. When someone commits such deep and ongoing harm that they destroy a relationship beyond repair, then the punishment of prison—isolating them from the community for a time because they have ostracized themselves through the gravity of their violence or cruelty and demonstrated no interest in making it right—may be the only appropriate consequence.

I also know that people who have committed horrific acts can change. I know it because I know of those people. I think of Shaka Senghor, Reginald Dwayne Betts, Phil Melendez, and many others convicted of violent offenses who have done deep work on themselves and who have committed to spending the rest of their lives working to make up for their mistakes. These individuals are doing incredible work healing communities, and they have supported many others in their transformation. Such healing occurs through relationship and engagement, the opposite of isolation.

"The thing that strikes me as most wrong with the justice system is that the deeper in it you go, the more isolated you become. That was true for my brother. He never got the support he needed. Children and adolescents make mistakes. That is part of growing up. Yet, when young people make mistakes and become involved in the justice system, it is a set up for failure," Marlena tells me. "When James first became involved in the system, he was not capable of causing the kind of harm that has led me to fear for my life today. Now, he is capable. The costs of that failure are too high for families like mine. And we are not the only ones. I talk to so many families whose story are like mine. We have to do better. No one should have to go through what I did."

What interventions could have saved the lives of Marlena's parents—and James's life, given that he will likely now die in prison? The first opportunity to rewrite the story came at school, as it did for Durrell Feaster. While James's impulsive or unfocused behavior in East San Jose was met with workaround solutions that allowed him to stay in the classroom, in Aptos his teachers more often responded by sending him to the principal's office or suspending him.

The difference between those two school experiences reflects a conundrum that parents of color find themselves often facing: Do we choose a school that is more culturally diverse where teachers may (sometimes, though certainly not always) relate to our children and treat them with tolerance, or do we choose a school that may be higher performing (because it is wealthier and whiter) but has less tolerance for real and perceived misbehavior?

Educator Christopher Emdin has written about how teachers who come from the same neighborhoods and backgrounds as their students are more likely to succeed at teaching.[6] He also believes that teachers who come from elsewhere can have more success if they actively learn about and become familiar with their students' communities: "If you want to be an aspiring teacher in urban education, you've got to leave the confines of that university and go into the hood. You've got to go in there and hang out at the barbershop, you've got to attend that black church, and you've got to view those folks that have the power to engage and just take notes on what they do. At our teacher education classes at my university, I've started a project where every single student that comes in there sits and watches rap concerts," Emdin says in his October 2013 TED talk.[7]

As with Durrell, it's not hard to imagine a school environment for James that would have served him better. A social and emotional learning program (SEL) would almost certainly have helped. As part of a "whole child education" philosophy, SEL programs train students in how to be self-aware and aware of others, how to set and achieve positive goals and make responsible decisions, and how to exhibit empathy and compassion for others in order to navigate relationships more successfully. Schools that adopt SEL see a drop in suspensions and expulsions, while students who receive SEL show "improved social and emotional skills, attitudes, behavior, and academic performance that reflected an 11-percentile-point gain in achievement."[8] A 2015 cost-benefit evaluation of SEL programs found that benefits outweigh the costs by a factor of eleven to one.[9] This is consistent with research demonstrating the enormous impact of healthy relationships on children and youth.

If James had attended a school with SEL, he might have been engaged in the process of designing discipline procedures at his school rather than just being a victim of them.[10] He might have been engaged in developing a new outdoor program for kids with ADHD. Perhaps this would have not just kept him in school, but helped other students as well.

At the Catholic high school I attended, I remember getting to do a ropes course, a series of physical challenges out in nature. I remember climbing the "giant's ladder" with a classmate and jumping out to catch a trapeze that was suspended forty feet above the ground. It's an example of ways adults provide environments for youth to positively challenge boundaries and rules, and their sense of what's possible. Making those kinds of experiences available is critical. Every student does better when those who struggle do well.

As with Durrell Feaster, a high school environment that was less prone to suspension and expulsion for minor infractions would have kept James out of the downward spiral into the juvenile and then adult criminal legal system. "When children attend schools that place a greater value on discipline and security than on knowledge and intellectual development," writes civil rights leader Angela Davis, "they are attending prep schools for prisons."[11] That's how it was for James.

Marlena says that James's mental illness was dramatically exacerbated by his repeated encounters with police. As it stands now, members of law enforcement are the default response in instances of mental health crises. In the event of an emergency, but also in the event of many non-emergencies, police are called to the scene. They are the "first responders." Yet police officers are only rarely trained to deal with people experiencing a mental health crisis. They have a set of tools available to them that are largely based on force, yet they are called upon to respond to situations that require other tactics and other skills. Many police officers themselves will be the first to admit that they can't arrest their way to community safety.

Most importantly, we need to broaden our understanding of, and budgets for, first responders—professionals with training in conflict resolution and in managing situations caused by mental illness and substance abuse. Specially trained first responders should be the first point of contact in myriad situations that police now struggle to handle appropriately. We need to transition from law enforcement responses to a more suitable public health response when circumstances arise from mental health conditions, thereby avoiding unnecessary arrests and detentions, and even fatal shootings. Community members and elected officials need to recognize the importance and benefits of creating these programs and be willing to divert funding or raise new revenues to support this vital work. City budgets should be geared toward advancing a public health approach to community safety.

People with mental illness are four and a half times more likely to be arrested than others, and are sixteen times more likely to be killed by police.[12] Because police are not equipped to respond to these crises, situations involving people with disabilities and mental illness can prove deadly. Joint partnerships involving mental health and advocacy agencies can respond much more effectively to crises than police alone. Crisis intervention team (CIT) protocols involve mental health providers and other medical professionals, who can provide immediate referral services and treatment alternatives to avoid arrest, incarceration, or involuntary psychiatric hospitalization. Compared to situations in which police alone were involved, responses involving CITs have higher rates of resolution, of making referrals to mental health treatment and immediately transporting the person to a health facility that can deal with a crisis, reducing incarceration. The CIT protocol is also associated with a reduced risk of injury from interactions with police.[13] Marlena believes that had a crisis intervention team been dispatched on the day of her parents' murders, it would have prevented their deaths.

Across America, suffering is increasing, amplified by the anxieties of job losses, insecure housing, and unaffordable healthcare. One in five adults in the US, almost 47 million people, experience some form of mental illness, while one in twenty-five, over eleven million adults, live their lives with a serious mental illness.[14] Approximately 10.2 million adults live with both mental illness and addiction.[15] Many people go untreated, while many others are treated with the big-pharma approach: medication. Yet many mental illnesses are linked to past trauma, where people's bodily integrity was violated and they were made to feel unsafe. While medications can play a role as a stabilizing force in moments of crisis, this form of treatment doesn't address rebuilding a sense of safety through self-awareness and positive relationships.

For the most severe of mental illnesses we have a serious shortage of care dating back to the 1960s, when many state-funded psychiatric facilities closed with the intention of providing treatment in more humane, less restrictive settings. But the community-based health centers and care facilities that were to take the place of those institutions never materialized, resulting in a public health crisis. Psychiatric experts recommend a minimum of fifty beds per 100,000 people; in 2010, the national average was closer to fourteen beds per 100,000, and in some places in the country, there were fewer than five.[16] Many of the private mental health hospitals still in operation do not accept insurance and can cost upwards of $30,000 per month, while a provision in the Medicare law prevents the use of federal funding for long-term care in an institution. As a result, many of the people who experience serious mental health crises wind up in the emergency room; but most hospitals are unable to keep them for more than seventy-two hours, at which point they're sent back out into the world. Many individuals who require intensive psychiatric care find themselves homeless or in prison.

"People in mental health crisis can't be put on a waiting list," Marlena says. "Their families need immediate support and interventions in order to maintain their safety. There needs to be somewhere to take people immediately so that they can become stabilized medically, emotionally, socially."

Today, the largest providers of mental health services are jails. According to a study published in 2017, "almost half of [state prison] inmates were diagnosed with a mental illness (48%), of whom, 29% had a serious mental illness (41% of all females and 27% of all males), and 26% had a history of a substance use disorder."[17] Other studies have found that approximately half of people in prison and jail meet DSM-IV criteria for substance abuse or dependence.[18] People with mental illnesses are disproportionately placed in solitary confinement in response to behavioral difficulties, but the confinement can cause their mental health to deteriorate further. They're also at a higher risk for abuse by other people in prison and correctional staff. Despite the need for treatment, only about a third of people in state prison and a sixth of people in jail who need mental health treatment report receiving it while incarcerated. The leading cause of death when exiting incarceration is drug overdose, illustrating the life-threatening risk incarceration poses for those who don't receive effective treatment while in custody. The environments within jails and prisons make them far more likely to worsen someone's mental state than improve it.

The reliance upon policing and imprisonment as opposed to medical care for mental illness and drug use endangers lives. We should not be blaming or punishing those with mental illness and substance abuse issues. We should not be burdening police officers with societal problems that we can solve. Instead we must directly address the public health and economic concerns that manifest in the forms of mental illness and substance use disorders. While the current conversation refers to these strategies as "alternatives," I think a better way to describe them is "imperatives." It is imperative for our well-being and safety that we move away from the framework of fear responses, to a new status quo: the culture of caring.

James was first arrested for possession of a small amount of marijuana. This is a direct result of the war on drugs, the federal initiative beginning in the 1980s that used "tough-on-crime" rhetoric and mandated long sentences for drug-related offenses, even those involving small amounts or first-time offenders. In 1980, there were just over forty thousand people incarcerated for drug offenses; by 2013, this number had increased to 489,000. The vast majority of drug arrests are for possession, not for selling.[19]

The decriminalization of drug possession would not just save young people like James from the trauma of youth prison; it would allow for reinvestment of millions of dollars into the development of much-needed drug treatment and harm reduction services. Many countries have decriminalized drug possession and consumption and, in place of these punitive measures, have developed advanced treatment options. With increased provision of treatment, these places have seen decreases in adolescent drug use and a decrease in drug-related deaths. As a result, major public health and human rights groups like the United Nations, the World Health Organization, the International Red Cross, the NAACP, and the American Civil Liberties Union have called for drug decriminalization as a public health measure.[20]

In 2014, California voters passed Proposition 47, the Safe Neighborhoods and Schools Act, which presents a model for reinvestment in prevention. After one year of implementation of Prop. 47, which reduced certain nonviolent, nonserious drug and property offenses from felonies to misdemeanors, more than thirteen thousand people had been resentenced and released. The savings of approximately $156 million in incarceration costs from just the first year has begun to be reinvested in drug treatment, mental health services, victim services, and K-12 programs for at-risk students.[21]

The decriminalization and legalization of marijuana could also be linked to a larger push to fund services and supports for communities hardest hit by mass incarceration. The Center for American Progress has argued that the revenue from the taxation of legalized marijuana should fund public sector jobs for communities of color that have been most harmed by the war on drugs.[22]

Even with drugs considered more serious than marijuana there is a movement afoot to reconsider framework-of-fear-style drug policies. The scope of the opioid crisis—in 2015, thirty-three thousand drug overdose-related deaths were caused by prescription pain relievers like hydrocodone and oxycodone, as well as heroin and illegally manufactured fentanyl— has overwhelmed law enforcement and led to more care-based public health approaches.[23] "The punishment of a disease wasn't working," says Leonard Campanello, who, as police chief of the city of Glouces-ter, Massachusetts, invited anyone needing help in overcoming an opi-ate addiction to come to his police station without fear of arrest and get placed in a detox facility "not in hours or days, but on the spot."[24] This approach has evolved into a nationwide initiative called police-assisted addiction and recovery initiative (PAARI), which almost four hundred police departments have adopted. So far, the places adopting this public health approach tend to be smaller, more homogenous (largely white) communities, where public officials including the police either personally know the people who are addicted, or have connections to them. Yet it illustrates the effectiveness of moving beyond Us vs. Them thinking and criminalization, toward policies of caring and healing.

Most of us have been trained to call the police first. Prior to the terrible day that James killed his parents, Marlena chose not to call 911 and in-stead called the local sheriff's department, believing it was the best way to help her family given the department's familiarity with her brother. This was a choice she later regretted, not only because it failed to send any responders at all, let alone the crisis intervention team Marlena believes could have stopped the murders, but also because a call to 911 would have been recorded, which would have created more accountability. But there is room for improvement with 911, our default emergency response and dispatch system.

At nearly six thousand call centers around the country, more than a hundred thousand workers receive over 240 million 911 calls each year. The call taker assigns the emergency a priority level from one to nine and decides whether to relay the information to police, fire, or medical responders. In her investigation into racial bias in 911 call centers, author and activist Rinku Sen noted that at "most call centers throughout the

U.S., both call takers and dispatchers are predominantly White."[25] According to Sen, "There is no universal regulation of 911 dispatch. Each center creates its own policies in conjunction with associated emergency departments, subject to state laws. While some statewide 911 dispatch centers exist, most counties have their own."

More funding, more training, higher wages, and higher standards for call workers could make the difference between tragedies and public safety. For example, in the case of Tamir Rice, the twelve-year-old boy shot to death by police in a public park in Cleveland, the officers had responded to a 911 call from someone else in the park. The caller told the dispatcher that the pellet gun Rice was playing with was probably fake and that he looked like a child, not an adult, but the dispatcher failed to pass this information along to the police. The dispatcher was suspended without pay for eight days as a result.[26] With more funding and more training, call takers could also talk people through life-saving procedures, from administering CPR to delivering babies, which could save lives before any first responders arrive.

We all need to be retrained to think differently about 911. Alternate assistance lines like 211 and 311 have been created, but are underfunded and undersold. The 211 number provides callers with information about social services for everyday needs but also in times of crisis. It can help with basic human needs by helping people obtain assistance with shelter, clothing, and utilities; by providing disaster response information and job training and employment services; and by helping people find support for elders and children and identify health and mental health resources.[27] Although the 211 service is available in all fifty states, in 2017 it received fifteen million requests (compared to the 240 million per year to 911).[28] The number 311 is dedicated to reporting such problems as abandoned vehicles or debris blocking the road, stolen vehicles, code and housing violations, nonworking streetlights or traffic lights, and noise complaints. There are also ways to divert calls away from the police even when someone does call 911. In Eugene, Oregon, a program called Cahoots has a mobile crisis intervention team that provides immediate stabilization in cases of urgent medical need and psychological crisis. The team "is wired into the 911 system" and is thus able to respond to most calls without police.[29]

We need public education campaigns and resources to support dispatch lines to divert calls to the appropriate services and experts. Everyone benefits—people in need of support are more likely to have someone to call and bystanders are less likely to fear their call will end with an inappropriate and potentially deadly response, while police have their calls narrowed to those that best suit their skill set.

Even if James had still wound up in prison as he did, things did not have to end the way they did for the family.

The experience of leaving prison has been compared to the experience of returning home from war. Even the very first night one is released can be difficult if not disastrous, as the harrowing story of Jessica St. Louis illustrates. She had spent just over ten days at Santa Rita County Jail in Dublin, California. It's not at all unusual for people to be released, as she was, in the dead of night, with little more to their name than a bus ticket. She was released at 1:30 a.m., but the subway didn't start running until 5 a.m., so Jessica bought drugs. She died of a drug overdose on the train platform. Santa Rita jail officials have consistently refused to provide Narcan (a brand of naloxone, an opiate overdose medication) to at-risk people whose drug use contributed to their being jailed in the first place. In fact, a new harm reduction initiative aimed at reducing fatalities from opiate overdoses is providing naloxone kits to *everyone* being released from prison, understanding that they are uniquely situated to encounter and avert overdoses.[30]

People who have been incarcerated have real challenges even finding places to sleep: in a survey conducted by my organization and others, 79 percent were denied housing based on a conviction history.[31] Finding employment is also extremely difficult: our survey revealed that three out of four people found finding employment after release difficult or nearly impossible. This was corroborated by numerous studies, including one published as "Rethinking Corrections: Rehabilitation, Reentry and Reintegration," which found that 60 percent of formerly incarcerated people were still unemployed a year after release and 67 percent of formerly incarcerated individuals were still unemployed or underemployed five years after release.[32]

Upon his release, James could have been enrolled in Santa Cruz County's Maintaining Ongoing Stability Through Treatment (MOST) program, a nationally recognized program that provides support with housing, jobs training, and psychotherapy for people with mental health needs who have been involved in the criminal justice system. Mental health counselors, psychologists, probation officers, psychiatrists, and correctional officers make up an individual's MOST team. They also provide support around specific issues related to the justice system like probation and court discharge planning. The goal is to involve the person in the community, and thereby reduce homelessness, time in jail or psychiatric facilities, probation violations, and new offenses. Unfortunately, although this excellent program is considered among "best practices" related to incarceration, a critical shortcoming of such programs is scale. Lack of funding means they are available for the lucky few rather than the broad masses.

So James was released without the supports that could have ultimately prevented the deaths of his parents, a lifetime of re-incarceration for him, and sadness and anxiety for his sister Marlena.

People who break the law need to be held accountable, yet part of being held truly accountable means having an opportunity to make amends and contribute. We have an obligation to make matters better whenever we can. This obligation is also to the people that incarcerated folks might harm upon release. Hurt people hurt people. But also true is that healed people heal people. If we are invested in a safer and more prosperous society, we need to take a hard look at where families face lose-lose scenarios and instead ensure that people have real choices and the support they need.

For Marlena's life after the death of her parents, what supports could a culture of care offer her that the current framework is failing to provide? Marlena has had to cope not just with the loss of her parents as team members in her parenting, but also with the lost days of work due to court dates. The kind of parental supports that would have helped Allen as a single father—universal, guaranteed, and unconditional monthly child allowance payments—would also help Marlena, who now struggles as a single mother who relied intensely on her parents to help raise her two sons. Additionally, a network of government-subsidized, good quality childcare facilities as proposed by Senator Elizabeth Warren would have helped Marlena with the care of her younger son when he was still too young to attend school. Warren's plan aims to improve wages for the workers of those child care centers while simultaneously allowing lower income families to afford them by having the government bear the costs.[33]

A culture of care also needs to provide support to victims after a crime. Trauma can arise not only from the violent act but also from interactions with law enforcement or the court process, as is the case for Marlena. If the trauma of victimization goes untreated, it can create a host of problems down the line, including substance abuse, mental illness, and homelessness. Traumatic experiences can affect an individual's ability to function effectively at work and to retain a job; as well as cause sleep disturbances, panic attacks, difficulty concentrating, and stress-related health problems.

During an adversarial court process, the survivor of the crime is used as a key chess piece in getting the wrongdoer convicted, but is generally abandoned as soon as the verdict is in. Helping survivors recover after the trial is not the focus of the criminal legal system or the overarching framework of fear. People who have witnessed and experienced violence and serious harm need grief counseling, trauma therapy, and support navigating the courts and the justice system, at a minimum. They might require shelter, legal services, time off from work, childcare, access to financial assistance or assistance getting victim's compensation.

The peace activist Aqeela Sherrills, who famously brokered a peace between rival gangs in the early 1990s in Los Angeles, comments: "When someone gets shot in our neighborhoods we deploy law enforcement in force but we don't deploy healers, therapists and counselors in force to help folks deal with the after effects of violence in our communities."[34]

According to a national survey of victims in 2016 by the Alliance for Safety and Justice, two out of three victims did not receive help following the incident.[35] Those who did often received the help from family, as opposed to any formal services. Danielle Sered and her organization Common Justice have drawn attention to the unmet needs of a particular group of survivors of violence: young men of color. Her 2014 report, *Young Men of Color and the Other Side of Harm: Addressing Disparities in Our Response to Violence*, identifies significant barriers that prevent young men of color from accessing victim services. These include social norms that make it less likely that young men will identify themselves as "victims" or be seen as such in our culture, as well as distrust of the justice system based on prior negative experiences with the criminal justice system. Sered concludes:

> Addressing these disparities also requires recasting a persistent and pervasive narrative that over-represents young men of color as aggressors or criminals. This narrative, which is often amplified by the media, includes the misperception that violence and pain somehow impact young men of color less profoundly than other victims, a distortion that may limit our ability to accurately recognize symptoms of trauma (such as being overly reactive to perceived threats) as natural human responses

to pain and fear rather than signs of character flaws or moral failure. Transforming this narrative matters, not only because young men of color internalize its negative messages, but because it can also powerfully shape how others see and treat them—with serious implications for social services, the criminal justice system, and the development of an equitable society more broadly.[36]

In Marlena's case, the trauma could extend to Marlena's sons even though she did her utmost to shield them from the media coverage of the murders. The whole family would benefit from supports for survivors of crimes that do not rely on law enforcement or adversarial court processes as the primary strategy. These supports need to be accessible to everyone—culturally as well as geographically.

Marlena's story is still unfolding as this book goes to print. She hopes that sharing the details of her family's story will help change the system to work better for others. I hope so too.

Here is a summary of my recommendations:

- We need to hire and train more teachers and administrators who look like students and can relate to their experiences, whether that means educators of color or educators who represent particular backgrounds and abilities—ideally people who live in the same neighborhoods as their students.

- Schools should implement SEL programs to set students up to succeed at relationships and collaboration. We also need to offer more physical education and outdoor learning opportunities, the better to engage students like James, who have a hard time sitting at a desk for extended periods. These programs pay for themselves in better outcomes for students.

- We need robust first responders who are trained and paid to handle incidents involving mental illness, substance abuse, and other issues not suited to a police response. This goes along with funding and promotion of emergency lines like 211 and 311, as well as alternative dispatch systems within 911 call centers.

- We need to continue the work of decriminalizing drug possession, instead reinvesting "war on drugs" resources into the social contract, and adopting a public health approach to substance abuse issues. This includes offering sophisticated treatment options for substance abuse nationwide, in big cities as in small towns.

- Clearly we need more resources and programs for mental health care, both in emergency and in everyday situations. People with mental health issues deserve help, not containment; we need beds in facilities equipped to give them the proper care.

- Reentry programs that provide support with housing and jobs training for all who are released from incarceration, and psychotherapy for those with mental health needs, are essential to reducing recidivism and helping people become productive and healthy members of their communities. Reentry programs should also support families as they help their loved ones return home and reintegrate.

- For survivors of all kinds of trauma, we must create a culture of care and provide access to mental, emotional, logistical, and financial supports beyond what is offered by the court system.

- In addition to a universal guaranteed allowance paid per child by the government, we should implement a government-subsidized network of childcare facilities that pay their workers well and offer good quality childcare while still being accessible to all families.

CHAPTER 7

ANITA

April 2019

I first meet Anita at a JJ's Fish and Chicken next to the laundromat. It's on the other side of the 980, the freeway that divides downtown Oakland from historically black West Oakland.

"When I first came to Oakland, in the 1990s, it was still a working-class town, affordable, plus I had family here. It was always: you knew somebody, somebody's mom or auntie; your grandmother had an extra room or had an extra property. I never had leases. I think the closest thing I had to one was on a napkin. And if I didn't have the rent on time, she worked with me, because that was family. That doesn't happen when a realty company owns everything."[1]

West Oakland and all of Oakland is changing and Anita can tell you all about not just the history of Oakland but her work to reshape its future. She tells me how the 10K redevelopment plan, an "urban renewal" plan aimed at bringing ten thousand new residents to the downtown area, brought in rich Hong Kong developers who bought up Oakland's Chinatown and pushed out many working-class Asian residents.

That evolution made it much more likely you would be renting from a company whose executives had never seen the place you live and had no connection to it. The gentrification that Anita describes anecdotally is part of a well-documented nationwide pattern. People often point to lack of rental units as the challenge facing renters, but it's just as much "the rise of investor-owned rental properties that dispossess communities from housing and places them under pressure of price speculation," as Dawn Phillips, formerly with the housing justice group Causa Justa::Just Cause notes.[2] In the wake of the mortgage crisis, this became one of the new strategies that housing investors focused on, "with a potential $1.5 trillion in such investments projected nationally."[3]

These are the forces Anita finds herself up against—she has a lot on her plate.

Sitting opposite her, behind my mountain of french fries, I get straight to the point. I tell her who I am, what my book is about, why I want to talk to her. I know she can see through the savviest politician's bullshit. She has squared off against them—city bureaucrats, frat boys, and two-bit hustlers alike—so I know to keep it one hunnit, as the youth say. Anita has plenty of reasons to be suspicious of someone's motivations.

It helps that my colleague Angelo, one of the community organizers working at the Ella Baker Center, introduces us. He has been getting to know her and the growing movement of unsheltered community members in Oakland. The term "unsheltered" refers to homeless people who are not using shelters for any number of reasons, from insufficient capacity to the lack of safety, privacy, and autonomy there. I remember being at a planning meeting for Restore Oakland in November 2018 when Angelo interrupted to tell me "they are trying to sweep the Housing and Dignity Village." There we were, laying out the vision for an Oakland where everyone has a sense of belonging and safety; meanwhile across town the city had sent a bulldozer and dozens of police in riot gear to clear a community of families.

Angelo and another coworker, Vince, left immediately to support the Village. But their efforts wouldn't be successful.

The next time Anita and I meet, any reservation she might have had about talking with me seems gone. We meet over Chinese takeout, as Anita takes me back years and decades and across oceans to the Philippines where her mom escaped an arranged marriage. She fled first to Manila, where she "hustled her way into a college education and got a teaching degree," and then to Los Angeles, with its well-established Filipino community, where she met and married a white man, Anita's father. Her dad was mentally unstable and found it impossible to hold down a job, but her mom was successful enough to eventually send all three of her kids to private school on her earnings alone. Her mom's many "hustles" in LA included selling Avon products, appearing on—and winning—television game shows like *Let's Make a Deal* and *The Price is Right*, and launching a successful food business selling frozen *lumpias*, the spring rolls popular in the Philippines.

Anita lights up when talking about her mom and about her own activism in college. She went to the University of California, Santa Barbara. Her first year, 1989, the student fees were around a hundred dollars per quarter and tuition for the year was less than $1,000. Today that sounds crazy cheap. But what *should* seem crazy is the ridiculous amount of debt that students now carry: the average student in the class of 2016 leaves with more than $37,000 in student loan debt.[4] You may have seen the images of not-quite-gleeful graduates with the amount they owe stickered across the top of their graduation caps. Whether they throw the caps in the air or not, they will still find themselves anchored by it.

The UC system now seems more geared toward supporting wealthy children from abroad, the sons and daughters of those wealthy Hong Kong investors, than the Anitas of the world. It didn't used to be that way. Working-class students could get a world-class education in the UC system.

Each year while Anita was in college, the fees went up, and each year she fought the hikes. She organized walkouts not just at her own school but across the UC and Cal State systems and in high schools too. "We shut down public education in California for one week." She also organized against the war in Iraq and the recruitment of students by the CIA on campus, at which point she was kicked out of UC Santa Barbara and banned from the entire UC system. It seems a point of pride for her. Anita doesn't shy away from conflict. She understands it as necessary for survival and evolution.

Anita had gotten what she needed from school, having served as the editor in chief of the school newspaper, and having studied with world-class radical thinkers like Chicano studies professor Chela Sandoval, black studies professor Cedric Robinson, and Asian American studies professor Diane Fujino, who introduced Anita to Japanese American activist Yuri Kochiyama.

"From a very early age, I had seen that things were not right, but I didn't have the language for it. I knew the violence and mental and emotional abuse I was seeing was not right. I didn't know what it was called, but I knew racism wasn't right. I knew poverty wasn't right, but I didn't have a language for it. I would talk about it in terms of *that's not fair. It's*

*not fair that people treat people like that because of their skin color. It's
not fair that some people are really rich and other people are poor.* It was
when I went to college that I got the language," Anita tells me.

> The first time I experienced homelessness, I was still in college, and I
> was super depressed. Within a three month period, my mom was mur-
> dered, I was gang-raped at a party—there was so much sexual violence
> on campus, rapes at the fraternities—and then my cousin got murdered.
> Those three things just pushed me over the edge. I ended up becoming
> a drug addict. I was still going to classes and doing the organizing, but
> I was using. I was in a really bad place, and I turned to drugs to cope.
> I ended up losing my housing. I was unhoused for about a year until I
> got my shit together.

Following her mother's death, Anita was in charge of her two younger
siblings. Child Protective Services (CPS) believed that Anita, who was
nineteen at the time, wasn't old enough to take care of them, and tried
to take her brother and sister away. Anita managed to persuade the principals of the private schools where her siblings were enrolled to waive
their tuition for the remainder of the school year, and to protect them
from CPS.

I'm amazed at how together she was in the aftermath of a crisis, that
she even thought of meeting with the principals of her siblings' schools.
Anita just shrugs "What else was I gonna do? I'm the eldest, so I was
already trained to be like the second mother of the house." She definitely
inherited her mother's hustle.

After college Anita continued her organizing work, mostly among
Filipino youth and farm workers. She did freelance writing for the *LA
Weekly*, the *Independent*, and other outlets. She founded a number of
grassroots political organizations, many of which exist to this day. Following in her mom's footsteps, she launched a successful business selling
lumpias and catering: "I could go to the nightclubs for a couple hours and
come home with $500 from selling lumpias." In the mid-1990s Anita was
offered a job organizing Filipino youth in San Francisco and Oakland, and
so she moved north.

For years Anita lived in apartments around Oakland that were
owned or managed by her family and extended family. She gave birth
to her daughter, Joyous. In 2013 she lucked into a rent-controlled unit
directly on Lake Merritt: an unheard-of $700 for a one bedroom with

utilities included, in a prime location. "It had been passed on to me by my ex-boyfriend, and when he needed a place to live down the road, I gave it back to him and moved out."

This corresponded with record spikes in rental prices in the Bay Area between 2011 and 2015. The same one-bedroom apartment in Oakland that cost about $1,200 per month in January 2011 cost more than $1,900 per month by January 2014 and more than $2,300 by January 2016, meaning the rent basically doubled within those five years.[5] The nationwide average increase in rents was 28.5 percent in the same period.[6] Alameda County (which includes Oakland) needs 60,173 more affordable rental homes to meet the needs of lowest income renters, according to a 2017 report by the California Housing Partnership.[7]

The shortage of homes priced for the lowest income levels is so extreme that nationwide, only thirty-five units are available for every hundred households that need them. But the housing crisis isn't limited to poor folks. Wages simply haven't kept pace with rising housing costs. The rule of thumb is that rent shouldn't exceed 30 percent of one's income, but fully half of American families are paying more than the recommended 30 percent for rent. Eleven million American households—including married couples with children, single folks just starting out, and elderly folks living alone—are paying *more than half* their income toward rent.

Evictions also contribute to homelessness. According to the Eviction Lab at Princeton University, which was created by sociologist Matthew Desmond while researching his landmark book *Evicted*, "There was roughly 1 eviction filing for every 17 renter households in the U.S. between 2000 and 2016. Approximately 1 in 40 renter households were evicted over this period. To put these numbers into perspective, at the peak of the financial crisis in 2010, slightly over one million foreclosures were completed nationally. By comparison, we see almost a million evictions against tenants every single year."[8] And this counts only formal evictions where data was available. "There is some evidence that "informal evictions" are more common than "formal," court-ordered evictions. Informal evictions are not captured in our dataset. Moreover, while we have tried to collect every recorded court-ordered eviction case, going back to 2000, some records were unavailable. Some courts seal eviction cases; others have not archived data; still others make recording eviction cases time-consuming and difficult."[9]

For Anita, as for many industrious businesspeople, a search for housing is made nearly impossible because of the nature of her work. Her catering business is mostly cash. "I have no proof of income. I have nothing on paper that shows that I'm worth anything. I don't qualify for anything in Oakland right now."

A friend offered Anita and her daughter part of a basement to live in, but the place had moisture and black mold issues, and at $1,000 per month—soon raised to $2,000—it just wasn't worth the trouble. Anita was homeless again, this time with her daughter, Joyous. But, as she told her daughter, and then me: "We're still better off than the majority of people who land on the streets. We have hella people who love us." As just one example, a friend who's a mechanic gave them a camper. "And I had the means to get it registered and insured. That's not a normal, typical situation when people are living in their cars." This means the city will be less likely to be able to list it as a nuisance and have it towed from city streets.

This once happened to a car I owned while I was away at college—after a neighbor called it in as a nuisance, the city towed it. I had payed $500 for it and the city wanted $900 to get it out of the tow yard. I just chalked it up as a loss. That is not so easily done when your car is also home for you and all your possessions. Anita knows that the camper is more security than many have right now on the streets of Oakland.

A 2017 survey found almost four thousand people are in need of shelter on any given night in Oakland, and only one shelter bed was available for every three people experiencing homelessness.[10] A 2018 report by the UN described the homeless situation in Oakland and San Francisco as "cruel and inhumane," the only two cities in the United States listed as part of the "global scandal" in housing.[11]

In January 2016, riding the crosstown bus early one morning, Anita noticed a huge number of homeless encampments that seemed like they'd sprung up overnight. She and Joyous cooked some food and brought it over. "We just kicked it and talked to people. By summertime it was seventy of us going to forty-five encampments. We were doing hot meals and provisions and advocacy: accompanying people to their doctor's appointments, taking people to the Oakland Police Department to try and get their property back, helping people fill out their paperwork to get an ID. As the need appeared, we'd respond." Feed the People was born.

That work spiraled into the first iteration of the Village. "We already knew the city wasn't going to take care of folks," says Anita. On the morning of January 20, 2017—while the rest of the world braced itself for the inauguration of Donald Trump—in the pouring rain, campers and tents were moved into a park named for Marcus Garvey, the Jamaican leader of the Pan-African Movement. Volunteers started a health and healing clinic at the site, with a hot home-cooked meal service, two hot showers, raised gardens, a computer lab, an adult education center, and a center for distributing donations to Oakland residents in need. The Village was open to all who needed services, whether they lived at the site or not. It was narcotics- and alcohol-free.

News of the encampment spread like wildfire throughout Oakland's homeless community who dubbed it "the Promised Land." Folks said that, unlike the city and nonprofits, the Village kept its promises. But on February 2, 2017, Oakland mayor Libby Schaaf ordered the site cleared.

A 2016 report by researchers at UC Berkeley on the ongoing criminalization of homeless people and the increasing number of vagrancy laws found that California cities continue to enact new anti-homeless laws in record numbers. In California's fifty-eight most populous cities, 592 laws establish 781 separate restrictions on standing, sitting, and resting in public places; on sleeping, camping, and lodging in public places, including in vehicles; on begging and panhandling; and even on sharing food with homeless people.[12] The report notes: "Anti-homeless laws represent a modern-day example of vagrancy laws that date back centuries. They are akin to Jim Crow laws, anti-Okie laws, sundown towns and 'ugly' laws, which were designed to expel, punish or otherwise discourage the presence of people deemed 'undesirable' in public spaces."[13]

The report also found that arrests of people experiencing homelessness continue to rise in spite of an improving economy, and that arrests of people experiencing homelessness are increasingly based on status, not behavior, meaning that while arrests for "drunkenness" and "disorderly conduct" went down significantly between 2000 and 2012, there was a 77 percent increase in arrests for "vagrancy" in that same period.[14]

For the next eight months, Anita and her allies spoke out about the need for housing, insisting that housing is a human right. "In September 2017, we got the city council to unanimously pass the shelter crisis declaration, which permitted and protected the efforts of the Village, and to unanimously pass the resolution to give us land." They were granted an acre and a half of land at another site, and re-established the Village.

But the city administration (at odds with the city council) kept trying to sabotage the effort. In October 2017 the city began clearing other encampments and herding the people from those sites to the Village. Anita tells me how it went down:

> City administrator Joe DeVries, under the direction of the mayor, shut down six encampments and put those folks on dump trucks—literally dump trucks, with all their belongings—drove them to us and dumped them. We spent months, from October 2017 to January 2018, trying to build community with these new arrivals. Come to find out they were from five rival gangs. The mayor herded five rival gangs onto the property that we had just been granted by the city of Oakland. Everything that we're trying to build has to do with either sobriety or recovery, and a lot of people out on the streets—they will want to stop using drugs but they're not in an environment where they can. And unlike the people we had previously gathered at the Village, they hadn't chosen to come there of their own free will. A big part of recovery or any transformation is—you need to have the agency. You have to want to be there. Our model is based on self-governance and autonomy. You're not a criminal, you're just someone who needs support. We tried to make it work. But all we ended up doing was trying to stop people from killing each other. We stopped a bunch of murders, but six people were murdered anyway. It was crazy. And it was the mayor that created these situations.[15]

Because of how unsafe the Village had become (on account of the mayor's meddling), Anita and other families with children moved to a new site, which they called the Housing and Dignity Village. "We were a group of unsheltered women who worked hard to turn an illegal dumping site into a community where we could safely sleep, eat, and provide some stability for our children. We provided meals, medical services, free winter clothing, and a community garden to anyone in the neighborhood."

Mayor Schaff, meanwhile, campaigned for reelection (elections were in the fall of 2018) with the promise that homelessness was a top priority and said that she'd work together with homeless people to come up with a solution. She was raising corporate donations for her own solution, which she would debut just after winning her new term—the Tuff Shed camps. During the mayor's press conference on the day she won, while Schaff was talking about making homelessness her priority, the Oakland Police were posting eviction notices at the Housing and Dignity Village.

This was the raid that my colleague Angelo had tried to help stop, in vain.

"They did not give us time to pack. They did not care that some residents were at work and their children were at school and would be returning to the destruction of their homes. They treated an intentional community designed to be a safe and sober space for women and children like a criminal enterprise," Anita wrote in an opinion piece published on *Medium*.[16]

In the belief that she knew best, Mayor Libby Schaaf opened the first Tuff Shed camp. Tuff Sheds are plastic storage units—"soaked in formaldehyde, arsenic and off-gassing polyurethane, toxic and uninhabitable," Anita notes—that are intended for use as garden tools or garages, measuring eight feet wide and ten feet long (at the second site erected by the city, the models were longer—fifteen feet long—to better accommodate two people inside). There are twenty sheds on a lot, with two residents per shed, at a cost of almost one million dollars: "$175,000 for the sheds, $550,000 for onsite staffing and services, and a $125,000 fund for helping residents land permanent housing," according to a local news source.[17]

Anita calls the sheds a waste of money and a purely "cosmetic" action, a part of what she calls the "homeless industrial complex," where people who have never been homeless make money from providing temporary, disempowering solutions for unsheltered people.

"Unlike our model, which is based on agency and autonomy, the city's model is super controlled," says Anita. "You have to sign in, sign out. You're not allowed to have visitors. You're not allowed to cook for yourself. The Oakland Police Department partners with the city to patrol and police the sites. Our model is to create a job program out of that, so that the folks living there actually get hired to do the security. Our model has the residents build their own housing, which we discovered is actually another step toward recovery. We hadn't planned that. It was something we witnessed: when people built their homes and then helped the next person build their home, they stayed off drugs, which was amazing."

She goes on, "The Tuff Sheds allow the mayor to say she's doing something. To get into the Tuff Sheds, you have to give up all your property. You're only allowed to bring in two duffle bags. You don't get to pick who your roommate is. They were putting men and women who didn't know each other in a Tuff Shed together, and all that separates you in this ten by eight thing is a plastic curtain. So we've documented women getting sexually assaulted and raped in the Tuff Sheds. Then they *and* their aggressor get kicked out. Women who go in there with their partners, if there's domestic violence, they *both* get kicked out. And there's no grievance process. Even in prison, if you get in trouble for something, you get to have a hearing or a challenge, but here there's no process. If they do kick you out, you don't get to get your property back."

Despite having been sabotaged and shut down by the city at multiple sites, Anita and her allies involved in the Dignity and Housing Village are pressing on. "We're now in a place where we're realizing there is no political will to build permanent housing for the working class. And there's no political will to really have approaches or solutions to homelessness that aren't just cosmetic." Anita's group, on the other hand, is setting up an organization to build permanent as well as temporary emergency housing. The staff will be 100 percent homeless people. "Once you get housed, you get a job, and you have one year to do your job before you train another homeless person to take your job. But you have to volunteer for the Village forever." She laughs, but she's serious. "A lot of folks are unemployable. But if we can help create jobs, and then give them the stability to get housed and then have them help other people who are homeless go through that process too, we develop leaders."

With her organizing savvy, her determination, and the hustle she inherited from her mother, Anita is still very much fighting for the rights and dignity of unsheltered people, including herself and her daughter. Nevertheless, looking back at earlier parts of her life, it's clear that there were various turning points where a culture of care would have made a big difference.

While she was still in college, Anita was hit with a succession of three horrendous tragedies: a rape and two murders in her family. Could more engaged community members and bystanders in each instance have prevented the violence? Could broader availability of mental health care and trauma therapy have stopped the harms endured by the people who turned around and then hurt Anita, her mother, and her cousin? Could a profound cultural shift around old patriarchal ideas about men's ownership of and rights to a woman's body have changed the way things played out? Would the availability of good, dignified work have made a difference to one of the murderers? It's hard to say how many of the deep shifts from a society based in fear to one based in care would have been necessary to prevent these three violent incidents.

Like the majority of people raped on campus, Anita did not report it (the American Civil Liberties Union estimates that a full 95 percent of campus rapes go unreported).[18] According to Anita, there was a culture of racism, as well as a culture of sexual misconduct at her school, both of which prevented her from coming forward and saying anything. In 2014 six students filed federal complaints against UC Santa Barbara, stating that the school "discouraged sexual assault survivors from reporting attacks, did not properly investigate allegations and impose sanctions, and created a hostile environment by failing to give survivors mandated academic accommodations, such as help with class scheduling and test extensions."[19] Given how often sexual assaults happen, educational institutions need to create an atmosphere in which survivors feel safe to come forward, and where they are taken seriously and are provided with the resources to heal. Campuses also need to hold people who commit rape and sexual assault responsible for their actions, and to convey to the student body how seriously they will deal with these kinds of harms.

The Campus PRISM (Promoting Restorative Initiatives for Sexual Misconduct) Project is a group of international practitioners and researchers who work with colleges to integrate restorative justice processes into the options available for students who have experienced sexual assault. PRISM takes a "whole campus" public health approach, utilizing three tiers of intervention. Tier one is preventative, designed to shift the culture on campuses by providing education to all students. Tier two is for when harm happens. It can be used for individual instances of sexual assault as well as for harms to the entire campus, such as when a group of students lead a "rape chant" or a fraternity hangs a sexist banner. Tier three is designed to support the reintegration of students who have been suspended to ensure that they follow through with their commitment to causing no further harm.[20]

In one example of a restorative justice response, a young woman in her freshman year who had been raped decided that the standard campus disciplinary process would further traumatize her, and chose instead to engage the student who had raped her in a healing process. She asked him to create a video with her in which each of them described the assault, and the two of them have presented it to various audiences, including his fraternity brothers and local high school students—a sort of "cautionary tale" to help other students understand the gravity of their actions.[21] While restorative justice is not for everyone, the option should be offered on all campuses.

After the tragedies, Anita turned to drugs to cope. RAINN—the Rape, Abuse and Incest National Network—cites substance abuse as one of the most common effects of sexual violence, alongside eating disorders, sleep disorders, and depression.[22] There are other reasons why college students use drugs, of course, ranging from the pressure of needing to pull all-nighters, to a culture of excessive partying. Things have actually gotten worse since Anita was in school. Nowadays college students are using prescription medications at record rates: both the stimulants prescribed for ADHD like Adderall and opioids like OxyContin. Use of stimulants in particular is so normalized that lots of students are unconcerned that they may become addicted.

There has been a corresponding increase in the number of treatment programs, from a few dozen in 2013 to around two hundred today, along with support from some state governments; New Jersey, West Virginia, and North Carolina, for example, provide grants for college recovery programs.[23] Obviously support for students with any kind of substance abuse issue is necessary, however. The treatment response is missing accountability for the real source of prescription drug abuse: the pharmaceutical industry. We need to hold those particular architects of anxiety responsible for massive harms to society.

Anita would have had one less thing to worry about if her college had been free—if higher education were publicly provided as a universal right—the way it is in many nations that are similarly economically situated. Instead she was weighed down with student debt. "We have an entire generation that is delaying or forgoing purchasing houses," Congresswoman Alexandria Ocasio-Cortez told *Time* magazine. "Our entire economy is slowing down due to the student-loan crisis."[24]

Elizabeth Warren and Bernie Sanders, 2020 presidential hopefuls, have made free higher education signature proposals, calling for the elimination of tuition and fees for undergraduates at all public colleges. Warren calls for the cancellation of up to $50,000 in student debt per person, and for student loans to be dischargeable in bankruptcy. The funding to cover her plan would come from the wealth tax previously described: 2 percent for net worth above $50 million, and 3 percent for those with more than $1 billion, generating $2.75 trillion in revenue over a decade.[25] While progressive politicians who advocate for free college tuition are derided as extreme by other politicians and media pundits, 79 percent of Democrats and 41 percent of Republicans support it.[26]

For Anita, there wasn't enough support in coping with the trauma, and she temporarily lost her housing. We need to understand this as a violation of her human rights. All people deserve the dignity of a home. Period.

In *Evicted*, Matthew Desmond writes: "We have affirmed provision in old age, twelve years of education, and basic nutrition to be the right of every citizen because we have recognized that human dignity depends on the fulfillment of these fundamental human needs. And it is hard to argue that housing is not a fundamental human need. Decent, affordable housing should be a basic right for everybody in this country. The reason is simple: without stable shelter, everything else falls apart."[27]

I consulted with Vanessa Moses, executive director of Causa Justa::Just Cause for her perspective on the housing crisis. Her organization's vision starts with the idea of human needs being more important than the interests of corporations: "We need to decommodify land use and housing," she says flat-out.[28] Viewing housing as a fundamental human right, as the Universal Declaration of Human Rights enshrines, means we have to stop allowing housing to be used as a tool of speculation and profiteering. The sentiment has been echoed by United Nations Special Rapporteur on the Right to Adequate Housing Leilani Farha, who was behind the 2018 report that called San Francisco and Oakland out for being part of a "global scandal." Farha has likewise called for a paradigm shift whereby housing is "once again seen as a human right rather than a commodity."[29]

How can we make the universal right to housing a reality? Just as land expropriation, redlining, and other forms of displacement were intentional policies of the government, so too can governments intentionally seek to transfer the ownership of land and housing back into the hands of *all* community members. Cities can directly support community control over land.

What if instead of kicking out the residents of the Dignity and Housing Village, the city used eminent domain over this vacant land? The city could take ownership of the land and transfer it to a limited equity cooperative (LEC) run by formerly unsheltered residents. LECs are democratic, member-run cooperative organizations that limit the equity individual homeowners can accumulate, thus preserving long-term affordability. In fact, Oakland could develop a citywide strategy to revitalize vacant lots, turning them over to LECs or community land trusts for development. Community land trusts are democratic, multistakeholder organizations that own the land for the permanent benefit of the community; they sell and rent homes with various resale restrictions in order to maintain long-term affordability.

Reversing the decades-long trends of commodification of housing and creating community ownership instead will take time, but in the interim we can use market-based mechanisms to make housing more immediately available to more people. Matthew Desmond calls for a universal housing voucher, and explains it like this:

> Every family below a certain income level would be eligible for a housing voucher. They could use that voucher to live anywhere they wanted, just as families can use food stamps to buy groceries virtually anywhere, as long as their housing was neither too expensive, big and luxurious nor too shabby and run-down. Their home would need to be decent, modest-sized and fairly priced. Program administrators could develop fine-grained analyses, borrowing from algorithms and other tools commonly used in the private market, to prevent landlords from charging too much and families from selecting more housing than they need. The family would dedicate 30% of their income to housing costs, with the voucher paying the rest. A universal voucher program would change the face of poverty in this country. Evictions would plummet and become rare occurrences. Homelessness would almost disappear. Families would immediately feel the income gains and be able to buy enough food, invest in themselves and their children through schooling or job training, and start modest savings. They would find stability and have a sense of ownership over their home and community. Universal housing programs have been successfully implemented all over the developed world.[20]

Currently, government support of housing is not meeting the need. The existing Section 8 "housing choice voucher" program functions like a lottery because there are long waiting lists that are opened up ("unfrozen") only every few years. If your family is lucky enough to get called up, you're allowed to look for an apartment up to a certain rent—"fair market rent"—an amount calculated by the Department of Housing that differs by region. Due to rising rents, voucher-holders are pushed farther out from the more expensive city center, often into buildings that are unsafe. According to a 2015 article in the *Atlantic*, "fair market rent" for New York City was $1,249 per month, "a price that would relegate voucher-holders to the neighborhood of Brownsville in Brooklyn, one of the most dangerous places in the city."[31] Meanwhile, the article continues,

> in much of the country, landlords can refuse to take Section 8 vouchers, even if the voucher covers the rent. And, unlike the landlords in poor

neighborhoods . . . many landlords of buildings in nicer neighborhoods will do anything to keep voucher-holders out. The result is that Section 8 traps families in the poorest neighborhoods. . . .

Though the landlords would say they refused the vouchers because they didn't want to deal with the paperwork, housing advocates say that property owners don't want Section 8 tenants (read: minorities) in buildings because they might drive away market-rate tenants.[32]

At a cost of nearly $20 billion, Section 8 currently serves only about 17 percent of low-income renters.[33] If it were to assist everyone earning less than 50 percent of regional median income, the cost would be about $41 billion, according to the Congressional Budget Office.[34] For that amount, we could just implement the universal housing voucher instead.

Many voices push for creation of affordable housing units by incentivizing builders through tax credits. It doesn't help matters when the president's tax reform bill significantly decreases the value of the low-income housing tax credit; the change could result in construction or renovation of 235,000 fewer affordable units over the next decade.[35] Certainly, as community members, we can pressure our local governments to mandate that higher percentages of new construction be allocated for the poorest members of our community. Everywhere you look in Oakland right now you see construction cranes. What if the city required that all large-scale development projects include community benefit agreements (CBAs) that support affordable housing? CBAs are legally enforceable contracts between developers and local residents, negotiated to ensure outcomes like mandated jobs for community members, environmental safeguards, or commitments to create a certain amount of affordable housing.

This has been done in Detroit. Long known as a city with high home-ownership rates for black residents, Detroit has an ongoing foreclosure crisis, which has led to renters actually outnumbering owners in 2017.[36] A group of community organizations mobilized Detroit voters in 2016 to pass a historic citywide community benefits ordinance that requires developers to enter into a CBA on all projects that cost more than $75 million and receive more than a million dollars in public investment. When a project meets those requirements, the city organizes community meetings over a three-month period to introduce the project to the impacted residents, determine potential impacts of the project, and establish benefits for the community. So far the process has secured $2.5 million to build sixty outdoor basketball courts in city parks and restore an abandoned school field for sports and recreation use, including a skate park, along with a commitment to provide more affordable rentals for low-income residents.[37] While some have complained that the Detroit ordinance is too weak and doesn't truly empower residents, others say that there's significant value in engagement and conversation among residents alone, and that it serves as a baseline for future CBAs.

Vanessa Moses believes we need to shift the emphasis away from building "affordable housing" as a silver-bullet solution. "Because of how long construction takes, the huge associated expense and the ongoing struggle over what constitutes 'affordable,' we will never just 'build our way out of the crisis,'" she tells me.

By utilizing available resources, we can avoid the need to build so much new housing. We can focus resources on renovating and utilizing existing housing. Across the country there is a lot of housing standing vacant, which, given the crisis in housing, is unconscionable and should be remedied accordingly. In November 2018, Oakland voters approved a tax on any property (residential as well as commercial and empty lots) that is not in use for more than fifty days. In December, the city sent out twenty-five thousand letters to non-owner-occupied properties warning them of the tax ($6,000 per year per parcel; $3,000 per year for condos, duplexes, and first-floor commercial space) if their property is deemed vacant.[38] Although results aren't in yet, the city's finance department estimates the tax could bring in $6 million to $10 million per year, deterring speculation and encouraging owners of vacant parcels to sell or develop their land, therefore unlocking sites for housing. San Francisco is considering following Oakland's lead and putting a vacant property tax on the November 2019 ballot.[39] The proceeds from these taxes should be used to fund housing projects that are controlled by communities.

We also need to emphasize protections and rights for tenants. Where people are already housed, we have to make it easier for them to stay. Renter protections are critical to preventing displacement and ensuring that homes are habitable, that rent increases are moderated, and that evictions come with due process. Rent control policies establish maximum annual rent increases and provide avenues for tenants to dispute increases that exceed those limits. Anita adds: "We need an immediate moratorium on evictions as they currently exist until the city creates a transparent and accountable encampment relocation process."

We can't allow landlords to evict tenants to make way for newer (wealthier and whiter) tenants. Tenants need lawyers to enforce tenants' rights. In the overwhelming majority of cases, landlords have lawyers and tenants do not. You have a right to counsel when your liberty is at stake, but not your home. This does not make sense. As Matthew Desmond notes: "Establishing publicly funded legal services for low-income families in housing court would be a cost-effective measure that would prevent homelessness, decrease evictions, and give poor families a fair shake."[40]

Anita got to know the members of the unsheltered communities in Oakland and the ways that they are being dehumanized and criminalized years after her initial experience of losing her housing during college. Although permanent housing for unsheltered people is the goal, we need to recognize their dignity and agency for as long as they are on the streets. Police harassment needs to stop, and we need to get rid of the myriad ridiculous "anti-homeless" laws that target people for things like loitering, sharing food, and camping. The 9th US Circuit Court of Appeals recently upheld the September 2018 ruling of a lower court that cities can't prosecute people for sleeping on the streets because it amounts to cruel and unusual punishment, which is unconstitutional.[41]

By some calculations, just providing people with a home is actually cheaper than dealing with all of the ways in which people's live fall apart without homes. Gordon Walker, director of Utah's Division of Community and Housing estimated that criminalizing Utah's unsheltered population cost about $20,000 per person in state services, jail time, and police costs. By adopting a housing first program, where the priority is to place people in permanent housing instead of locking them up or sweeping them away, Utah saved millions and dramatically improved the lives of unsheltered people in the state.[42]

Finally, any program to provide housing has to refuse what Anita calls the "homeless industrial complex," created by people with no experience of homelessness as a way to make profit. Instead, like the organization Anita and her allies are launching, every aspect of a project can serve to empower and train people, which contributes to healing and long-term stability, and greater safety for everyone.

Here is a summary of my recommendations:

- College campuses need to create cultures of accountability. They need to discourage a climate of sexual violence, encourage reporting of assaults, and hold people who commit rape and sexual assault responsible for their actions. Using the

PRISM program, they should offer restorative justice as an option for survivors, in order to ensure healing.

- We should eliminate all fees and tuitions for undergraduates at public colleges and universities. Higher education should be publicly provided as a universal right, the way it is in many nations that are similarly economically situated. This would keep student debt from holding so many young people back from security.

- We need to treat substance abuse on campus as the public health issue it is and address the rampant overuse of prescription medications on campus.

- State and local governments should pass resolutions and other policies that enshrine housing a human right. They can also establish policies that enable the scaling of community-controlled housing.

- Reversing decades-long trends of redlining, as well as "urban renewal" and federal highway development that expropriated and demolished many homes, local governments can use eminent domain for good, creating land banks to turn vacant lands into community-controlled housing developments.

- While the community-controlled development of land proceeds, market-based mechanisms and renter protections should be used to keep people in their homes. This means a universal housing voucher program, rent-control policies, publicly funded legal services for low-income families, and "just cause" eviction ordinances that limit the reasons a landlord can use to kick someone out of their rental property and set penalties for when unjustified evictions occur.

- Both laws and cultural attitudes related to homeless and unsheltered individuals must change, ensuring they have dignity as well as opportunities for work and participation in society.

CONCLUSION

WE THE PEOPLE

As I began writing this book, consensus around the untenable nature of our incarceration system in America seemed certain. Steadily, over the decade leading up to 2016, there had been a sea change, a shift toward decarceration (the opposite of incarceration), a movement to reduce the number of prisons, people in prison, and prison sentences.

Public support for punishment had been dropping since the mid-1990s, as measured by attitudes toward the death penalty and law enforcement authority, as well as toward harsh judicial sentencing and spending for police enforcement.[1] This shift has happened thanks in large part to the work of community organizers across the country. Six states were leading the nation in decarceration: New Jersey has seen a 37 percent decline in prison populations since 1999, Alaska a 33 percent decline since 2006, New York a 31 percent decline since 1999, Vermont a 29 percent decline since 2009, Connecticut a 28 percent decline since 2007, and my home state, California, a 25 percent decline since 2006. Even in the South, where there are exceptionally high rates of incarceration, there were double-digit declines in a number of states in 2008, including in Mississippi (14 percent since 2008), South Carolina (13 percent since 2009), Alabama (12 percent since 2102), and Louisiana (11 percent since 2012). Meanwhile the federal prison population declined 13 percent between 2011 and 2016.[2]

There was even a healthy conversation about prison abolition, a notion that previously seemed suited only for science fiction. In her book *Are Prisons Obsolete?*, lifelong civil rights activist Angela Davis writes:

"Prison abolitionists are dismissed as utopians and idealists whose ideas are at best unrealistic and impracticable, and, at worst, mystifying and foolish. This is a measure of how difficult it is to envision a social order that does not rely on the threat of sequestering people in dreadful places designed to separate them from their communities and families. The prison is considered so 'natural' that it is extremely hard to imagine life without it."[3] Yet suddenly a number of people were contemplating life, and a country, without prisons.

For financial reasons, many agreed, our levels of incarceration are untenable. It costs a hell of a lot to keep millions of people behind bars and under surveillance, not to mention the costs resulting from lost earnings and reduced tax base. For moral reasons, others noted, the culture of prisons is an abomination, leading to family-wide and community-wide trauma. For reasons of justice and the founding promise of America, some said, our incarceration nation was the antithesis of liberty and equality for all.

The rationales were disparate, as described by sociologist Patrick Sharkey in *Uneasy Peace*, but they united the unlikeliest of bedfellows, from the Black Lives Matter movement to Newt Gingrich, Rand Paul, and Ted Cruz; from prison guards to families of victims of violent crime; and from conservative organizations such as Koch Industries and Americans for Tax Reform to progressive or liberal organizations, such as the Center for American Progress and the American Civil Liberties Union. Republicans might not believe that locking up people convicted of nonviolent drug offenses has intentionally disproportionately targeted and harmed people of color, in what Michelle Alexander calls "the New Jim Crow," but they understood that the system costs too much and threatens family values. All these voices from across the map—from generally opposing sides of the spectrum—agreed that the current system wasn't producing its stated goals of safety, accountability, and healing.

What they couldn't agree on is what to replace it with.

For example, one potential future path involves electronic monitoring (EM), constant "intensive supervision"—what professor and activist James Kilgore has called "e-carceration."[4] It's basically a virtual cage. Shackled to your ankle or wrist is a GPS tracker that limits your movement to your house or neighborhood, preventing you from getting a job, attending school, and visiting loved ones. Some of the trackers monitor your blood alcohol level at regular intervals or use a camera that literally watches your every move. Unsurprisingly, people of color are much more likely to be on EM. "Digital prisons are to mass incarceration what Jim

Crow was to slavery," comments Michelle Alexander.[5] EM is a favorite tool of US Immigration and Customs Enforcement, with thirty thousand immigrants subject to electronic monitoring.[6] For those solely concerned with government spending, EM provides a neat solution because it shifts the costs of incarceration from the government to those who are monitored—they are required to lease bracelets from private companies at a cost of about $300 per month.[7] According to research by *Colorlines*, the four major producers of EM made $200 million on trackers in 2018, and the market keeps expanding.[8]

Ending mass incarceration does not mean we ensure safety, fairness, and opportunity. In fact, if you look at how the criminal legal system has evolved since its inception, you find that it has morphed every fifty years or so, yet remained consistent in its worst features. The constant feature of our nation's framework of fear has been that it has reinforced white supremacy and the systemic deprivation, scapegoating, and subjugation of people of color.

In the context of widespread bipartisan agreement that incarceration has gone too far, a window opened for creation of a new plan to ensure safety and security. We had a once-in-several-generations opportunity to replace the system of scapegoating and punishment with a plan that would actually result in long-term safety and security. Would we finally recognize that public safety starts with resources and relationships? Would we figure out more satisfactory ways of holding people accountable for their actions and for healing our communities?

This was the need I felt I should address, standing on the shoulders of the many giants who had written about the problems of incarceration—from activists and academics to incarcerated folks and formerly incarcerated folks. There was Ruth Wilson Gilmore's *Golden Gulag* in 2006, Mumia Abu-Jamal's *Jailhouse Lawyers* in 2009, *The New Jim Crow* by Michelle Alexander in 2012, *Just Mercy* by Bryan Stevenson in 2014, Shaka Senghor's *Writing My Wrongs* in 2016, and 2018's *Decarcerating America* by Ernest Drucker, to name just a few.

For me, the focus was never incarceration. Of course I believe that given prison sentences that are twice the international average, and rates of violence and poverty unparalleled in similar OECD countries, the United States needs to declare a national emergency: federal prison sentences should be cut in half and resources saved from the shortened prison sentences should be diverted to support people leaving prison and the communities to which they are returning.

Yet when I chose to study law and to work at organizations involved in criminal justice reform, it was not because I was interested in the law, the courts, or judges, or prisons, or jails. I was and am interested in the well-being of families and communities, most especially my own community of Oakland. The questions before me were: how do we achieve safety and accountability in America, if not through the old framework of fear? And, further, could a new model of public safety more effectively handle the harms that our current system is totally failing to address, whether that means systemic racism or poverty or sexual abuse, and all the real harms, hurts, and threats in between?

What came next, after our era of incarceration, was very much up for grabs, and the window of opportunity was not infinite.

And then, America elected its forty-fifth president.

Trump and his revolving cast of Justice Department officials have doubled down on policies of othering. They have taken Us vs. Them and made it national policy. The government is blatantly conveying the sentiment that might makes right and we are not all created equal. There is rampant scapegoating, intimidation, violence. They are separating children from their families and putting babies in cages. The president of the United States excuses the actions of neo-Nazis and calls them "fine people." The divides between Americans seem insurmountable. Our social fabric is hanging by a thread as authoritarianism and dehumanization gain more and more ground.

Under fascism, the dynamics of true democracy are reversed. Whereas in real democracy, individual people are empowered to choose and can hold their elected officials accountable, in fascism, individuals give up their power to the strongman who promises to save them.

At this point, I felt this book needed to include an additional thread: if a fear-based system paved the way to creeping authoritarianism, could a transformed justice system, a culture of care, pave the way to real democracy? Can we take the opportunity that justice reform presents and create true democracy?

Among the most fundamental differences between democracy and fascism is the vision of how we get to safety. Under fascist ideology, safety is achieved through the separation of people seen as superior beings from those who are viewed as less than human. This distinction is enforced violently up to and including extermination. The vision of safety under democracy is that we are safer and better off when more people are involved in governing. Part of the idea behind democracy is that no one individual can alone correctly account for the needs of all of the individuals in the collective. Implicit in this idea is that there is a common good.

Is our democracy up to the task of keeping us safe, given the internal divisions among us? At perhaps no other time in our history as a country has there been a greater fear that there will be no reconciling the chasm that separates us. There is deep skepticism that any re-examination of the origins of the country or its history could help bridge this chasm. And yet at no other time in history has there been a greater sense that we must. If we are going to create safe communities and a safe country, we have to change how we think about ourselves. We can't fall prey to Us vs. Them mythology as the answer. We need to embrace what john powell calls the "bigger We." We need to heal the divides and the trauma.

Participation in our democracy goes beyond the voting booth. Of course elections matter. Of course we must participate in them in order to use the levers we have as ordinary people to try to create a better and safer society for all of us. But elections alone will not be enough. The problem runs deeper than the forty-fifth president. Can we legitimately claim that the politics of hate are a new phenomenon? I think we need to ask: are the foundations of the country solidly rooted in democracy? Is this a rise of fascism, or its resurgence? The United States is lauded as one of the first democratic nations because the founding fathers were trying to escape the rule of monarchs. Yet the system of slavery and the dispossession of Native people's land was justified by a belief in white supremacy, which was enforced through violence. If fascism existed as a term when the nation was founded, we might well have called it that.

Our democratic experiment is very new. There have been less than a hundred years of adult universal suffrage in this country. Since our founding, anyone who wanted to be included in the governance of society had to fight for that inclusion. A powerful minority has always been adept at maintaining their control. Since the founding of this country, the notion of "versus" has been key to our identity and safety. Man vs. nature. American vs. un-American. Good guys vs. bad guys. Profit vs. workers. The architects of anxiety called it safety when one of these sides defeated the other. But whether we are looking at violence, chaotic weather and natural disasters, or economics, safety doesn't come from standing alone. If safety is anything, it is relationship and connection. It is because we have built our institutions as if safety comes from separation that we now find ourselves hanging by a thread. Now We the People need to roll up our sleeves and hold our institutions accountable to all of us.

Real safety happens when we bridge the divides and build relationships with each other, overcoming suspicion and distrust.

Real safety comes from strategic, smart investments—meaning resources directed toward our stability and well-being.

Real safety addresses the harms that the current system is failing to tackle, and holds people accountable for those harms while still holding them in community.

Real safety results from reinstating full humanity and agency for everyone who has been dehumanized and traumatized, so they can participate fully in society.

If we are able to transform our old system and create a culture of caring and healing in its place, we may have an actual shot at creating real democracy for the first time.

ACKNOWLEDGMENTS

A powerful dream, awake from sleep. An envelope folding in on itself, time warped. Here is how it went: I was playing with my kids, watching my kids. We are at a mall and there is a parking lot. The background is I have this fear of parking lots. I am worried that my kids will be hit by a car in a parking lot. People generally drive slower in parking lots so it is not completely rational but it is there nonetheless. I am watching my kids on the sidewalk near this parking lot, when I observe young men hiding something behind a bench. Is it drugs? Always subconsciously there are thoughts of safety when I am with my kids. Did I imagine it? Was an ancestor run over by a street car? Was he tied down and then run over because he was running bootleg? This is a story I've heard. Are these young men outside selling drugs? Do I have drugs on me? Then the police are on the scene and they are listening to the conversation of these young men. But we are no longer in a time that is now and I am no longer with my kids. We know that the police will make something up. These young men will be sent up the river or they will be sold down river. The writing is all over the walls of my dream. And I am left sobbing uncontrollably as I stand with these young men who will be falsely accused. And as I stand with them for some reason I thank them through tears because I know that the trauma of our ancestors is in us. And if we know the stories and tell them, then it is those stories that give us resilience. So, I would like to start by thanking my ancestors, my grandparents and my parents; my wife and life partner, Saru; my kids, Akeela and Lina; and my brother and sister.

My grandfather Bernard Norris and grandmother Annie Mae Norris were both born in a little town called Osyka, in Mississippi, near the border of Louisiana. They grew up together in Osyka. My grandfather worked on the trains throughout the South. They went from Louisiana to Texas to Southern California, to the Central Valley and finally to San Francisco.

My father's mother, Annie Mae, always held the family together and was one of the strongest women I have ever met. I still remember fishing with her at Clear Lake and feeling totally at peace. She let me eat rice and peanut butter and jelly sandwiches because I was a picky eater. She was such a solid presence, and raised five children and helped raise some grandkids too.

My father's father called me "fishin' buddy" because I used to like to go fishing with him and my grandma too. Despite carrying a lot of responsibility, he always seemed cool, calm, and collected.

My mother's father, William Thomas Dunn, a San Francisco native, was always there for me. He always seemed to just take things in stride and go with the flow. He always had a sports magazine for me and a joke to tell. He played baseball in the Pacific League, which took him to Vancouver, where he met my grandmother. They moved together back to San Francisco.

My mother's mother, Fenella Dunn, is an amazing person. She is one of the most kind, brilliant, caring, and thoughtful people I know. She kept the family connected by keeping us in contact with one another. She helped me get through high school and college. She has always been incredibly generous and concerned with others.

My mother is like the sun. Clouds or not, rain or not, you know the sun is there despite it all. Where would I be without my mom? She took on the world to keep us safe and to give us a chance at happiness.

When I was three or four years old, I managed to accidentally lock my dad out of the house. He climbed under the crawl space to get back in. That is the determination of the best dad I could ever ask for.

My wife is a bad-ass. She is fierce, she is determined, she is a mama bear to our kids, and she will take you down if you mess with us. I am so glad to be in a partnership, in a relationship, and on too-infrequent date nights with her! She loves so intensely, she feels so deeply, she cares for the world and all the creatures in it. Saru, will you go out with me?

To my daughters, Akeela and Lina, I will always be in awe of you. I hope to be the dad you deserve and thank you for continuing to hold me accountable.

My older brother Toreano, when I turned thirteen years old, gave me a copy of *The Autobiography of Malcolm X*. That was the earliest step on my path toward trying to reshape the world around me toward justice. I have appreciated his support every step along that path.

During summers in high school, my older sister Satise let me stay with her while she was at school at the University of California at Santa Cruz. Who lets her little brother tag along at college? I'll tell you who! My sister. She is a co-conspirator, an artist, and a teacher who inspires me to dream big.

Paige Bence and John Lee are like second parents to me. I spent so many nights at their home, it felt like my own. I would like to thank my Uncle Bernard, Aunt Carolyn, and Uncle Quincy for their support in providing interviews and just being uncles and aunts and great people.

Ariane Conrad, Book Doula Extraordinaire, believed I had this book in me. At first, I wasn't sure I did, and then I starting feeling myself and wanted to cover safety, democracy, relationships, trauma, fascism, racism, and some other topics, too, all in one book. She helped me discern, write, and secure a publishing contract for *this* book. I am grateful for her friendship and guidance. Thanks also go to Emily Paul who volunteered research support.

Helene Atwan and the team at Beacon believed in this book. I am proud to join the ranks of Beacon's fearless, truth-telling authors.

I want to thank all those who shared their stories with me and whose stories I was welcomed to share, above all Durrell and Allen Feaster, Marlena and James Henderson, Anita De Asis Miralle, as well as DeVone Boggan, Bill Lindsay, Sam Vaughn, Taryn Ishida, and Vanessa Moses.

I would also like to thank Diana Frappier and Van Jones for founding this amazing institution that is the Ella Baker Center for Human Rights. I would like to thank them for seeing my potential to grow and for their persistence in making change daily. I hope we honor your legacy, Miss Ella Jo Baker.

The Levi Strauss Foundation and Prime Movers/Hunt Alternatives provided support for the writing of this book and without that support, I wouldn't be writing these acknowledgments.

There are many colleagues and comrades from whom I have learned so much and with whom I have sometimes disagreed, which is its own kind of learning: NTanya Lee, Steve Williams, Mei-ying Williams, Ying-sun Ho, Jakada Imani, Nicole Lee, Lenore Anderson, Bernadette Armand, Jennifer Kim, Nwamaka Agbo, Max Rameau, Grace Bauer, Gina Womack, Malkia Cyril, Eric Mann, Patrisse Cullors, Mark Anthony Johnson,

Damon Azali-Rojas, Manuel Criollo, Maria Del Carmen Verdu, Joseph Jordan, Ajamu Dillahunt, Bryan Stevenson, and Michelle Alexander top a list too long to print here. When you are making your way to understand that a different world is possible, it is helpful to know that there are those who have already seen it and are actively dreaming and scheming to bring it into being.

Toward a more just world. Toward a more safe world.

NOTES

INTRODUCTION: US VS. THEM

1. Nina Martin and Renee Montagne, "U.S. Has the Worst Rate of Maternal Deaths in the Developed World," May 12, 2017, https://www.npr.org/2017/05/12 /528098789/u-s-has-the-worst-rate-of-maternal-deaths-in-the-developed-world; "Easing the Dangers of Childbirth for Black Women," editorial, *New York Times*, April 20, 2018, https://www.nytimes.com/2018/04/20/opinion/childbirth-black -women-mortality.html. Also see the 2018 MBRRACE-UK report on maternal mortality (*Saving Lives, Improving Mothers' Care: Lessons Learned to Inform Maternity Care from the UK and Ireland Confidential Enquiries into Maternal Deaths and Morbidity 2014–16*, November 2018), which found "black women are five times more likely and Asian women are twice as likely to die" from complications of pregnancy and childbirth compared to white women.

2. Ashish Thakrar, "Child Mortality in the US and 19 OECD Comparator Nations," *Health Affairs*, January 2018.

3. Alan B. Cibils et al., "Argentina Since Default: The IMF and the Depression," Center for Economic and Policy Research, September 2002, http://cepr.net/documents /publications/argentina_2002_09_03.htm, accessed May 17, 2019.

4. Klaus Friedrich Veigel, "The Great Unraveling: Argentina 1973–1991," in *Governed by Emergency: Economic Policy-Making in Argentina, 1973–1991* (Princeton, NJ: Princeton University, 2005).

5. Barry Glassner, *The Culture of Fear: Why Americans Are Afraid of the Wrong Things* (orig. 1999; New York: Basic Books, 2018), xi–xii.

6. Umair Haque, "The Birth of Predatory Capitalism," *Medium*, March 3, 2019, https://eand.co/the-birth-of-predatory-capitalism-6d443eda03.

7. John Anthony Powell, *Racing to Justice: Transforming Our Conceptions of Self and Other to Build an Inclusive Society* (Bloomington: Indiana University Press, 2012). Quote is from his blog, http://www.johnapowell.org/blog.

8. Jason Stanley, *How Fascism Works: The Politics of Us and Them* (New York: Random House, 2018). Quote from Sean Illing, "How Fascism Works," *Vox*,

December 15, 2018, https://www.vox.com/2018/9/19/17847110/how-fascism
-works-donald-trump-jason-stanley.

9. Lawson Fusao Inada and Patricia Wakida, *Only What We Could Carry:
The Japanese American Internment Experience* (Berkeley, CA: Heyday Books,
2000).

10. "The U.S. has a staggering 2.3 million people behind bars, but even this
number doesn't capture the true scale of our correctional system. For a complete
picture of our criminal justice system, it's more accurate to look at the 6.7 million
people under correctional control, which includes not only incarceration but also
probation and parole." From Alexi Jones, "Correctional Control 2018," Prison Policy
Initiative, December 2018, https://www.prisonpolicy.org/reports/correctional
control2018.html.

11. Cody Cain, "Taxing the Rich Was a Pillar of Our Modern Society," *Huffington Post*, August 13, 2015, https://www.huffpost.com/entry/taxing-the-rich-was
-a-pil_b_7977654. Data from "U.S. Federal Individual Income Tax Rates History,
1862 2013 (Nominal and Inflation-Adjusted Brackets)," https://taxfoundation.org
/us-federal-individual-income-tax-rates-history-1913-2013-nominal-and-inflation
-adjusted-brackets.

CHAPTER 1: WHO AND WHAT HARMS US

1. Robert O. Self, *American Babylon: Race and the Struggle for Postwar Oakland* (Princeton, NJ: Princeton University Press, 2003), 104.

2. Martin Ricard, "San Leandro Report Details Racist Past," *East Bay Times*,
August 17, 2016, https://www.eastbaytimes.com/2007/06/02/san-leandro-report
-details-racist-past.

3. Ishmael Reed, *Blues City: A Walk in Oakland* (New York: Crown, 2003), 19.

4. Reed, *Blues City*, 20.

5. Self, *American Babylon*, 12.

6. Matthew Desmond, *Evicted: Poverty and Profit in the American City* (New
York: Crown, 2016), 24.

7. Center on Juvenile and Criminal Justice, "California Youth Crime Decline:
The Untold Story," September 2006, 10, https://www.prisonpolicy.org/scans/cjcj
/CAYouthCrimeSept06.pdf.

8. Jeannette Wicks-Lim, "The Great Recession in Black Wealth," *Dollars &
Sense/Truthout*, February 14, 2012, http://www.dollarsandsense.org/archives/2012
/0112wicks-lim.html.

9. Lovemme Corazón, *Trauma Queen: A Memoir* (Toronto: Biyuti, 2013), 7.

10. MEY, "Trauma Queen: An Autostraddle Review and Interview," *Autostraddle*, June 11, 2013, https://www.autostraddle.com/trauma-queen-an-autostraddle
-book-review-and-interview-179954.

11. "22 Year Old Ohio Trans Woman Stabbed to Death by Father," PghLesbian,
February 15, 2015, http://www.pghlesbian.com/2015/02/22-year-old-ohio-trans
-woman-stabbed-to-death-by-father.

12. National Center for Transgender Equality, https://transequality.org/issues
/housing-homelessness.

13. Diana Tourjee, "The Murder of Keisha Jenkins and the Violent Reality for Trans Women of Color," *Vice*, November 10, 2015, https://www.vice.com/en_us/article/9ae4yp/the-murder-of-keisha-jenkins-and-the-violent-reality-for-trans-women-of-color.

14. Janet Mock, *Redefining Realness: My Path to Womanhood, Identity, Love & So Much More* (New York: Atria, 2014), 213–14.

15. Mock, *Redefining Realness*, 207.

16. Peyton Goddard and Dianne Goddard (with Carol Cujec), *I Am Intelligent: From Heartbreak to Healing—A Mother and Daughter's Journey Through Autism* (Guilford, CT: Skirt! Press, 2012). All biographical material in this vignette is from *I Am Intelligent* and Peyton's personal website. All quotes from Peyton are accurate to her expression, despite sometimes being divergent from standard grammar, spelling, or vocabulary.

17. Peyton Goddard (website), http://peytongoddard.com. In fact, Peyton enrolled in college in 1998 and graduated four years later as the valedictorian with a nearly 4.0 GPA.

18. Goddard and Goddard, *I Am Intelligent*, xii.

19. Joseph Shapiro, "The Sexual Assault Epidemic No One Talks About," NPR, January 8, 2018, https://www.npr.org/2018/01/08/570224090/the-sexual-assault-epidemic-no-one-talks-about.

20. Shapiro, "The Sexual Assault Epidemic No One Talks About."

21. "Peyton's Biography," http://peytongoddard.com/index.php/peytons-biography.

22. Ursula Buffay, "For Women Restaurant Workers, Sexual Harassment Starts with the Day You're Hired," *In These Times*, November 9, 2017, http://inthesetimes.com/working/entry/20680/for_women_in_restaurant_work_sexual_harassment_starts_with_hiring.

23. Buffay, "For Women Restaurant Workers."

24. Restaurant Opportunities Centers United and Forward Together, *The Glass Floor: Sexual Harassment in the Restaurant Industry* (October 7, 2014), https://rocunited.org/wp-content/uploads/2014/10/REPORT_The-Glass-Floor-Sexual-Harassment-in-the-Restaurant-Industry2.pdf.

25. Restaurant Opportunities Centers United and Forward Together, *The Glass Floor*.

26. Bryce Covert, "When Harassment Is the Price of a Job," *Nation*, February 7, 2018, https://www.thenation.com/article/when-harassment-is-the-price-of-a-job.

27. Covert, "When Harassment Is the Price of a Job."

28. Restaurant Opportunities Centers United and Forward Together, *The Glass Floor*.

29. Buffay, "For Women Restaurant Workers."

30. Virginia Chamlee, "Teen Chipotle Worker Wins $7.65M in Sexual Harassment Suit," *Eater*, September 29, 2016, https://www.eater.com/2016/9/29/13104528/chipotle-teen-7-million-judgment.

31. Covert, "When Harassment Is the Price of a Job."

32. In prison, Madoff "cornered the hot chocolate market. He bought up every package of Swiss Miss from the commissary and sold it for a profit in the prison yard." From Caroline Halleman, "What Life Is Like for Bernie Madoff in Prison,"

Town & Country, January 13, 2017, https://www.townandcountrymag.com/society
/money-and-power/news/a9249/bernie-madoff-life-in-prison.

33. Paddy Hillyard and Steve Tombs, "Beyond Criminology," in *Criminal Obsessions: Why Harm Matters More Than Crime*, ed. Hillyard et al. (London: Crime and Society Foundation, 2005), 13–14.

34. Haque, "Birth of Predatory Capitalism."

35. Haque, "Birth of Predatory Capitalism."

36. Emmie Martin, "Only 39% of Americans Have Enough Savings to Cover a $1,000 Emergency," CNBC, January 18, 2018, https://www.cnbc.com/2018/01/18
/few-americans-have-enough-savings-to-cover-a-1000-emergency.html.

37. Terry Gross, "First-Ever Evictions Database Shows: 'We're in the Middle of a Housing Crisis,'" *Fresh Air*, NPR, April 12, 2018, https://www.npr.org/2018/04/12
/601783346/first-ever-evictions-database-shows-were-in-the-middle-of-a-housing
-crisis.

38. "Each year, nearly 900,000 Americans die prematurely from the five leading causes of death—yet 20 percent to 40 percent of the deaths from each cause could be prevented, according to a 2014 study from the Centers for Disease Control and Prevention." *Morbidity and Mortality Weekly Report*, May 1, 2014, Centers for Disease Control and Prevention, https://www.cdc.gov/media/releases/2014/p0501-preventable
-deaths.html.

39. Edgar Villanueva, *Decolonizing Wealth: Indigenous Wisdom to Heal Divides and Restore Balance* (Oakland: Berrett-Koehler, 2018), 26.

40. Robin DiAngelo, *White Fragility: Why It's So Hard for White People to Talk About Racism* (Boston: Beacon Press, 2018).

41. Mimi Kim, phone interview by the author, April 10, 2018.

42. P. R. Lockhart, "What Serena Williams's Scary Childbirth Story Says About Medical Treatment of Black Women," *Vox*, January 11, 2018, https://www.vox.com
/identities/2018/1/11/16879984/serena-williams-childbirth-scare-black-women.

43. Villanueva, *Decolonizing Wealth*, 32.

44. bell hooks, *The Will to Change: Men, Masculinity and Love* (New York: Atria, 2004), 27.

45. "Women and the Law," Harvard Business School, https://www.library.hbs
.edu/hc/wcs/collections/women_law, accessed April 17, 2019.

46. Senator Kamala Harris pushed Supreme Court nominee Brett Kavanaugh to answer questions about abortion rights during his confirmation hearing on September 5, 2018. C-SPAN footage posted on YouTube, https://www.youtube.com/watch?v
=b6g-zycRv8Q, accessed April 3, 2019.

47. Annie Lowrey, "Women May Earn Just 49 Cents on the Dollar," *Atlantic*, November 28, 2018, https://www.theatlantic.com/ideas/archive/2018/11/how-big
-male-female-wage-gap-really/576877. The article cites research by social scientists Stephen Rose and Heidi Hartmann published by the Institute for Women's Policy Research, https://iwpr.org/women-earn-just-half-of-what-men-earn-over-15-years.

48. Lowrey, "Women May Earn Just 49 Cents on the Dollar."

49. "Transgender Workers at Greater Risk for Unemployment and Poverty," Human Rights Commission, September 26, 2013, in *A Broken Bargain: Discrimination, Fewer Benefits, and More Taxes for LGBT Workers*, https://www.hrc.org/blog
/transgender-workers-at-greater-risk-for-unemployment-and-poverty.

50. Anna Aizer, "The Gender Wage Gap and Domestic Violence," *American Economic Review* 100, no. 4 (September 2010): 1847–59.

51. Michael Paymar, *Violent No More: Helping Men End Domestic Abuse* (Nashville: Hunter House, 2000), 174.

52. John DeVore, "We Need to Start Seeing Powerful Men for What They Are," *Medium*, December 21, 2018, https://medium.com/s/story/we-need-to-start-seeing -powerful-men-for-what-they-are-e5ce79a226a9.

53. "Intentional Homicide Victims," *United Nations Office on Drugs and Crime*, https://dataunodc.un.org/crime/intentional-homicide-victims, accessed August 20, 2018.

54. J. Pete Blair, M. Hunter Martaindale, and Terry Nichols, "Active Shooter Events from 2000 to 2012," https://leb.fbi.gov/articles/featured-articles/active-shooter -events-from-2000-to-2012, cited in National Center for Victims of Crime Fact Sheet on Mass Casualty, https://ovc.ncjrs.gov/ncvrw2018/info_flyers/fact_sheets /2018NCVRW_MassCasualty_508_QC.pdf, accessed July 2, 2018.

55. Saeed Ahmed and Christina Walker, "There Has Been, on Average, 1 School Shooting Every Week This Year," CNN, May 25, 2018, https://edition.cnn.com /2018/03/02/us/school-shootings-2018-list-trnd/index.html.

56. Kashmira Gander, "More Children Were Shot Dead in 2017 Than On-Duty Police Officers and Active Duty Military, Study Says," *Newsweek*, March 21, 2019, https://www.newsweek.com/kids-and-guns-alarming-rise-firearm-deaths-among -american-children-1370866.

57. US Department of Health and Human Services, Children's Bureau, National Child Abuse and Neglect Data System (NCANDS), http://www.acf.hhs.gov/pro- grams/cb/resource/about-ncands, cited in the fact sheet "Child Maltreatment," in the Child Trends DataBank, https://www.childtrends.org, accessed July 3, 2018.

58. Fact sheet "Child, Youth and Teen Victimization," National Center for Vic- tims of Crime, http://victimsofcrime.org/docs/default-source/ncvrw2015/2015ncvrw _stats_children.pdf?sfvrsn=2, accessed July 3, 2018.

59. David Finkelhor, *Polyvictimization: Children's Exposure to Multiple Types of Violence, Crime and Abuse* (Washington, DC: Office of Juvenile Justice and Delinquency Prevention, Office of Justice Programs, 2011), 2, cited in the fact sheet "Child, Youth and Teen Victimization."

60. generationFIVE, *Ending Child Sexual Abuse: A Transformative Justice Re- port* (June 2017), http://www.generationfive.org/wp-content/uploads/2017/06 /Transformative-Justice-Handbook.pdf.

61. generationFIVE, *Ending Child Sexual Abuse.*

62. generationFIVE, *Ending Child Sexual Abuse.*

63. Nicole S. Dahmen and Raluca Cozma, eds., *Media Takes: On Aging* (New York: International Longevity Center, 2009).

64. Matthew J. Breidling et al., *Prevalence and Characteristics of Sexual Vio- lence, Stalking, and Intimate Partner Violence Victimization—National Intimate Partner and Sexual Violence Survey, United States, 2011* (Atlanta: Centers for Disease Control and Prevention, 2014).

65. Breidling et al., *Prevalence and Characteristics of Sexual Violence, Stalking, and Intimate Partner Violence Victimization.*

66. Jen Christensen, "Killings of Transgender People in the US Saw Another High Year," CNN, January 17, 2019, https://edition.cnn.com/2019/01/16/health /transgender-deaths-2018/index.html.

67. Danielle Sered, *Until We Reckon: Violence, Mass Incarceration, and a Road to Repair* (New York: New Press, 2019).

68. Sered, *Until We Reckon*, 14.

69. "The Practices We Need: #metoo and Transformative Justice Part 2," How to Survive the End of the World Podcast, https://soundcloud.com/endoftheworldshow /the-practices-we-need-metoo-and-transformative-justice-part-2/s-CovZV, accessed November 9, 2018.

70. Bessel van der Kolk, *The Body Keeps the Score: Brain, Mind and Body in the Healing of Trauma* (New York: Viking, 2014), 210.

71. Jimmy Tobias, "US Official Reveals Atlantic Drilling Plan While Hailing Trump's Ability to Distract Public," *Guardian*, March 14, 2019, https://www.the guardian.com/environment/2019/mar/14/offshore-drilling-trump-official-reveals -plan-and-distractions-delight.

CHAPTER 2: THE FRAMEWORK OF FEAR

1. Jacob Soboroff, "Surge in Children Separated at Border Floods Facility for Undocumented Immigrants," NBC, June 16, 2018, https://www.nbcnews.com/news /us-news/surge-children-separated-border-floods-facility-undocumented-immigrants -n883001.

2. "In part because it's hard to collect data on them, undocumented immigrants have been the subjects of few studies, including those related to crime. But Pew Research Center recently released estimates of undocumented populations sorted by metro area, which the Marshall Project has compared with local crime rates published by the FBI." From Anna Flagg, "Is There a Connection Between Undocumented Immigrants and Crime?," Marshall Project, May 13, 2019, https://www.themarshallproject.org /2019/05/13/is-there-a-connection-between-undocumented-immigrants-and-crime?.

3. Michelle Mark, "'My Son Is Traumatized': Heartbreaking Video Shows a Young Immigrant Child Squirming Away from His Mother After Being Reunited After Months of Separation," *Insider*, August 25, 2018, https://www.insider.com /family-reunification-heartbreaking-video-2018-8.

4. Video of Hillary Clinton speech at Keene State College, New Hampshire, January 25, 1996, https://www.youtube.com/watch?v=ALXulkoT8cg.

5. John DiIulio Jr., "The Coming of the Super Predators," *Weekly Standard*, November 27, 1995. Also see William J. Bennett, John P. Walters, and John DiIulio Jr., *Body Count: Moral Poverty . . . and How to Win America's War Against Crime and Drugs* (New York: Simon & Schuster, 1996).

6. John DiIulio Jr., "My Black Crime Problem, and Ours," *City Journal* (Spring 1996), https://www.city-journal.org/html/my-black-crime-problem-and-ours -11773.html.

7. George L. Kelling and James Q. Wilson, "Broken Windows: The Police and Neighborhood Safety," *Atlantic*, March 1982.

8. John DiIulio Jr., "How to Stop the Coming Crime Wave," Manhattan Institute, 1996.

9. Nathan J. Robinson, *Superpredator: Bill Clinton's Use and Abuse of Black America* (West Somerville, MA: Current Affairs Press, 2016). Excerpted in "Bill Clinton, Superpredator," *Jacobin*, September 2016, https://www.jacobinmag.com /2016/09/bill-clinton-hillary-superpredators-crime-welfare-african-americans.

10. Howard N. Snyder and Melissa Sickmund, *Juvenile Offenders and Victims: 1999 National Report* (National Center for Juvenile Justice, September 1999), http:// www.ncjj.org/pdf/1999%20natl%20report.pdf.

11. Council of Juvenile Correctional Administrators, *Toolkit: Reducing the Use of Isolation*, March 2015, http://cjca.net/index.php/resources/cjca-publications/107 -toolkit/751-cjca-toolkit-for-reducing-the-use-of-isolation.

12. Human Rights Watch, *Branded for Life: Florida's Prosecution of Children as Adults Under Its 'Direct File' Statute* (April 10, 2014), https://www.hrw.org/report /2014/04/10/branded-life/floridas-prosecution-children-adults-under-its-direct -file-statute.

13. Rachel Barth, "Prisons Want to Rebrand Solitary Confinement," *Business Insider*, April 11, 2014, http://www.businessinsider.com/prisons-want-to-rebrand -solitary-confinement-2014.

14. Barth, "Prisons Want to Rebrand Solitary Confinement."

15. Jennifer Gonnerman, "Kalief Browder, 1993–2015," *New Yorker*, June 7, 2015, https://www.newyorker.com/news/news-desk/kalief-browder-1993-2015.

16. Selena Teji, "Goodbye Preston," Center on Juvenile & Criminal Justice, June 10, 2011, http://www.cjcj.org/news/5374.

17. Brief of Jeffrey Fagan, et al., Miller v. Alabama, Np. 10-9646, 63 So. 3d 676.

18. In 2001, as the newly appointed director of the White House Office of Faith-Based and Community Issues under George W. Bush, DiIulio conceded "that he wished he had never become the 1990's intellectual pillar for putting violent juveniles in prison and condemning them as "superpredators.' . . . 'I'm sorry for any unintended consequences,' Mr. DiIluio said today. 'But I am not responsible for teenagers' going to prison.'" Elizabeth Becker, "As Ex-Theorist on Young 'Super-predators,' Bush Aide Has Regrets," *New York Times*, February 9, 2001, https:// www.nytimes.com/2001/02/09/us/as-ex-theorist-on-young-superpredators-bush -aide-has-regrets.html.

19. Inada and Wakida, *Only What We Could Carry*, xix.

20. *Children of the Camps: Internment History*, PBS, 1999, https://www.pbs.org /childofcamp/history.

21. Michi Weglyn, *Years of Infamy: The Untold Story of America's Concentra-tion Camps* (New York: Morrow, 1976).

22. Ann Binlot, "Japanese Internment Camp Survivors Reflect on America's Dark Past 75 Years Later," *Document*, May 24, 2017, http://www.documentjournal .com/2017/05/japanese-internment-camp-survivors-reflect-on-americas-dark-past -75-years-later.

23. "Children of the Camps: Internment History," PBS.

24. Inada and Wakida, *Only What We Could Carry*, xix.

25. Donna K. Nagata, *Legacy of Injustice: Exploring the Cross-Generational Impact of the Japanese American Internment* (New York: Springer, 1993). Cited in "Children of the Camps: Internment History," PBS.

26. Vanessa Rancano, "'We've Been There': Native Americans Remember Their Own Family Separations" PRI, August 14, 2018, https://www.pri.org/stories /2018-08-14/we-ve-been-there-native-americans-remember-their-own-family -separations.

27. US Office of Indian Affairs, *Annual Report of the Commissioner of Indian Affairs, for the Year 1891*, part 1 (Washington, DC: GPO, 1891), http://digital .library.wisc.edu/1711.dl/History.AnnRep91p1.

28. Rancano, "'We've Been There.'"

29. Charla Bear, "American Indian Boarding Schools Haunt Many," NPR, May 12, 2008, https://www.npr.org/templates/story/story.php?storyId=16516865.

30. Vinnie Rotondaro, "Boarding Schools: A Black Hole of Native American History," Indian Country Today, September 19, 2015, https://newsmaven.io/indian countrytoday/archive/boarding-schools-a-black-hole-of-native-american-history -dD8_HeergoumF_IDjvkyUA.

31. Villanueva, *Decolonizing Wealth*, 30.

32. Michael Tadman, *Speculators and Slaves: Masters, Traders, and Slaves in the Old South* (Madison: University of Wisconsin Press, 1989).

33. Dylan Matthews, "23 Charts and Maps That Show the World Is Getting Much, Much Better," *Vox*, October 17, 2018, https://www.vox.com/2014/11/24 /7272929/global-poverty-health-crime-literacy-good-news. Citing "Crime in the United States," US Department of Justice, https://ucr.fbi.gov/crime-in-the-u.s/2016 /crime-in-the-u.s.-2016/tables/table-1.

34. "Assault Death Rates 1960–2013," Kieran Healy, October 1, 2015, https:// kieranhealy.org/blog/archives/2015/10/01/assault-death-rates-1960-2013.

35. Andrew Dugan, "In U.S., 37% Do Not Feel Safe Walking at Night Near Home," Gallup, November 24, 2014, https://news.gallup.com/poll/179558/not-feel -safe-walking-night-near-home.aspx.

36. Betsy Cooper et al., "How Immigration and Concerns about Cultural Change Are Shaping the 2016 Election," PRRI, June 23, 2016, https://www.prri .org/research/prri-brookings-poll-immigration-economy-trade-terrorism -presidential-race.

37. Daniel Sullivan, Mark J. Landau, and Zachary K. Rothschild, "An Existential Function of Enemyship," *Journal of Personality and Social Psychology* 98, no. 3 (2010): 434–49, http://lemmalab.com/wp-content/uploads/2017/01/Sullivan _enemyship_JPSP-2010.pdf.

38. Kate M. McQuade, "Victim-Offender Relationship," *The Encyclopedia of Criminology and Criminal Justice* (New York: Springer, 2014), https://onlinelibrary .wiley.com/doi/full/10.1002/9781118517383.wbeccj131.

39. "Expanded Homicide Data: Crime in the United States 2011," US Department of Justice, https://ucr.fbi.gov/crime-in-the-u.s/2011/crime-in-the-u.s.-2011 /offenses-known-to-law-enforcement/expanded/expanded-homicide-data.

40. Julia Ainsley and Robert Windrem, "New Report Says Most U.S. Terrorists Foreign Born, but Check the Fine Print," NBC, January 16, 2018, https://www .nbcnews.com/news/us-news/new-report-says-most-u-s-terrorists-foreign-born -check-n838041.

41. Sered, *Until We Reckon*.

42. Brian Thompson, "The Racial Wealth Gap: Addressing America's Most Pressing Epidemic," *Forbes*, February 18, 2018, https://www.forbes.com/sites /brianthompson1/2018/02/18/the-racial-wealth-gap-addressing-americas-most -pressing-epidemic/#3ff2b4c7a48a.

43. Thompson, "The Racial Wealth Gap."

44. Historians point out that the interest deduction for home mortgages was not intended to encourage home ownership. The deduction was created with the birth of the income tax in 1913—a tax designed explicitly to hit only the richest individuals, a group for whom homeownership rates were not a social concern. In 1913, when interest deductions started, Congress "certainly wasn't thinking of the interest deduction as a stepping-stone to middle-class home ownership, because the tax excluded the first $3,000 (or for married couples, $4,000) of income; less than 1 percent of the population earned more than that." *United States National Educational and Social Development Policy Handbook, Vol. 2: Social Policy: Important Programs and Regulations* (Washington, DC: Global Investment Center, 2015), 121. Moreover, during that era, most people who purchased homes paid up front rather than taking out a mortgage. Rather, the reason for the deduction was that in a nation of small proprietors, it was more difficult to separate business and personal expenses, and so it was simpler to just allow deduction of all interest. See Bruce Bartlett, "The Sacrosanct Mortgage Interest Deduction," *New York Times*, August 6, 2013.

45. "Quarterly Residential Vacancies and Homeownership, First Quarter 2019," US Census Bureau, https://www.census.gov/housing/hvs/files/currenthvspress.pdf, accessed May 23, 2019.

46. Jarrid Green and Thomas M. Hanna, "Community Control of Land and Housing," Democracy Collaborative, August 20, 2018, https://democracycollaborative.org /content/community-control-land-and-housing-exploring-strategies-combating -displacement-expanding.

47. Maya Brennan and Martha Galvez, "Housing as a Platform," Urban Institute, September 2017.

48. Emily Ekins, *Policing in America: Understanding Public Attitudes Toward the Police; Results from a National Survey*, Cato Institute, December 7, 2016, chapter 3, "Personal Contact with the Police and Justice System," https://www.cato.org /policing-in-america/chapter-3/personal-contact-police-and-justice-system.

49. "Factsheet: The NYPD Muslim Surveillance Program," ACLU.org, https:// www.aclu.org/other/factsheet-nypd-muslim-surveillance-program.

50. Scott Shane, "Amid Details on Torture, Data on 26 Who Were Held in Error," *New York Times*, December 12, 2014, https://www.nytimes.com/2014/12/13 /us/politics/amid-details-on-torture-data-on-26-held-in-error-.html.

51. Niaz Kasravi et al., *Born Suspect: Stop-and-Frisk Abuses & the Continued Fight to End Racial Profiling in America*, NAACP, 2014, https://www.prisonpolicy .org/scans/naacp/Born_Suspect_Report_final_web.pdf.

52. Kasravi et al., *Born Suspect*.

53. "Stop and Frisk Data," New York Civil Liberties Union, https://www.nyclu .org/en/stop-and-frisk-data, accessed April 27, 2018.

54. Center for Constitutional Rights, "Landmark Decision: Judge Rules NYPD Stop and Frisk Practices Unconstitutional, Racially Discriminatory," August 12,

2013, https://ccrjustice.org/home/press-center/press-releases/landmark-decision-judge-rules-nypd-stop-and-frisk-practices.

55. Janine Jackson, "The FBI Appears to Be Engaged in a Modern-Day Version of COINTELPRO," Fairness and Accuracy in Reporting, April 19, 2019, https://fair.org/home/the-fbi-appears-to-be-engaged-in-a-modern-day-version-of-cointelpro.

56. Juan Del Toro et al., "The Criminogenic and Psychological Effects of Police Stops on Adolescent Black and Latino Boys," *Proceedings of the National Academy of Sciences* 116, no. 17 (2019): 8261–8, cited in Tom Jacobs, "'Proactive Policing' Could Be Creating Criminals," *Pacific Standard*, April 9, 2019, https://psmag.com/social-justice/proactive-policing-could-be-creating-criminals.

57. Michelle Alexander, "The Newest Jim Crow," *New York Times*, November 8, 2018, https://www.nytimes.com/2018/11/08/opinion/sunday/criminal-justice-reforms-race-technology.html.

58. Jessica McCrory Calarco, "'Free Range' Parenting's Unfair Double Standard," *Atlantic*, April 3, 2018, https://www.theatlantic.com/family/archive/2018/04/free-range-parenting/557051.

59. Diane Redleaf, letter to the editor, "Legalizing 'Free-Range' Parenting Is a Step in the Right Direction," *Atlantic*, April 12, 2018, https://www.theatlantic.com/letters/archive/2018/04/letters-free-range-parenting/557558.

60. Alexi Jones, *Correctional Control 2018* (Prison Policy Initiative, December 2018), https://www.prisonpolicy.org/reports/correctionalcontrol2018.html; Wendy Sawyer and Peter Wagner, *Mass Incarceration: The Whole Pie 2019* (Prison Policy Initiative, March, 2019), https://www.prisonpolicy.org/reports/pie2019.html.

61. National Research Council, *The Growth of Incarceration in the United States: Exploring Causes and Consequences* (Washington, DC: National Academies Press, 2014), 33.

62. Beth Griffith, "Return of Military Equipment Causes Frustration Among Some Officers," The 109, February 9, 2016, https://m.the109.org/2016/02/09/recall-of-military-equipment-causes-frustration-among-some-officers.

63. Eli Hager, "When 'Violent Offenders' Commit Nonviolent Crimes," Marshall Project, April 3, 2019, https://www.themarshallproject.org/2019/04/03/when-violent-offenders-commit-nonviolent-crimes.

64. John Pfaff, *Locked In: The True Causes of Mass Incarceration—and How to Achieve Real Reform* (New York: Basic Books, 2017), 6.

65. "No Safe Place: The Criminalization of Homelessness in U.S. Cities," National Law Center on Homelessness and Poverty, February 2019, https://nlchp.org/wp-content/uploads/2019/02/No_Safe_Place.pdf.

66. Sawyer and Wagner, "Mass Incarceration."

67. Interview with john a. powell, *On Being*, May 10, 2018, https://onbeing.org/programs/john-a-powell-opening-the-question-of-race-to-the-question-of-belonging.

68. Rhitu Chatterjee, "Americans Are a Lonely Lot, and Young People Bear the Heaviest Burden," NPR, May 1, 2018, https://www.npr.org/sections/health-shots/2018/05/01/606588504/americans-are-a-lonely-lot-and-young-people-bear-the-heaviest-burden.

69. "Most common" means the highest number of Americans has zero confidants. The *average* number of confidants is thrown off by those highly social folks

who have many confidants, making the average number two confidants per person. Miller McPherson, Lynn Smith-Lovin, and Matthew E. Brashears, "Social Isolation in America: Changes in Core Discussion Networks over Two Decades," *American Sociological Review* (June 1, 2006), https://doi.org/10.1177/000312240607100301.

70. J. Wesley Boyd, "Solitary Confinement: Torture, Pure and Simple," *Psychology Today* blog, January 15, 2018, https://www.psychologytoday.com/us/blog/almost-addicted/201801/solitary-confinement-torture-pure-and-simple.

71. Christopher Uggen, Ryan Larson, and Sarah Shannon, "6 Million Lost Voters: State-Level Estimates of Felony Disenfranchisement, 2016," Sentencing Project, October 6, 2016, http://www.sentencingproject.org/publications/6-million-lost-voters-state-level-estimates-felony-disenfranchisement-2016.

72. Uggen, Larson, and Shannon, "6 Million Lost Voters."

73. So-called "good character" provisions in occupational licensing rules block potential applicants even if they've been out prison for years and even if their criminal history has little or nothing to do with the licensed profession. See Ashley Nerbovig, "License to Clip," Marshall Project, July 10, 2018, https://www.themarshallproject.org/2018/07/10/license-to-clip.

74. Nick Sibilla, "Inmates Who Volunteer to Fight California's Largest Fires Denied Access to Jobs on Release," *USA Today*, August 20, 2018, https://eu.usatoday.com/story/opinion/2018/08/20/californias-volunteer-inmate-firefighters-denied-jobs-after-release-column/987677002.

75. Bryan Stevenson, *Just Mercy: A Story of Justice and Redemption* (New York: Spiegel and Grau, 2014), 290.

CHAPTER 3: ADDRESSING HARMS

1. Micah Uetricht, "Accused Torturer Jon Burge Died Last Week, but His Legacy of Brutal, Racist Policing Lives On in Chicago," *Intercept*, September 25, 2018, https://theintercept.com/2018/09/25/jon-burge-chicago-police-torture.

2. Natalie Y. Moore, "Payback," Marshall Project, October 30, 2018, https://www.themarshallproject.org/2018/10/30/payback.

3. Katara Patton, "I Lived Through Hell: Ronald Kitchen Shares His Story of Surviving Jon Burge's Torture Ring," *Chicago Defender*, August 1, 2018, https://chicagodefender.com/i-lived-through-hell-ronald-kitchen-shares-his-story-of-surviving-jon-burges-torture-ring.

4. Students for Human Rights, "Chicago Police Torture Ring Timeline," based on information from the People's Law Office, https://www.stetson.edu/law/studyabroad/netherlands/media/Trk2-Week4-Scully-1_Chicago-Police-Torture-Timeline.pdf. See also G. Flint Taylor, "Federal Appeals Court Rejects Torture Survivor's Case," *In These Times*, June 26, 2014, http://inthesetimes.com/article/16881/federal_appeals_court_rejects_torture_survivors_case.

5. Office of Professional Standards, *Burge Investigation (Goldston) Report*, November 2, 1990, document available at https://peopleslawoffice.com/wp-content/uploads/2012/02/Goldston-Report-with-11.2.90-Coversheet.pdf, accessed July 23, 2019.

6. Uetricht, "Accused Torturer Jon Burge Died Last Week."

7. Students for Human Rights, "Chicago Police Torture Ring Timeline."

8. Uetricht, "Accused Torturer Jon Burge Died Last Week."

9. Moore, "Payback."

10. Yana Kunichoff and Sarah Macaraeg, "How Chicago Became the First City to Make Reparations to Victims of Police Violence," *Yes*, May 21, 2017, https://www.yesmagazine.org/issues/science/how-chicago-became-the-first-city-to-make-reparations-to-victims-of-police-violence-20170321.

11. Moore, "Payback."

12. Kunichoff and Macaraeg, "How Chicago Became the First City to Make Reparations to Victims of Police Violence."

13. Max Gluckman, "The Ideas in Barotse Jurisprudence," *Yale Law Journal* (1967), https://www.jstor.org/stable/795040?seq=1#page_scan_tab_contents, accessed August 20, 2018.

14. Robert Yazzie, "Navajo Justice," *Yes*, September 30, 2000, https://www.yesmagazine.org/issues/is-it-time-to-close-the-prisons/navajo-justice.

15. "He Hīnātore ki te Ao Māori: A Glimpse into the Maori World: Maori Perspectives on Justice," New Zealand Ministry of Justice, March 2001, https://www.justice.govt.nz/assets/Documents/Publications/he-hinatora-ki-te-ao-maori.pdf.

16. Michael McCullough, "The Forgiveness Instinct," *Greater Good*, March 1, 2008, https://greatergood.berkeley.edu/article/item/forgiveness_instinct.

17. McCullough, "The Forgiveness Instinct."

18. sujatha baliga, Sia Henry, and Georgia Valentine, *Restorative Community Conferencing* (Impact Justice, Summer 2017), https://impactjustice.org/wp-content/uploads/CWW_RJreport.pdf.

19. Melissa Jeltsen, "Joe Biden's Proudest Achievement Looks a Lot More Complicated in 2020," *Huffington Post*, April 7, 2019, https://www.huffpost.com/entry/joe-biden-violence-against-women-act_n_5c7d4097e4b0614614dd02b8.

20. Angelina Chapin, "Why Would a Woman Want to Talk with the Man Who Abused Her?," *Cut*, May 2017, https://www.thecut.com/2017/05/a-better-man-film-restorative-justice-and-domestic-abuse.html.

21. generationFIVE, *Ending Child Sexual Abuse*.

22. Audrey Carlsen et al., "#MeToo Brought Down 201 Powerful Men. Nearly Half of Their Replacements are Women," *New York Times*, October 29, 2018, https://www.nytimes.com/interactive/2018/10/23/us/metoo-replacements.html.

23. "A Brief History of PBIS with Rob Horner," Association for Persons with Severe Handicaps (TASH) podcast, January 27, 2016, https://tash.org/news/a-brief-history-of-pbis-with-rob-horner.

24. "PBIS/RJ Integration at School Sites," University of Vermont, http://www.uvm.edu/~cdci/best/pbswebsite/RJandPBIS.pdf.

25. Human Rights Watch, *Truth and Partial Justice in Argentina* (April 1990), https://www.hrw.org/sites/default/files/reports/argen914full.pdf.

26. David Smith et al., "Special Report: Truth, Justice and Reconciliation: An Examination of How Countries Around the World Affected by Civil War or Internal Conflict Have Approached Justice," *Guardian*, June 24, 2014, https://www.theguardian.com/world/2014/jun/24/truth-justice-reconciliation-civil-war-conflict.

27. Bilal Qureshi, "From Wrong to Right: A U.S. Apology for Japanese Internment," NPR, August 9, 2013, https://www.npr.org/sections/codeswitch/2013/08/09/210138278/japanese-internment-redress.

28. "History," Japanese American Citizens League, https://jacl.org/about/history, accessed December 28, 2018.

29. Ta-Nehisi Coates, "The Case for Reparations," *Atlantic*, June 2014, https://www.theatlantic.com/magazine/archive/2014/06/the-case-for-reparations/361631.

CHAPTER 4: PREVENTING HARMS

1. David Debolt, "Richmond City Manager Bill Lindsay to Retire," *East Bay Express*, March 8, 2018, https://www.eastbaytimes.com/2018/03/08/richmond-city-manager-bill-lindsay-to-retire.

2. Bill Lindsay, interview by the author, May 18, 2018.

3. Lindsay, interview.

4. DeVone Boggan, interview by the author, March 20, 2018. All information in this story is derived from the interviews with Lindsay and Boggan.

5. Jason Motlagh, "A Radical Approach to Gun Crime: Paying People Not to Kill Each Other," *Guardian*, June 9, 2016, https://www.theguardian.com/us-news/2016/jun/09/richmond-california-ons-gun-crime.

6. Julius Thibodeaux, "Want to Prevent Gun Violence in Hard-Hit Communities? Invest in Peace," *Sacramento Bee*, May 12, 2019, https://www.sacbee.com/opinion/california-forum/article230231924.html.

7. Rachel Huget et al., "Cost Benefit Analysis: Operation Peacemaker," University of Southern California, Sol Price School of Public Policy, 2016, https://www.advancepeace.org/wp-content/uploads/2017/04/6-USC_ONS_CBA.pdf.

8. Brett Samuels, "Poll: Most NRA Members Support Comprehensive Background Checks," *Hill*, March 8, 2018, https://thehill.com/blogs/blog-briefing-room/377455-poll-most-nra-members-support-comprehensive-background-checks.

9. Ian Urbina, "A Look at California Gun Laws, Among the Toughest in the Nation," *New York Times*, November 8, 2018, https://www.nytimes.com/2018/11/08/us/california-gun-laws.html.

10. Patrick Sharkey, *Uneasy Peace: The Great Crime Decline, the Renewal of City Life, and the Next War on Violence* (New York: W. W. Norton, 2018), 162.

11. To be exact, Prop. 13 rolled back assessments for homes and businesses to 1976 levels and capped annual tax increases at 2 percent.

12. Joe Garofoli, "Proposition 13 Is No Longer Off Limits in California," *San Francisco Chronicle*, December 27, 2018, https://www.sfchronicle.com/politics/article/Proposition-13-is-no-longer-off-limits-in-13492400.php.

13. "The Lock-In Effect of California's Proposition 13," National Bureau of Economic Research, https://www.nber.org/digest/apr05/w11108.html, accessed July 23, 2019.

14. "State Spending on Corrections and Education," University of California, https://www.universityofcalifornia.edu/infocenter/california-expenditures-corrections-and-public-education, accessed May 18, 2019.

15. Additionally, the president of the CCPOA at the time, Mike Jimenez, had had a personal awakening after his teenage son went through the criminal legal system. See Sasha Abramsky, "When Prison Guards Go Soft," *Mother Jones*, July/August 2008, https://www.motherjones.com/politics/2008/07/when-prison-guards-go-soft.

16. *$80B*: In 2014 the Hamilton Project, part of the centrist think tank the Brookings Institution, reported total corrections expenditures as "more than $80 billion in

2010. When including expenditures for police protection and judicial and legal services, the direct costs of crime rise to $261 billion. . . . More than 57% of direct cash outlays for corrections came from state governments, compared to 10% from the federal government and nearly 33% from local governments. . . . Each U.S. resident on average contributed $260 to corrections expenditures in 2010, which stands in stark contrast to the $77 each resident contributed in 1980." From Melissa S. Kearney and Benjamin H. Harris, "Ten Economic Facts about Crime and Incarceration in the U.S.," Brookings Institution, May 1, 2014, https://www.brookings.edu/research/ten-economic-facts-about-crime-and-incarceration-in-the-united-states. *$1.2T:* A 2016 report from Washington University in St. Louis came up with an even more devastating price tag, maintaining that corrections spending figures ignore the costs borne by incarcerated persons, families, children, and communities. For example, prisoners' absence from employment resulted in an average annual $23,286 ($33,066 in 2014 dollars) in lost productivity, yielding $24.6 billion in lost wages per year nationwide. The injuries people sustain while incarcerated have further costs, as do their higher mortality rates, which lead to lifelong lost wages. The study concluded that for "every dollar in corrections spending, there's another 10 dollars of other types of costs to families, children and communities," yielding a grand total "annual economic burden" in the amount of $1.2 trillion. From Michael McLaughlin et al., "The Economic Burden of Incarceration in the U.S.," Concordance Institute for Advancing Social Justice, Washington University in St. Louis, July 2016, https://joinnia.com/wp-content/uploads/2017/02/The-Economic-Burden-of-Incarceration-in-the-US-2016.pdf.

17. David Roodman, "Reasonable Doubt: A New Look at Whether Prison Growth Cuts Crime," Open Philanthropy Project, September 25, 2017, https://www.openphilanthropy.org/blog/reasonable-doubt-new-look-whether-prison-growth-cuts-crime.

18. Steven Brill, "Is America Any Safer?," *Atlantic,* September 2016, https://www.theatlantic.com/magazine/archive/2016/09/are-we-any-safer/492761.

19. Cody Cain, "Taxing the Rich Was a Pillar of Our Modern Society," *Huffington Post,* August 13, 2015, https://www.huffpost.com/entry/taxing-the-rich-was-a-pil_b_7977654. Data from "U.S. Federal Individual Income Tax Rates History, 1862–2013 (Nominal and Inflation-Adjusted Brackets)," https://taxfoundation.org/us-federal-individual-income-tax-rates-history-1913-2013-nominal-and-inflation-adjusted-brackets, accessed April 14, 2019.

20. Matthew Yglesias, "Elizabeth Warren's Proposed Tax on Enormous Fortunes, Explained," *Vox,* January 24, 2019, https://www.vox.com/policy-and-politics/2019/1/24/18196275/elizabeth-warren-wealth-tax.

21. Alexandria Ocasio-Cortez (@AOC), Twitter, March 13, 2019, https://twitter.com/AOC.

22. Alexandria Ocasio-Cortez (@AOC), Twitter, March 16, 2019, https://twitter.com/AOC.

23. DeVone Boggan, interview by the author, March 20, 2018.

24. MEY, "Trauma Queen: An Autostraddle Review and Interview."

25. Jane Jacobs, *The Death and Life of Great American Cities* (New York: Random House, 1961).

26. Cindy Martinez, conversation with the author, March 2018.

27. Van der Kolk, *The Body Keeps the Score*, 95.

28. Robert D. Putnam, "The Strange Disappearance of Civic America," *American Prospect*, no. 24 (Winter 1996), http://epn.org/prospect/24/24putn.html. The essay is one of two that led to Putnam's 2000 book *Bowling Alone*.

29. Thomas Sander and Robert Putnam, "Still Bowling Alone? The Post 9/11 Split," *Journal of Democracy* 21, no. 1 (January 2010): 9–16, https://sites.hks.harvard.edu/ocpa/pdf/still%20bowling%20alone.pdf.

30. Based on the May 2014 Allstate/National Journal Heartland Monitor Poll, cited in "Only One Percent of Americans," *Atlantic*, May 9, 2014, https://www.theatlantic.com/business/archive/2014/05/only-one-percent-of-americans-are-really-politically-active/425286.

31. Eric M. Uslaner and Mitchell Brown, "Inequality, Trust and Civic Engagement," *American Politics Research* 31 (2003), https://www.russellsage.org/sites/all/files/u4/Uslaner%20and%20Brown.pdf.

32. Uggen, Larson, and Shannon, "6 Million Lost Voters."

33. Union of Concerned Scientists, "To Defend Public Health, Protect Voting Rights," October 2, 2018, https://www.ucsusa.org/news/press-release/voting-rights-healthy-democracy.

34. Sean Kates, Jonathan M. Ladd, and Joshua A. Tucker, "New Poll Shows Dissatisfaction with American Democracy, Especially Among the Young," *Vox*, October 31, 2018, https://www.vox.com/mischiefs-of-faction/2018/10/31/18042060/poll-dissatisfaction-american-democracy-young, citing the 2018 American Institutional Confidence Poll, sponsored by the John S. and James L. Knight Foundation and Georgetown University's Baker Center for Leadership & Governance, conducted in June and July 2018. This is a large sample poll (5,400 respondents), which asked a series of questions about support for American national institutions and for democratic norms and principles.

35. Sharkey, *Uneasy Peace*, 53–54. Based on Patrick Sharkey et al., "Community and the Crime Decline: The Causal Effect of Local Nonprofit Formation on Violent Crime," *American Sociological Review* (2018).

CHAPTER 5: ALLEN AND DURRELL

1. Allen Feaster, interviews by the author in September 2018. All information in this story is provided by these interviews.

2. Teji, "Goodbye Preston."

3. Teji, "Goodbye Preston."

4. Dwyer Gunn, "Non-White School Districts Get $23 Billion Less Funding Than White Ones," *Pacific Standard*, February 26, 2019, https://psmag.com/education/nonwhite-school-districts-get-23-billion-less-funding-than-white-ones. Based on research by EdBuild, a nonprofit analyzing school funding. "Non-White School Districts Get $23 Billion Less than White Districts Despite Serving the Same Number of Students," EdBuild, https://edbuild.org/content/23-billion, accessed July 23, 2019.

5. Katy Tur, "Principal Fires Security Guards to Hire Art Teachers—and Transforms Elementary School," NBC News, May 1, 2013, http://dailynightly.nbcnews.com/_news/2013/05/01/18005192-principal-fires-security-guards-to-hire-art-teachers-and-transforms-elementary-school?lite.

6. James Vaznis, "City Unveils Plan for Schools," *Boston Globe*, November 19, 2009, http://archive.boston.com/news/education/k_12/articles/2009/11/19/city_unveils_plan_for_schools.

7. Orchard Gardens website, https://www.bostonpublicschools.org/school/orchard-gardens-k-8-school.

8. Sarah Spinks, "Adolescent Brains are Works in Progress," *Frontline*, PBS, January 31, 2002, https://www.pbs.org/wgbh/pages/frontline/shows/teenbrain/work/adolescent.html.

9. Taryn Ishida, executive director of Californians for Justice, interview by author, May 15, 2019, citing findings of the organization's youth-led action research that surveyed two thousand students and sixty-five school leaders across California, Californians for Justice Relationship Centered Schools, https://caljustice.org/our-work/rcs, accessed January 25, 2018.

10. Stephanie Chen, "Girl's Arrest for Doodling Raises Concerns About Zero Tolerance," CNN, February 18, 2010, http://edition.cnn.com/2010/CRIME/02/18/new.york.doodle.arrest/index.html?hpt=C1.

11. 'Pop Tart Suspension Should Be Upheld, School Official Says," CBS News, July 1, 2014, https://www.cbsnews.com/news/examiner-recommends-school-board-uphold-pop-tart-suspension.

12. Jessica Chasmar, "10-Year-Old Pennsylvania Boy Suspended for Pretend Bow-and-Arrow Shooting," *Washington Times*, December 11, 2013, https://www.washingtontimes.com/news/2013/dec/11/10-year-old-pennsylvania-boy-suspended-imitating-b.

13. Stacy Teicher Khadaroo, "Restorative Justice: One High School's Path to Reducing Suspensions by Half," *Christian Science Monitor*, March 31, 2013, https://www.minnpost.com/christian-science-monitor/2013/04/restorative-justice-one-high-schools-path-reducing-suspensions-hal.

14. "Civil Rights Data Collection: Revealing New Truths About Our Nation's Schools," US Department of Education, March 12, 2012, http://www2.ed.gov/about/offices/list/ocr/docs/crdc-2012-data-summary.pdf.

15. Angel Jackson, *Repairing the Breach: A Brief History of Youth of Color in the Justice System* (Oakland, CA: W. Haywood Burns Institute for Justice Fairness & Equity, 2016), https://www.burnsinstitute.org/publications/repairing-the-breach-pdf.

16. Sometimes also called multisystemic therapy (MST).

17. "No Place for Kids," Annie E. Casey Foundation, 2011, https://www.aecf.org/m/resourcedoc/aecf-NoPlaceForKidsFullReport-2011.pdf, 17.

18. Van der Kolk, *The Body Keeps the Score*, 170.

19. Joe VerValin, "The Case for Universal Child Allowance in the United States," *Cornell Policy Review*, October 5, 2018, http://www.cornellpolicyreview.com/universal-child-allowance.

20. US Department of Labor, Apprenticeship Toolkit, Frequently Asked Questions, https://www.dol.gov/apprenticeship/toolkit/toolkitfaq.htm, accessed May 3, 2019.

21. "No Place for Kids," Annie E. Casey Foundation, 2011, https://www.aecf.org/m/resourcedoc/aecf-NoPlaceForKidsFullReport-2011.pdf.

22. "Sticker Shock: Calculating the Full Price Tag for Youth Incarceration," Justice Policy Institute, December 9, 2014, http://www.justicepolicy.org/uploads/justicepolicy/documents/sticker_shock_final_v2.pdf.

23. Justice for Families, "Families Unlocking Futures: Solutions to the Crisis in Juvenile Justice," May 2013, http://www.justice4families.org//wp-content/uploads/2013/05/J4F-Families-Unlocking-Futures.pdf.

24. "Momentum Builds in States to End the Youth Prison Model," Annie E. Casey Foundation, January 25, 2018, https://www.aecf.org/blog/momentum-builds-in-states-to-end-the-youth-prison-model; Don Thompson, "California Governor Seeks to Transform Youth Prisons," *AP News*, January 23, 2019, https://apnews.com/7306ab2ee9384aca81c97eff9a3b15df.

25. Youth Correctional Leaders for Justice, "Statement on Ending Youth Prisons," April 7, 2019, https://yclj.org/statement.

26. Allen Feaster, interview by the author, September 10, 2018.

27. As I write, the agency is up for another rebranding and new name, a surefire sign of a failing institution.

28. Carolyn McClanahan, "People Are Raising $650 Million on GoFundMe Each Year to Attack Rising Healthcare Costs," *Forbes*, August 13, 2018, https://www.forbes.com/sites/carolynmcclanahan/2018/08/13/using-gofundme-to-attack-health-care-costs/#a167e4228598.

29. Scott D. Ramsey and Veena Shankaran, "Financial Toxicity: 1 in 3 Cancer Patients Have to Turn to Friends or Family to Pay for Care," Stat News, November 2, 2016, https://www.statnews.com/2016/11/02/cancer-treatment-financial-toxicity.

30. Dan Witters, "U.S. Uninsured Rate Rises to Four-Year High," Gallup, January 23, 2019, https://news.gallup.com/poll/246134/uninsured-rate-rises-four-year-high.aspx.

31. Kaiser Family Foundation, "New Kaiser/New York Times Survey Finds One in Five Working-Age Americans With Health Insurance Report Problems Paying Medical Bills," January 5, 2016, https://www.kff.org/health-costs/press-release/new-kaisernew-york-times-survey-finds-one-in-five-working-age-americans-with-health-insurance-report-problems-paying-medical-bills.

CHAPTER 6: MARLENA AND JAMES

1. Marlena Henderson, interview by the author, May 17, 2018. All information in this story is derived from this interview unless otherwise noted.

2. Saneta deVuono-powell, Chris Schweidler, Alicia Walters, and Azadeh Zohrabi, *Who Pays? The True Cost of Incarceration on Families* (Oakland, CA: Ella Baker Center, Forward Together, Research Action Design, 2015), https://ellabakercenter.org/sites/default/files/downloads/who-pays.pdf.

3. Prior to the sixty-day hunger strike in the summer of 2013, people in SHU got one-fourth the maximum monthly canteen draw, telephone calls on an emergency basis only, limited yard access and no other recreational activities, and receipt of one package of thirty pounds maximum weight per year.

4. James Ridgeway and Jean Casella, "America's 10 Worst Prisons: Pelican Bay," *Mother Jones*, May 18, 2013, https://www.motherjones.com/politics/2013/05/10-worst-prisons-america-pelican-bay.

5. Van der Kolk, *The Body Keeps the Score*, 210.

6. Christopher Emdin, *For White Folks Who Teach in the Hood . . . and the Rest of Y'all Too: Reality Pedagogy and Urban Education* (Boston: Beacon Press, 2016).

7. Christopher Emdin, "Teach Teachers How to Create Magic," TEDx talk, October 2013, https://www.ted.com/talks/christopher_emdin_teach_teachers_how_to_create_magic.

8. Joseph A. Durlak et al., "The Impact of Enhancing Students' Social and Emotional Learning," *Child Development*, January/February 2011, http://www.casel.org/wp-content/uploads/2016/01/meta-analysis-child-development-1.pdf.

9. Clive Belfied et al., "The Economic Value of Social and Emotional Learning," Center for Benefit-Cost Studies in Education, Teachers College, Columbia University, February 2015 (revised), 46, http://blogs.edweek.org/edweek/rulesforengagement/SEL-Revised.pdf.

10. See Monique Morris, *Pushout: The Criminalization of Black Girls in Schools* (New York: New Press, 2016). In Chapter 5, "Repairing Relationships, Rebuilding Connections," Morris argues for a collaborative approach to establishing school norms and discipline that includes student voices.

11. Angela Y. Davis, *Are Prisons Obsolete?* (New York: Seven Stories Press, 2003), 39.

12. Doris A. Fuller et al., "Overlooked in the Undercounted: The Role of Mental Illness in Fatal Law Enforcement Encounters," Treatment Advocacy Center, December 2015, https://www.treatmentadvocacycenter.org/storage/documents/overlooked-in-the-undercounted.pdf.

13. "Crisis Intervention Team Programs," National Alliance on Mental Illness, https://www.nami.org/Get-Involved/Crisis-Intervention-Team-(CIT)-Programs, accessed July 7, 2018.

14. "Mental Health by the Numbers," fact sheet from National Alliance on Mental Illness, https://www.nami.org/Learn-More/Mental-Health-By-the-Numbers, based on data from the National Institute of Mental Health, accessed May 22, 2019.

15. "Mental Health Facts in America," National Alliance on Mental Illness, https://www.nami.org/NAMI/media/NAMI-Media/Infographics/GeneralMIIFacts.pdf.

16. Jenny Gold, "A Dearth of Hospital Beds for Patients in Psychiatric Crisis," Kaiser Health News, April 12, 2016, https://khn.org/news/a-dearth-of-hospital-beds-for-patients-in-psychiatric-crisis. Data in the article drawn from Doris A. Fuller et al., "Going, Going, Gone: Trends and Consequences of Eliminating State Psychiatric Beds," Treatment Advocacy Center, 2016, https://www.treatmentadvocacycenter.org/storage/documents/going-going-gone.pdf.

17. Tala Al-Rousan et al., "Inside the Nation's Largest Mental Health Institution: A Prevalence Study in a State Prison System," BioMed Central Public Health, April 20, 2017, https://www.ncbi.nlm.nih.gov/pmc/articles/PMC5397789.

18. "Incarceration and Mental Health," Center for Prisoner Health and Human Rights, https://www.prisonerhealth.org/educational-resources/factsheets-2/incarceration-and-mental-health, accessed September 25, 2018.

19. "Incarceration, Substance Abuse, and Addiction," Center for Prisoner Health and Human Rights, https://www.prisonerhealth.org/educational-resources/factsheets-2/incarceration-substance-abuse-and-addiction, accessed September 25, 2018.

20. Suchitra Rajogopalan, "United Nations and World Health Organization Call for Drug Decriminalization," Drug Policy Alliance, June 29, 2017, http://www.drugpolicy.org/blog/united-nations-and-world-health-organization-call-drug-decriminalization.

21. Drug Policy Alliance, "One Year Later and the Experts Agree: California's Landmark Criminal Justice Reform Measure, Proposition 47 Is a Success," November 2, 2015, http://www.drugpolicy.org/news/2015/11/one-year-later-and-experts -agree-californias-landmark-criminal-justice-reform-measure-p.

22. Maritza Perez et al., "Using Marijuana Revenue to Create Jobs," Center for American Progress, May 20, 2019, https://www.americanprogress.org/issues /criminal-justice/reports/2019/05/20/470031/using-marijuana-revenue-create-jobs.

23. Nazgol Ghandnoosh and Casey Anderson, "Opioids: Treating an Illness, Ending a War," Sentencing Project, December 13, 2017, https://www.sentencing project.org/publications/opioids-treating-illness-ending-war.

24. Erick Trickey, "'The Police Aren't Just Getting You in Trouble. They Actually Care,'" *Politico*, June 2, 2018, https://www.politico.com/magazine/story/2018 /06/02/the-police-arent-just-getting-you-in-trouble-they-actually-care-218586.

25. Rinku Sen, "Can 9-1-1 Protocols Protect Us from 'Barbecue Beckys'?," *Maven*, February 8, 2019, https://mavenroundtable.io/rinkusen/should-i-call-the-cops/can -9-1-1-protocols-protect-us-from-barbecue-beckys-QiUNFDCtp0-mqGp8zbsbPw.

26. Sen, "Can 9-1-1 Protocols Protect Us From 'Barbecue Beckys'?"

27. "What Is 211?," Helpline Center, https://www.helplinecenter.org/2-1-1 -community-resources/what-is-211, accessed July 23, 2019.

28. "2-1-1," Wikipedia, https://en.wikipedia.org/wiki/2-1-1, accessed July 23, 2019.

29. Sigal Samuel, "Calling the Cops on Someone Can Go Terribly Wrong. Here's a Better Idea. What If We Sent Mental Health Experts Instead of Police?," *Vox*, July 1, 2019, https://www.vox.com/future-perfect/2019/7/1/20677523/mental -health-police-cahoots-oregon-oakland-sweden.

30. Michelle Chen, "The Formerly Incarcerated Are Becoming Opioid-Overdose First Responders," *Nation*, April 3, 2018, https://www.thenation.com/article/the -formerly-incarcerated-are-becoming-opioid-overdose-first-responders.

31. DeVuono-powell et al., *Who Pays?*

32. Lior Gideon and Hung-En Sung, eds., *Rethinking Corrections: Rehabilitation, Reentry, and Reintegration* (Los Angeles: SAGE, 2010), 332.

33. Sarah Kliff, "Elizabeth Warren's Universal Child Care Plan, Explained," *Vox*, February 22, 2019, https://www.vox.com/policy-and-politics/2019/2/22/18234606 /warren-child-care-universal-2020.

34. Aqeela Sherrills's tweet posted by Crime Survivors for Safety and Justice (@CSSJustice), "When someone gets shot in our neighborhoods we deploy law enforcement in force but we don't deploy healers, therapists & counselors in force to help folks deal with the after-effects of violence in our communities. #Survivors-Speak," Twitter, https://twitter.com/CSSJustice/status/981740311650037762.

35. "Crime Survivors Speak," Alliance for Safety and Justice, 2016, https://www .allianceforsafetyandjustice.org/wp-content/uploads/documents/Crime%20Survivors %20Speak%20Report.pdf.

36. Danielle Sered, *Young Men of Color and the Other Side of Harm: Addressing Disparities in Our Response to Violence* (New York: Vera Institute of Justice, December 2014), https://storage.googleapis.com/vera-web-assets/downloads /Publications/young-men-of-color-and-the-other-side-of-harm-addressing -disparities-in-our-responses-to-violence/legacy_downloads/men-of-color-as -victims-of-violence-v3.pdf.

CHAPTER 7: ANITA

1. Anita De Asis Miralle, interview by the author, April 17, 2019. All information in this story is from this interview unless otherwise noted.

2. Dawn Phillips et al., "Development Without Displacement," Causa Justa::Just Cause, April 7, 2015, https://cjjc.org/wp-content/uploads/2015/11/development-without-displacement.pdf.

3. Phillips et al., "Development without Displacement."

4. Zach Friedman, "Student Loan Debt Statistics in 2018: A $1.5 Trillion Crisis," *Forbes*, June 13, 2018, https://www.forbes.com/sites/zackfriedman/2018/06/13/student-loan-debt-statistics-2018/#2dbbdf37310f.

5. "Rent Trend Data in Oakland, California," Rent Jungle, https://www.rentjungle.com/average-rent-in-oakland-rent-trends, accessed May 1, 2019.

6. Based on data from RealPage, a real estate analytics firm, cited in Julie Littman, "Rents in Bay Area Major Metros Increased by About 50% Since 2010," Bisnow, April 3, 2018, https://www.bisnow.com/san-francisco/news/multifamily/rents-in-bay-area-major-metros-increased-by-about-50-since-2010-86847.

7. "Alameda County Renters in Crisis: A Call for Action," California Housing Partnership, May 2017, http://1po8d91kdoco3rlxhmhtydpr.wpengine.netdna-cdn.com/wp-content/uploads/2017/05/Alameda-County-2017.pdf.

8. Eviction Lab, Princeton University, https://evictionlab.org/national-estimates.

9. Eviction Lab.

10. "EveryOne Counts! 2017 Alameda County's Homeless Persons Point-In-Time Count," EveryOneHome, http://everyonehome.org/wp-content/uploads/2016/02/Homeless-Count-Notes-5-22-17-w-EdC-edits-1.pdf.

11. Lisa Fernandez, "UN Report Singles Out Homeless Conditions in Oakland, San Francisco as 'Cruel and Inhumane,'" KTVU.com, October 24, 2018, http://www.ktvu.com/news/un-report-singles-out-homeless-conditions-in-oakland-san-francisco-as-cruel-and-inhumane-.

12. "California's New Vagrancy Laws: The Growing Enactment and Enforcement of Anti-Homeless Laws in the Golden State," Berkeley Law Policy Advocacy Clinic, University of California, June 2016, http://ssrn.com/abstract=2794386.

13. "California's New Vagrancy Laws."

14. "California's New Vagrancy Laws."

15. Anita De Asis Miralle, interview by the author, April 17, 2019.

16. Anita De Asis Miralle, "Criminalizing the Unsheltered Is Not the Solution to Oakland's Housing Crisis," *Medium*, May 8, 2019, https://medium.com/ellabakercenter/https-medium-com-ellabakercenter-criminalizing-the-unsheltered-3a7f12209aa5.

17. Marisa Kendall, "Homeless Greet Oakland's Tuff Sheds with Hesitation, Hope," *Mercury News*, May 8, 2018, https://www.mercurynews.com/2018/05/08/homeless-greet-new-tuff-sheds-with-hesitation-hope.

18. Suzanne Ito, "New Report Shows 95% of Campus Rapes Go Unreported," ACLU, February 25, 2010, https://www.aclu.org/blog/smart-justice/mass-incarceration/new-report-shows-95-campus-rapes-go-unreported?redirect=blog/speakeasy/new-report-shows-95-campus-rapes-go-unreported.

19. Katie J. M. Baker, "UCSB Is One of Four New Schools Accused of Mishandling Rape Cases," *BuzzFeed News*, September 3, 2014, https://www.buzzfeednews

.com/article/katiejmbaker/ucsb-is-one-of-four-new-schools-accused-of-mishandling
-rape.

20. Campus PRISM Project Briefing Paper, December 2017, https://www
.skidmore.edu/campusrj/documents/Next-Steps-for-RJ-Campus-PRISM.pdf.

21. Tovia Smith, "After Assault, Some Campuses Focus on Healing over
Punishment," NPR, July 25, 2017, https://www.npr.org/2017/07/25/539334346
/restorative-justice-an-alternative-to-the-process-campuses-use-for-sexual-assault.

22. "Effects of Sexual Violence," RAINN, https://www.rainn.org/effects
-sexual-violence, accessed February 27, 2019.

23. Kelly Field, "A New Challenge for Colleges: Opioid-Addicted Students,"
Hechinger Report, September 13, 2018, https://hechingerreport.org/a-new-challenge
-for-colleges-opioid-addicted-students.

24. Charlotte Alter, "'Change Is Closer Than We Think.' Inside Alexandria
Ocasio-Cortez's Unlikely Rise," *Time*, March 21, 2019, http://time.com/longform
/alexandria-ocasio-cortez-profile.

25. Andy Kroll, "Elizabeth Warren Wants to Wipe Out Student Debt for 42
Million Americans," *Rolling Stone*, April 22, 2019, https://www.rollingstone.com
/politics/politics-news/elizabeth-warren-wants-to-wipe-out-student-debt-for-42
-million-americans-825006.

26. Margery Eagan, "'Extremists' Like Warren and Ocasio-Cortez Are Actually
Closer to What Most Americans Want," *Boston Globe*, January 10, 2019, https://
www.bostonglobe.com/opinion/2019/01/10/extremists-like-warren-and-ocasio
-cortez-are-actually-closer-what-most-americans-want/JgoFtRMY5IbMMaDZld
7wnK/story.html.

27. Desmond, *Evicted*.

28. Vanessa Moses, email exchange with the author, April 29, 2019.

29. Patrick Butler, "'Housing Should Be Seen as a Right. Not a Commodity,'"
Guardian, February 28, 2017, https://www.theguardian.com/society/2017/feb/28
/luxury-real-estate-housing-crisis-un-homelessness.

30. Desmond, *Evicted*.

31. Alana Semuels, "How Housing Policy Is Failing America's Poor," *Atlantic*,
June 24, 2015, https://www.theatlantic.com/business/archive/2015/06/section-8-is
-failing/396650.

32. Semuels, "How Housing Policy Is Failing America's Poor."

33. Jake Blumgart, "What an Affordable Housing Moonshot Would Look Like,"
Slate, July 1, 2016, https://slate.com/business/2016/07/its-time-for-universal
-housing-vouchers.html.

34. Blumgart, "What an Affordable Housing Moonshot Would Look Like."

35. Michael Novogradac, "Final Tax Reform Bill Would Reduce Affordable
Rental Housing Production by Nearly 235,000 Homes," Tax Reform Resource Center,
Novogradac, December 19, 2017, https://www.novoco.com/notes-from-novogradac
/final-tax-reform-bill-would-reduce-affordable-rental-housing-production-nearly
-235000-homes.

36. Jarrid Green and Thomas M. Hanna, "Community Control of Land and Housing," Democracy Collaborative, August 20, 2018, https://democracycollaborative
.org/content/community-control-land-and-housing-exploring-strategies-combating
-displacement-expanding.

37. "Community Benefits Ordinance," City of Detroit, https://detroitmi.gov
/departments/planning-and-development-department/citywide-initiatives
/community-benefits-ordinance, accessed May 23, 2019.

38. Kathleen Pender, "Oakland's Vacant-Property Tax Takes Effect, Sparking
Hope—and Alarm," *San Francisco Chronicle*, January 26, 2019, https://www
.sfchronicle.com/business/networth/article/Oakland-s-vacant-property-tax-takes
-effect-13563273.php.

39. Pender, "Oakland's Vacant-Property Tax Takes Effect."

40. Desmond, *Evicted*, 303.

41. Rebecca Boone, "Court: Cities Can't Prosecute People for Sleeping on
Streets," *AP News*, September 5, 2018, https://www.apnews.com/3964861076af
417a9734bfc4aa1eefdd.

42. Terence McCoy, "The Surprisingly Simple Way Utah Solved Chronic Homelessness and Saved Millions," *Sydney Morning Herald*, April 18, 2015, https://www
.smh.com.au/world/the-surprisingly-simple-way-utah-solved-chronic-homelessness
-and-saved-millions-20150418-1mnrvh.html.

CONCLUSION: WE THE PEOPLE

1. Mark Ramirez, "Punitive Sentiment," *Criminology* 52, no. 2 (2013): 338,
http://www.public.asu.edu/~mdramir/punitive-sentiment-project.html.

2. Nazgol Ghandnoosh, "Can We Wait 75 Years to Cut the Prison Population
in Half?," Sentencing Project, March 2018, https://www.sentencingproject.org
/publications/can-wait-75-years-cut-prison-population-half.

3. Davis, *Are Prisons Obsolete?*, 9–10.

4. See Challenging E-Carceration: The Voice of the Monitored, https://www
.challengingecarceration.org, accessed July 23, 2019. See also James Kilgore and
Emmett Sanders, "Ankle Monitors Aren't Humane. They're Another Kind of Jail,"
Wired, August 4, 2018, https://www.wired.com/story/opinion-ankle-monitors-are
-another-kind-of-jail.

5. Alexander, "The Newest Jim Crow."

6. "Electronic Monitoring Is a Form of Incarceration," Center for Media Justice,
https://centerformediajustice.org/wp-content/uploads/2018/03/electronic-monitoring
-infographic-final.pdf, accessed November 15, 2018.

7. Eric Markowitz, "Chain Gang 2.0," *International Business Times*, September
21, 2015, https://www.ibtimes.com/chain-gang-20-if-you-cant-afford-gps-ankle
-bracelet-you-get-thrown-jail-2065283.

8. Myaisha Hayes, "#NoMoreShackles: Why Electronic Monitoring Devices Are
Another Form of Prison," *Colorlines*, December 5, 2018, https://www.colorlines
.com/articles/nomoreshackles-why-electronic-monitoring-devices-are-another
-form-prison-op-ed.

INDEX

Buffett, Warren, 88
Burge, Jon, 63–66
Burke, Tarana, 34, 75

Cahoots (crisis intervention program),
130
Calarco, Jessica McCrory, 54
California: anti-vagrancy laws in, 142;
decarceration in, 154; framework
of fear in, 87–89. *See also* Oakland,
California
California Correctional Peace Officers
Association (CCPOA), 88
California Housing Partnership, 140
Californians for Justice (CFJ), 105
California Youth Authority (CYA), 43,
99–100, 112, 113, 120
Campanello, Leonard, 129
Campus PRISM (Promoting Restor-
ative Initiatives for Sexual Miscon-
duct) Project, 146, 153
Canada, Truth and Reconciliation Com-
mission, 78
capitalism, harms from, 28–30
carceral state, punishment and, 55–56.
See also incarceration
care-based models of safety, 9–11
Carter, Jimmy, 79
"The Case for Reparations" (Coates), 79
case studies. *See* Feaster, Allen and
Durrell; Henderson, Marlena and
James; Miralle, Anita De Asis
Causa Justa::Just Cause, 18–19, 148
CBAs (community benefit agreements),
150
CCPOA (California Correctional Peace
Officers Association), 88
Center for American Progress, 128–29
Center for Juvenile and Criminal
Justice, 112
CFJ (Californians for Justice), 105
Chicago, restorative justice in, 63–66, 78
Chicago Torture Justice Center, 66
children: child abuse, prevalence of, 27;
childcare facilities, government-
subsidized network of, 132, 135;

immigrant children, treatment of,
40–41; as Japanese American in-
ternees, 44; killed by gun violence,
35; maltreatment of, 35–36, 48, 74;
in slavery, 46; as superpredators,
41–43; threats to safety of, anxiety
about, 5; traumas to, 2
Child Tax Credit, 109
Child Tax Exemption, 109
Chile: Commission for Truth and
Reconciliation, 78; Commission
on Political Imprisonment and
Torture, 78
CIT (crisis intervention team) protocols, 126
civic engagement, increasing, 92–96
Civil Liberties Act (1988), 78–79
Clements, Mark, 65
Clinton, Bill, 9, 42
Clinton, Hillary, 9, 41, 42
Coates, Ta-Nehisi, 79
Common Justice, 133
communities: in accountability, 67–70,
74, 77–78; community benefit
agreements, 150; community engagement, need for, 92–96; community guardians, 87; community land
trusts, 148; teachers' knowledge of,
124, 134
Community Works (Oakland), 80
computer algorithms, profiling by, 53–54
confidants, numbers of, 57, 173–74n69
conflict management, through distancing, 106
Connecticut, decarceration in, 154
Cook, Joyce, 111
Corazón, Lovemme, 20, 58
Cornell Policy Review, support for
report on parenting, 109
corporations: corporate accountability,
restorative justice and, 77; corporate crimes, lack of punishment for,
26–27
corrections expenditures, 176–77n16
crimes: community engagement's
impact on, 95; disconnect of harms

from, 25–28; expanded criminal
liability, 55; fear of, 47; spending
on, 176–77n16. *See also* harms
criminal legal system, 25–27, 58, 69,
73–74, 106, 133, 156
crisis intervention team (CIT) protocols, 126
cultural deprivation, 52
culture of care, 10, 123, 132–34
The Culture of Fear (Glassner), 6
CYA (California Youth Authority), 43,
99–100, 112, 113, 120

Dalbo, Frank, 22
Daley, Richard M., 64, 65
Davis, Angela, 125, 154–55
deaths, preventable, 167n38
decarceration, 89, 154
Decolonizing Wealth (Villanueva), 30
dehumanization, practices of, under
Trump, 41
demagogues, conditions supporting rise
of, 6–7
democracy, 93, 157–58
Department of Justice. *See* Justice
Department
deprivation, as component of frame-
work of fear, 49–52
Desmond, Matthew, 16–17, 140, 148,
149, 152
Detroit, community benefit agreements
in, 150–51
DeVore, John, 34
DeVries, Joe, 143
DiAngelo, Robin, 31
DiIulio, John, 42, 43, 170n18
domestic violence, 27, 33–34, 73
Drucker, Ernest, 156
drug possession, decriminalization of,
128–29, 134–35
Duarte, Lourdes, 111
Durrell. *See* Feaster, Allen and Durrell

Eastmont Mall (Oakland), 16–17
economy: economic deprivation, 50–52;
economic inequality, growth of,
10; financialization of, 29; Great

Depression (Argentina), 3; Great
Recession, 19, 29; inclusivity in, 89
education. *See* schools
elderly, violence against, 36
electronic monitoring (EM), 155–56
Ella Baker Center for Human Rights,
4, 80, 92
Emanuel, Rahm, 65, 66
Emdin, Christopher, 123
eminent domain, 153
enemies, external, systemic harms
versus, 48
Enron Corporation, 26
Equal Employment Opportunity Commission, litigation of cases by, 25
Evicted (Desmond), 16–17, 140, 148
Eviction Lab (Princeton University),
140
evictions, 30, 140, 149, 151, 153

facilitated communication (FC), 22
families: domestic violence, 27, 33–34,
73; family separations, as isolation,
58; parents, support for, 109, 116;
restorative justice in, 72–74. *See
also* children; *specific case studies*
Families for Books Not Bars, 99,
110–11, 112, 113
Farha, Leilani, 148
fascism, 6, 7, 157–58
FC (facilitated communication), 22
fear: culture of, 6–9; fear-based models
of safety, care-based models versus,
9–11. *See also* framework of fear
Feaster, Allen and Durrell (case study),
99–114; Allen, spirit of, 115–16;
Allen's illness and death, 113–14;
anti-youth prisons activism of,
110–13; possible alternative realities for, 103–10; recommendations
based on story of, 116–17; story of,
99–103
Federal Housing Authority, redlining
by, 50–51
Feed the People, 141–42
Festival at the Lake (Oakland), 17
fight or flight response, 6

ABOUT THE AUTHOR

EURYDICE THOMAS

Zach Norris is the executive director of the Ella Baker Center for Human Rights and a cofounder of Restore Oakland, a community advocacy and training center that will empower Bay Area community members to transform local economic and justice systems and make a safe and secure future possible for themselves and for their families. Zach is also a cofounder of Justice for Families, a national alliance of family-driven organizations working to end our nation's youth incarceration epidemic.

Zach helped build California's first statewide network for families of incarcerated youth, which led the effort to close five youth prisons in the state, passed legislation to enable families to stay in contact with their loved ones, and defeated Prop 6, a destructive and ineffective criminal justice ballot measure.

In addition to being a Harvard University graduate and a New York University–educated attorney, Zach is also a graduate of the Labor Community Strategy Center's National School for Strategic Organizing in Los Angeles, California, and was a 2011 Soros Justice Fellow. He is a former board member at Witness for Peace and Just Cause Oakland and currently serves on the Justice for Families board. Zach was a recipient of the American Constitution Society's David Carliner Public Interest Award in 2015, and he is a member of the 2016 class of the Levi Strauss Foundation's Pioneers of Justice.

Zach is married to author and labor organizer Saru Jayaraman; they have two daughters, whom they are raising in Oakland, California.

The Ella Baker Center for Human Rights is a nonprofit organization based in Oakland, California, working to advance racial and economic justice to ensure dignity and opportunity for low-income people and people of color. Founded by Van Jones, Diana Frappier, and Mike McLoone in 1996, the Ella Baker Center has been on the front lines of campaigns for police oversight, the green jobs movement, promoting civic engagement, violence prevention through youth leadership, and transforming juvenile justice systems in California. The Ella Baker Center works to build people-powered movements to end mass incarceration, criminalization, and state violence through Truth and Reinvestment—moving resources away from failed criminal justice policies and toward family-driven solutions that improve public health, safety, and prosperity for all communities.